Usable Security

History, Themes, and Challenges

Synthesis Lectures on Information Security, Privacy, and Trust

Editors
Elisa Bertino, *Purdue University*
Ravi Sandhu, *University of Texas, San Antonio*

The Synthesis Lectures Series on Information Security, Privacy, and Trust publishes 50- to 100-page publications on topics pertaining to all aspects of the theory and practice of Information Security, Privacy, and Trust. The scope largely follows the purview of premier computer security research journals such as ACM Transactions on Information and System Security, IEEE Transactions on Dependable and Secure Computing and Journal of Cryptology, and premier research conferences, such as ACM CCS, ACM SACMAT, ACM AsiaCCS, ACM CODASPY, IEEE Security and Privacy, IEEE Computer Security Foundations, ACSAC, ESORICS, Crypto, EuroCrypt and AsiaCrypt. In addition to the research topics typically covered in such journals and conferences, the series also solicits lectures on legal, policy, social, business, and economic issues addressed to a technical audience of scientists and engineers. Lectures on significant industry developments by leading practitioners are also solicited.

Usable Security: History, Themes, and Challenges
Simson Garfinkel and Heather Richter Lipford
2014

Reversible Digital Watermarking: Theory and Practices
Ruchira Naskar and Rajat Subhra Chakraborty
2014

Mobile Platform Security
N. Asokan, Lucas Davi, Alexandra Dmitrienko, Stephan Heuser, Kari Kostiainen, Elena Reshetova, and Ahmad-Reza Sadeghi
2013

Security and Trust in Online Social Networks
Barbara Carminati, Elena Ferrari, and Marco Viviani
2013

ABSTRACT

There has been roughly 15 years of research into approaches for aligning research in Human Computer Interaction with computer Security, more colloquially known as "usable security." Although usability and security were once thought to be inherently antagonistic, today there is wide consensus that systems that are not usable will inevitably suffer security failures when they are deployed into the real world. Only by simultaneously addressing both usability and security concerns will we be able to build systems that are truly secure.

This book presents the historical context of the work to date on usable security and privacy, creates a taxonomy for organizing that work, outlines current research objectives, presents lessons learned, and makes suggestions for future research.

KEYWORDS

usable privacy and security, passwords, device pairing, privacy, authentication, privacy policies

Contents

Acknowledgments

Figure Credits

Figure 2.1	Based on Jermyn et al. The design and analysis of graphical passwords. *SSYM'99 Proceedings of the 8th conference on USENIX Security Symposium*, Volume 8, Pages 1–15. Copyright © 1999, USENIX Association Berkeley, CA, USA.
Figures 3.1, 3.2	Based on Florencio, D. and Herley, C. A large-scale study of web password habits. *WWW '07 Proceedings of the 16th international conference on World Wide Web*, pages 657–666. Copyright © 2007, Association for Computing Machinery, Inc. DOI: 10.1145/1242572.1242661
Figure 3.3	From Ur et al. How does your password measure up? The effect of strength meters on password creation. *Security '12 Proceedings of the 21st USENIX conference on Security symposium.* Copyright © 2012, USENIX Association Berkeley, CA, USA. Reprinted with permission.
Figure 3.4	From Munroe, R. Password strength. *XKCD: A webcomic of romance, sarcasm, math, and language.* Used with permission. http://xkcd.com/936/
Figure 3.5	Based on Bonneau et al. The quest to replace passwords: A framework for comparative evaluation of web authentication schemes. *2012 IEEE Symposium on Security and Privacy (SP)*, pages 553–567. Copyright © 2012 IEEE. DOI: 10.1109/SP.2012.44
Figures 3.6, 3.7, 3.8	Based on user images from Daniel McCarney, David Barrera, Jeremy Clark, Sonia Chiasson, and Paul C. van Oorschot. 2012. Tapas: design, implementation, and usability evaluation of a password manager. In *Proceedings of the 28th Annual Computer Security Applications Conference (ACSAC '12)*. ACM, New York, NY, USA, 89–98. Used with Permission.

user interface and usability engineering, which emerged during the same period, addressed other issues.

The past decade has seen a dramatic increase in attention to usable privacy and security (UPS). Less than a dozen papers on the topic were published between the first mention of "psychological acceptability" and the first usable security workshop [Patrick et al., 2003]. Since then, hundreds of papers on usable security have appeared in peer-reviewed literature, with multiple workshops and one standing conference on the topic. Much of the motivation for this work has been the development of consumer e-Commerce applications and the corresponding increase in cyber attacks of all kinds that took place in the first decade of the 21st century. Today more than ever, it is clear that we cannot secure computer systems unless we pay attention to the human element.

Today, the majority of the world's population are users of email and social media [Reaney, 2012]. Early hopes that people who grew up immersed with information and communications technology (ICT) would somehow understand it as "digital natives" [Prensky, 2001] have been shown to be largely unfounded [Selwyn, 2009]. For example, Kurkovsky and Syta [2010] surveyed over 330 young people aged 18–25 who had grown up with the technology and found that, even though they were aware of privacy and security threats that they faced as a result of using mobile phones, the majority did not take technical measures to protect themselves. Although 80% of the survey respondents were aware that phones could be locked with a PIN, only 29% employed PIN locks. "Young people participating in our survey rank malware and wireless attacks as the least likely causes of compromising or losing private data stored on their mobile phones, but the vast majority admits that they do not understand the technology basics, which questions their ability to reasonably evaluate such threats."

Indeed, users are increasingly besieged by contradictory rules governing passwords, encryption, and mobile computing. The result is a simultaneous decrease in both usability and security, and an increase in frustration and user disengagement. Passwords must be so long and complex that they cannot be guessed and, as a result, users reuse the same password at multiple sites, making them less secure [Gaw and Felten, 2006]. Financial institutions will not encrypt sensitive information sent over the Internet by email because they think users cannot cope with encrypted or digitally signed messages, and as a result, they send email to customers telling them to go to websites to check for secure messages—a practice that makes users more vulnerable to phishing attacks [Jakobsson and Myers, 2006]. Internet marketing and promotion is the primary way that users find out about the need to secure their devices, yet these same channels are also one of the primary ways that malware comes to be installed on mobile devices and self-managed computer systems [Li et al., 2012, Oberheide and Jahanian, 2010]. Users are conflicted between following security requirements and getting their work done [Beautement et al., 2008].

To be sure, there have been some successes in usable security. Today, anti-phishing technology is widely deployed, two-factor authentication is available from many vendors, and many wireless access points are now encrypted [Ho et al., 2010, RSA Security, 2008]. However, usable privacy and security is a young field, with much research only just now beginning to have an impact on real-world practices. With this in mind, we aim to provide the first comprehensive survey of this field, to provide the context of where this field has focused, in order to project what challenges and opportunities lie ahead. We hope that this document will serve as a road map for future research in this important field.

1.1   WHY USABLE PRIVACY AND SECURITY IS HARD

Modern society depends on computers, and that dependence comes with risks. Security research exists largely for the purpose of reducing the risks related to deliberate attacks. Until the mid-1990s, most research in security was focused on technical issues—for example, developing basic cryptographic protocols and bug-free implementations. As public adoption of networked computers increased dramatically in the 1990s, attackers quickly learned that they could evade many technical protection measures by directly targeting users. Meanwhile, users frequently did not employ the available technical solutions because they were too difficult to use.

Today there has been clear success in a few specific areas of secure computer operation. For example, end-user systems are more secure and easier-to-use than their predecessors, and many users are able to rely on managed cloud-based services and mobile devices that automatically apply security patches, rather than having to maintain their own secure systems.

At the same time, the threats facing users and organizations have increased dramatically. The increased reliance on computing systems, combined with the increase in storage densities, means that a single attacker or incident can have far greater consequences then in the past. Many more devices also need securing and, as a result, the uses of passwords have also multiplied: today televisions, cable and Internet TV adapters, telephones, and even electronic door locks can all have passwords where none of these devices had them a decade ago. Since security software cannot always make the correct decision on behalf of users, users are routinely forced to be aware of security and privacy issues and to make decisions for themselves. And they need to manage the privacy and security of their personal information, shared on an ever-growing set of social media, mobile, and cloud computing platforms, against threats that ten years ago were less apparent. For example, the widespread use of advertiser-supported communications platforms means that the privacy interests of users may be directly opposed to the interests of the organizations providing the service.

One of the early influential papers in usable security [Whitten and Tygar, 1999] identified five properties that made usable security "problematic." They were:

1. **The Unmotivated User Property:** "People do not generally sit down at their computers wanting to manage their security; rather, they want to send email, browse web pages, or download software, and they want security in place to protect them while they do those things."

2. **The Abstraction Property:** "[S]ecurity policies…are systems of abstract rules. …The creation and management of such rules is an activity that programmers take for granted, but which may be alien and unintuitive to many members of the wider user population."

3. **The Lack of Feedback Property:** "The need to prevent dangerous errors makes it imperative to provide good feedback to the user, but providing good feedback for security management is a difficult problem."

4. **The Barn Door Property:** "Once a secret has been left accidentally unprotected, even for a short time, there is no way to be sure that it has not already been read by an attacker."

5. **The Weakest Link Property:** "If an [attacker] can exploit a single error, the game is up. This means that users need to be guided to attend to all aspects of their security, not left to proceed through random exploration as they might with a word processor or a spreadsheet [application]."

Although more than a decade old, this list still provides valuable insight. It captures the idea that protecting privacy and security is a practical problem for users, but it is just one of many that users must negotiate in order to accomplish their goals [Beautement et al., 2008, Dourish et al., 2004]. Such broad goals compound the UPS problem, making if difficult for security technologies to flexibly be balanced and applied across a broad range of contexts.

1.2 WHY USABLE SECURITY RESEARCH IS HARD

Systems that cost more to operate because of poor usability or poor security should be at a disadvantage. Likewise, vendors naturally wish to increase the usability and the security of their computer systems (although perhaps not both at the same time). As a result, we expect that both the usability and security of computer systems should naturally increase over time due to market forces.

The goal of academic research in usable security should be to help speed the discovery (and therefore the adoption) of techniques that simultaneously improve both usability and security. Research does this by developing underlying theories that are both explanatory and generative, discovering and validating new techniques, and creating pedagogies for training future practitioners. Ideally, research should allow new UPS techniques to be rapidly tested and either improved or discarded in the lab, rather than having developers test those ideas on unwitting customers.

Confounding this goal are challenges that arise when performing UPS research—many of which are not present in either pure usability or pure security research. In writing this review we have identified several of these challenges, which we identify below:

1. **The Interdisciplinary Challenge:** The usable security field is inherently interdisciplinary, mixing the methods and outcomes of Human Computer Interaction (HCI) with the very different methods and outcomes of information security and privacy. Often, it is easier for specialists to work in one area or the other, rather than trying to blend the two.

2. **The Challenge of Familiarity:** We suspect that research in UPS is complicated by research on devices that people use every day. Because developers and security experts alike must have some familiarity with UPS problems, and may even have tried to solve some of them, they may believe that solutions are impossible. Worse, solutions that are elegant and intuitive frequently appear obvious after the fact, which minimizes the challenging work in producing them. As a result, major advances are frequently under-appreciated.

3. **The Interrelation Challenge:** Usable technologies frequently impact the underlying security and privacy mechanisms. Often a "simple" system is either not secure at all or is very secure—but not very usable. We do not believe usability and security are necessarily in conflict, merely that the goals of security and usability interact in complex ways with each other, presenting trade-offs and design decisions that must be balanced to provide the most effective overall solution. This interrelation makes understanding those trade-offs more challenging than considering each in isolation.

4. **The User Evaluation Challenge:** While users can be interviewed or tested to determine the usability of a system, users are not in a position to evaluate the security of the system or of their own behavior. Yet, perceptions of security also have an important impact on the way that technology is used and the extent to which it is adopted. For example, Sun et al. [2011] evaluated why users refused to use the OpenID single sign-on system and found that many rejected the system because they thought it was less secure than typing a password. In fact, OpenID may make the user less susceptible to phishing because the password is typed less often. However, OpenID may introduce new security vulnerabilities because of protocol complexity or implementation errors. The inability of users to evaluate security properties complicates experimental design. Additionally, while user studies traditionally rely on user reports or observations to infer usability problems with systems, users are generally not able to describe accurately security problems they have experienced [Rader et al., 2012].

5. **The Ecological Validity Challenge:** A second evaluation challenge is evaluating the use of usable security systems. Because security is a secondary task, there are fears that alerting the user to the purpose of the study may prime the user and result in skewed results. Social scientists use the phrase "ecological validity" to describe the extent to which research findings can be generalized to settings outside the laboratory. Serious concerns regarding ecological validity have been raised on many UPS studies because subjects are frequently primed to consider security (whereas outside the laboratory they may not be), and because laboratory studies necessarily expose subjects to significantly higher rates of attack than people experience in the wild. This issue of ecological validity is addressed directly by Fahl et al. [2013], who found that priming was not an issue in a password study, but priming might still be at issue in other domains. Another concern is that the primary purpose of security systems is to defeat intentional attacks, so realistic evaluation of usable security systems should require that the systems (and the people using them) be subject to realistic attacks. Yet, such attacks

are still relatively rare for any individual, thus participants may suspect that such attacks are part of the study, or may not expect them to be possible during a study.

6. **The Adversary Modeling Challenge:** Unlike traditional work in HCI, security exists in the context of an adversary whose goals are aligned against those of the user. This creates a challenge for researchers, who need to reason about and model the way that adversaries will attack users. It likewise makes it difficult to understand how user behaviors can be leveraged to attack systems. Users' perceptions of adversaries can also impact their behavior [Wash, 2010]. For example, users may think that their accounts are not interesting to a hacker, who they expect are after "bigger fish," and as a result may not be willing to expend significant effort in protecting their accounts.

7. **The Technology Velocity Challenge:** Another challenge in this field is the speed with which the underlying technology keeps changing. Current UPS research must be done with current operating systems, current web browsers, and current websites. It is hard to replicate work because the underlying technology keeps evolving and because there is an acceptance bias against replication. Studies done with toy systems may be replicable, but they lack external validity. Finally, review committees may be hesitant to publish studies performed on software that is no longer in use. Jaferian et al. discuss this problem in detail [Jaferian et al., 2011].

8. **The Customer Challenge:** Who is the customer for research in usable security? Should researchers target the security of groups or of individuals? How are the results of research integrated or sold? Is usable security something that is added to existing products or built into new ones? Whose role is it to educate in this field? Who is responsible for paying for it? Is computer security like public health? Are secure systems a public good? If so, is usability an inherent part of security, or is it something else?

   Answering these questions is critical for sustaining UPS as a field. Usability is something that computer vendors have traditionally competed with, while security is traditionally seen as a core infrastructure that should be shared. Vendors do not compete on who has the more secure Secure Socket Layer/Trusted Layer Security (SSL/TLS) implementation, for example; should security user interfaces be similarly standardized?

   The customer challenge directly impacts how UPS research should be funded. Security research has traditionally been funded to solve specific problems or create new capabilities, whereas the goal of usability research typically results in design guidelines and an understanding of how to create better tools.

Despite the challenges, a substantial amount of usable security research has been performed over the past decade. This research has resulted in improved techniques and systems that have made the world a safer, more trustworthy and better place.

1.3   THIS BOOK

This book traces the growing interest and major themes that have emerged over the past 15 years in usable privacy and security research (UPS). Our goal is to present these efforts not as a series of individual contributions, but as a systematic body of work produced by a global research community that spans academia and industry. To that end, we distinguish validated research findings from the many other publications in the area. Finally, we outline a clear agenda for future research.

To date, the agenda of the UPS community has been remarkably consistent: the design, construction, and deployment of systems that people can use to secure computers and personal information. Much of this work has required applied research in perception, risk analysis [Sheng et al., 2010], and other cognitive factors. Transitioning work from the research lab to industry has been uneven. In some cases, commercial adoption has clearly been influenced by the academic research, and we discuss these examples when known. In others, its unclear how much impact the research has had on consumer technologies.

Much of the research is young, and its impact is still unclear. For example, graphical authentication has been a major theme in usable security for the past decade, with numerous schemes, papers, student projects, and patents [Biddle et al., 2012]. Much of this research might have seemed inconsequential—until Google deployed graphical authentication on Android phones and Microsoft put it in Windows 8. Thus, our goal is to survey the broad set of research themes, whether the results have yet transitioned to practice or not.

Looking forward, this book explores the challenges and opportunities facing the community of usable privacy and security researchers over the next decade. These challenges include: crafting a community-wide research agenda; identifying opportunities to make the research relevant to industry; shining attention on important but underrepresented topics; and crafting an approach for teaching usable security to students and practitioners.

1.4   METHODOLOGY

To create this book, we began by reviewing and categorizing every paper that has been published at the Symposium on Usable Privacy and Security (SOUPS), the Usability, Psychology, and Security (UPSEC) workshops, the Workshop on Usable Security (USEC), and the workshops on security at the ACM Human Factors and Computing Systems (CHI) conferences. We also performed an in-depth literature review using the ACM and IEEE digital libraries, as well as reviewing the lists of publications on websites of major researchers in the field and the HCISec Bibliography (Ponnurangam 2008). We performed keyword searches through the last five years of papers presented at the ACM Conference on Computer and Communications Security (ACM CCS), CHI and the ACM Symposium on User Interface Software and Technology (UIST), as well as the IEEE Security and Privacy and USENIX Security conferences. We also extensively traced references. Obviously (and unfortunately), such as this cannot list every notable publication in the field. Nevertheless, we have done our best to include the field's significant publications. We invite the authors of publications that we have missed to notify us; we will maintain an updated list on our website.

1.5   SCOPE

Some aspects of usable security will not be covered by this book.

This book will largely avoid reviewing how software implementation errors may compromise user security or privacy. This is an important part of the overall security picture, but covering it here would expand this book to include literature in programming practices, formal specifications, bug-finding, software validation, and other topics that have been widely discussed elsewhere.

A related difficulty in discussing implementation errors is that it is often not possible to distinguish an actual *error* from policy disagreements between developers. For example, popular web browsers do not consistently implement so-called "private browsing modes," but it is unclear if the differences are intentional or not [Aggarwal et al., 2010].

Additionally, while many research themes overlap with those in traditional information security and privacy, we will focus primarily on work that has occurred within the UPS community, with results that focus on users' needs, evaluations, and impact. For example, while there is a large literature on access control, we focus on the work that understands how users share and protect information and utilize access control systems, of which there is considerably less.

1.6   DEFINITIONS

1.6.1   SECURITY

There are many definitions for computer security, information security, cybersecurity, and related topics. The International Organization for Standards (ISO) and International Electrotechnical Commission (IEC) have developed a series of information security standards in the ISO/IEC 27000 series. Common to many of these definitions is the notion that security includes the "preservation of confidentiality, integrity and availability of information" [ISO/IEC, 2012]—the so-called "CIA" model. The standard goes on to say that implementing this model typically requires other properties, "such as authenticity, accountability, non-repudiation, and reliability can also be involved." That is, information security assures that private information will not be unintentionally released or modified, and that it will be available for use when it is needed.

In the first issue of *Security & Privacy Magazine*, Matt Bishop provides an expansive definition of computer security that includes the security of network infrastructure, such as routers and domain servers, as well as end points (e.g., computers) [Bishop, 2003]. He describes security as a process which identifies security requirements, develops policy to assure those requirements, and mechanisms to implement that policy. Bishop's description of security contains a significant amount of software assurance: not only must a firewall be properly configured to implement the desired policy, but it must be properly implemented "so that it will not fail in its intended task."

For our purpose of understanding usable privacy and security research, these definitions are overly expansive, because they include not just security, but *reliability engineering*, *safety engineering*, and other elements required for ongoing and unsurprising operation of computer systems.

ISO/IEC 2382-8 has a more limited definition, defining computer security as "the protection of *data* and *resources* from accidental or malicious acts, usually by taking appropriate actions." It adds: "NOTE: these acts may be modification, destruction, access, disclosure, or acquisition if not authorized." [ISO/IEC, 1998]

This definition does a better job of capturing what makes usable privacy and security hard— an adversary that that can attack the users of computers or otherwise exploit usability problems. Sometimes the adversary is a hostile, malicious adversary; sometimes the adversary is the authorized user, who compromises systems or their data by accident.

1.6.2 USABILITY

Usability is defined as "the extent to which a product can be used by specified users to achieve specified goals with effectiveness, efficiency, and satisfaction in a specified context of use" (ISO 9241). Shneiderman [2003] further characterizes usability of a system or interface as involving the following concerns:

- **Learn-Ability:** The time for typical users to learn the actions relevant to a set of tasks

- **Efficiency:** How long it takes users to perform typical tasks

- **Errors:** The rate of errors users make when performing tasks

- **Memorability:** How users can retain their knowledge of the system over time

- **Subjective Satisfaction:** How users like the various aspects of the system

Thus, there is no single metric for determining the usability of a system and comparing designs or systems against each other. Evaluating usability requires understanding the users, their needs and tasks, and how well the system meets those various aspects. The field of Human Computer Interaction advocates achieving usable systems through various user-centered design practices that focus on determining usability requirements early in the life cycle of a product, and iteratively prototyping and evaluating whether designs achieve those requirements. Much like security, usability is a non-functional requirement that is best addressed throughout the creation of a product rather than added on after the fact.

1.6.3 PRIVACY

The concepts and enforcement of privacy have a long history, built upon early legal definitions, such as Warren and Brandeis in the U.S. detailing the right of individuals to "be let alone" [Warren and Brandeis, 1890]. Within computing, much work in privacy has focused on data privacy, reflecting the right of an individual to control the accuracy, use, and distribution of digital information about themselves [Westin, 1970]. Social perspectives define privacy as a boundary regulation process, where people regulate their interaction with others [Altman, 1974]. Other definitions emphasize the contextual nature of privacy, where what is considered private vs. public information is dependent on the norms of behavior of a situation [Nissenbaum, 2004]. Thus, privacy is a rich and difficult-to-define concept, with differing needs and concepts depending on the domain.

One of the challenges of addressing privacy within UPS is that HCI researchers and security researchers have different views of the appropriate needs and mechanisms for providing privacy. Often, security mechanisms ensure that privacy is maintained. For example, access control policies and encryption can ensure information is seen only by those with permission, and protected from others. Yet, end users often do not make the distinction between security and privacy tasks. For end users, both security and privacy technologies are about protecting a person and their information from those who should not have it, and allowing access to services and people who are desired. Thus, research on privacy, even from a social and behavioral perspective, can help to inform the design of security mechanisms that meet user needs.

1.7 RELATED SURVEYS AND STUDIES

Although this is the first survey of UPS as a field that we are aware of, other surveys have covered specific areas of the UPS enterprise in greater depth.

Iachello and Hong [2007] summarize privacy in HCI with a comprehensive survey with 30 years of references appearing between 1977 and 2007, a total of more than 300 references in all. The authors note that the primary challenge of addressing privacy has been the need to expand traditional HCI concerns, such as cognitive science, to include new domains, such as economics and law. The authors identify five challenges facing HCI practitioners that wish to address privacy concerns.

- The development of better interaction techniques and standard defaults that users can easily understand,

- The development of stronger analysis techniques and survey tools,

- The documentation of the effectiveness of design tools, and the creation of a 'privacy toolbox,'

- The development of organizational support for managing personal data, and

- The development of a rigorous theory of acceptance dynamics of users, specifically related to privacy. [Iachello and Hong, 2007]

Since that survey in 2007, the research on privacy has continued to expand. One reason is that many of the prototype systems in social and mobile computing that earlier work investigated have become common, everyday applications. Researchers are now able to investigate many more real-world perceptions, needs, and behaviors because these devices and applications are widely used and integrated into hundreds of millions of people's lives. Thus, we highlight some of this more recent work in social media, mobile and location-based systems, and Web privacy in this book.

Biddle et al. [2012] presented a comprehensive survey of the first 12 years of graphical authentication techniques. They concluded that there are "few schemes that deliver on the original promise of addressing the known problems with text passwords." Forward progress, the authors suggest, requires that research "be conducted and presented in a manner allowing systematic examination and comparison of each scheme's main characteristics, showing how each meets the usability and security requirements of specific target environments."

Arguably Biddle et al. [2012]'s plea was taken up by Bonneau et al. [2012b], a meta analysis that evaluated "two decades of proposals to replace text passwords for general-purpose user authentication on the web using a broad set of 25 usability, deployability, and security benefits that an ideal scheme might provide." The authors conclude that "graphical and cognitive schemes offer only minor improvements over passwords and thus have little hopes of displacing them." Although these conclusions are important in their own right, the authors' lasting contribution is likely to be the detailed methodology that is developed and presented for comparing different authentication schemes.

Hidalgo and Alvarez [2011] presented a 70-page analysis of the Completely Automated Public Turing test to tell Computers and Humans Apart (CAPTCHA), a technique designed for the purpose of making computers easy to use by people, and harder to use by malicious bots. The authors presented CAPTCHA history, their design, evaluation, and subversion. We present a minimal treatment of CAPTCAHs in Section 3.1.7.

There have been a few studies or reports advocating the need for a usable security research agenda. As mentioned in the introduction, U.S. Department of Homeland Security [2009] resulted from a series of meetings with security experts in 2008. Concurrently with the DHS project, The U.S. National Academies convened a workshop on Usability, Security, and Privacy of Computer Systems; the workshop report was published in Steering Committe on the Usability, Security, and Privacy of Computer Systems [2010].

C H A P T E R   2

A Brief History of Usable Privacy and Security Research

In this chapter we discuss the major arc of UPS research over the past four decades.

2.1   EARLY WORK (1975–1995)

Saltzer and Schroeder's seminal 1975 work on the design of computer security mechanisms is widely seen as the first to observe that computer systems must be usable to be secure. The paper identified "psychological acceptability" as one of eight design principles for building systems that can protect information.[1]

Saltzer and Schroeder [1975] provided this definition:

> **Psychological Acceptability:** It is essential that the human interface be designed for ease of use, so that users routinely and automatically apply the protection mechanisms correctly. Also, to the extent that the user's mental image of his protection goals matches the mechanisms he must use, mistakes will be minimized. If he must translate his image of his protection needs into a radically different specification language, he will make errors.

That is, there are two aspects of psychological acceptability: user interfaces that promote ease-of-use; and correspondence between internal system mechanisms and user mental models. Norman [1983] makes a similar observation, presenting design rules for accommodating user error. Computer users tend to make two kinds of errors: *slips*, when the user's intention is correct but an error was made in the execution; and *mistakes*, in which the user's intended action was itself in error.

Following Saltzer and Schroeder [1975], academics gave minimal attention to the usability of security mechanisms. The sole exception being the usability of password authentication schemes, and here, usability and security were seen as inherently in conflict. Morris and Thompson [1979]'s article "Password Security" noted that the goal of passwords was to provide "security at minimal inconvenience to the users of the system" Nielsen [1993, p. 42] notes in a somewhat resigned tone that security realities frequently require that systems be made less helpful than they might otherwise be; the example is password authentication, which must give the same feedback

---

[1] In 2009, Saltzer and Kaashoek revisited the 1975 design principles, taking the opportunity to substitute the name "Principle of Least Astonishment" for "psychological acceptability" [Saltzer and Kaashoek, 2009]; we use the original terminology.

whether the username is valid or not, otherwise an attacker can probe the system to determine a list of valid usernames, and then target those usernames for a password-guessing attack. (Today the costs and benefits have changed significantly: it has become so easy for attackers to learn usernames that system security must be based entirely on the password, and, as a result, many systems will provide users with feedback as to whether or not the password is valid either in the interest of usability or as a consequence of implementing another security scheme.)

Security and usability need not be inherently contradictory—not even when it comes to passwords, as we discuss below. Over the past two decades we have learned that they can be aligned, but that success requires attention to both.

Karat [1989] showed how human-factors engineering approaches developed for mainframe applications—techniques that included user interviews, paper mock-ups, user studies of prototypes, and eventual field studies—could be applied equally well to security applications, improving their usability without negatively impacting their security. The application was a single-sign-on solution that had been developed by IBM for internal use. Significantly, the paper was presented at the annual meeting of the Human Factors Society, rather than at a security conference: the security community at the time had little interest in usability issues.

2.2   THE BIRTH OF UPS (1995–2000)

In 1996, Zurko and Simon published a position paper "User-Centered Security" at the New Security Paradigm Workshop [Zurko and Simon, 1996] that identified three categories for researchers to explore in pursuing a "user-friendly" security agenda: "applying usability testing and techniques to secure systems; developing security models and mechanisms for user-friendly systems; and considering user needs as a primary design goal at the start of secure system development."

Zurko and Simon's argument was market-centered: "users will not purchase or use security products they cannot understand." To create understandable systems, they proposed an agenda consisting of: usability testing; model-building; and addressing UPS issues during design, rather than adding it as an afterthought.

The need to have clearly articulated models and mechanisms, and to address issues during the design phase, had long been identified as key requirements for both building secure systems and for building systems that were usable. The key difference proposed by Zurko and Simon was applying these ideas concurrently—and specifically applying usability requirements on the secure design. Perhaps the most radical idea, at least for the security community, was the need to conduct formal usability testing of security mechanisms to establish not their usability, *per se*, but their security. This represented a significant departure from the established practice of security designers creating terminology, user interfaces, and other security mechanisms that were assumed to be understandable and easy-to-use, and then loosing those new mechanisms on users—sometimes world-wide—without any testing at all.

Today we can expand Zurko and Simon's agenda to include case studies, large-scale data collection from the field (both of user actions and current security threats), and the analysis of economic motivations. Also required are research on techniques for transferring research from the laboratory into the marketplace—perhaps a usability problem of a different kind.

In 1999 three landmark UPS papers set the UPS research agenda for the following decade.

- "Why Johnny Can't Encrypt: a usability evaluation of PGP 5.0" [Whitten and Tygar, 1999] reported the results of usability testing of an email encryption tool for the Macintosh operating system that had received very positive views in the popular press. "Johnny" is one of the first research publications in which a commercially available security tool was subject to laboratory testing by someone other than the tool's creator. The study subjects were given a scenario that they could only complete by using and understanding the encryption software.

  None of the "Johnny" subjects were able to complete the task. Seven sent email messages encrypted with their own public keys (the messages could not be read by the recipient); three accidentally emailed the secret without encryption; one forgot their passphrase during the test, and one was unable to encrypt anything at all. Clearly the task—using PGP 5.0—was too difficult for the subjects. This was taken as the first scientific validation of the widespread perception that even easy-to-use email encryption programs were too complex to be used by the general public.

  Ironically, one of the critical elements missing from the "Johnny" test was an adversary. That is, "Johnny" was literally a usability test of a piece of security software. As such, it tested to see if the software protected users against a passive, eavesdropping adversary, but it did not test to see if the software could protect the users against an adversary that employed active measures to read the contents of their confidential email messages. We will return to this issue in Section 5.2.

- "Users are Not the Enemy" [Adams and Sasse, 1999] discussed how users are frequently blamed for compromising system security—for example, by choosing bad passwords. The authors performed a study of factors impacting compliance with corporate password policies at two organizations in the U.K. The study was motivated by previous research that found that users were generally picking poor passwords (short and easy-to-guess) and that they were not changing the passwords unless forced to do so. Even when technical measures attempt to enforce stronger security practices (e.g., rejecting dictionary words and forcing users to change passwords), many users find ways to overcome these measures (e.g., by picking minor variants of dictionary words, and by toggling between a set of favorite passwords). The purpose of the Adams and Sasse project was to find out why users were being so hostile to security.

  The authors found that users were frequently challenged to comply with conflicting requirements of their organizations. For example, many users had to remember multiple passwords and change them frequently, which resulted in users picking passwords that were easy to guess. But the authors also found that users had confused and often incorrect beliefs regarding what makes a password weak or strong, and that users did not understand the actual threats to computer security that their organizations faced. "Users are often told as little as possible because security departments see them as "inherently insecure." One clear finding from this study is that inadequate knowledge of password procedures, content, and cracking lies at the root of users' "insecure" behaviors."

The paper argued that users can become the first line of defense when the rationale for security measures are explained to the users. This article laid the framework for more than a decade of field studies of users—security in the wild—which verges at times on ethnography. The valuable purpose behind this line of inquiry is to give security professionals both qualitative and quantitative data about security as it is in the world, rather than security as it is imagined by security professionals.

- "The Design and Analysis of Graphical Passwords" [Jermyn et al., 1999] introduced to a broad audience the idea of using graphical passwords as an alternative authentication scheme with a working prototype called "Draw A Secret," in which the user authenticated by drawing a design with a stylus or finger on a matrix displayed on a touch screen (Figure 2.1). (See Section 3.1.3 for a discussion of graphical authentication schemes.)

The primary usability problem that DAS attempts to resolve is the difficulty entering passwords on portable devices. (Jermyn et al. were concerned with personal digital assistants (PDAs), as smart phones were not widely available in 1999.) The authors suggested that their scheme might actually be more secure than passwords, since it is possible for users to chose more complex drawings than passwords, and it should be more difficult for an adversary to build a dictionary of popular drawings, since the stronger security of PDAs would make password sniffing more difficult. These conjectures turned out to be wrong. Because DAS transformed complex drawings into a sequence of grid crossing (for matching), the resulting strings had considerably less variation than the original drawings. Worse, users favored simple drawings over complex ones, so it turned out to be relatively straightforward to build a dictionary of popular drawings. Subsequent research in graphical passwords found that allowing users to choose their own graphical passwords ("user choice") invariably results in graphical passwords that have similar diversity problems to text passwords, resulting in passwords that are easier to guess or crack [Oorschot and Thorpe, 2008, Thorpe and van Oorschot, 2004].

These papers neatly bracketed the usable security agenda for the following decade: understanding and improving technical failings of today's security tools; user modeling; and the developing and evaluation of authentication approaches. As a set, they see the computer systems of the day as having overall good usability, but not for the specific mechanisms that relate to security, and see users as being not the "enemy" of security but as reasonable actors whose short-term goal is to get their job done and for whom maintaining security and privacy are not primary tasks.

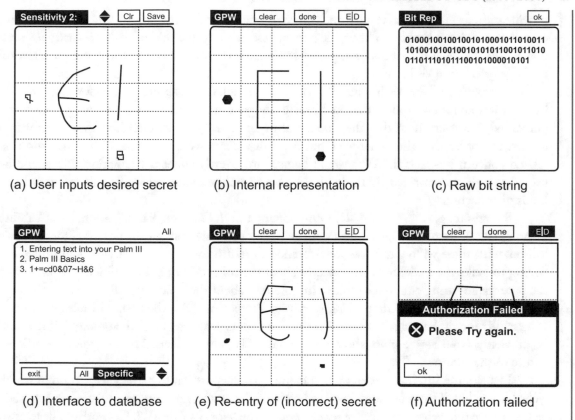

(a) User inputs desired secret

(b) Internal representation

(c) Raw bit string

(d) Interface to database

(e) Re-entry of (incorrect) secret

(f) Authorization failed

Figure 2.1: "A password is created by drawing the secret on the display as shown in (a). Both the internal representation of the input password showing the cells covered by the user's drawing and the derived key are depicted in (b) and (c), respectively. To apply a symmetric cryptographic function to records in the database (shown in (d)), the user selects the records and then re-inputs the DAS password. If the encryption of a known cleartext with the input password matches the stored ciphertext created during initialization, then the symmetric cryptographic routine, $E_k(x)$, is applied to the selected Records. Otherwise the user is prompted to re-enter the DAS secret." (Jermyn et al. [1999, Figure 3].)

These papers also presented a hopeful, optimistic view of the usable security: the belief that through the application of scientific, user-centered research, it should be possible to create a new generation of systems that are both more secure and easier-to-use.

At the same time that work was progressing on usable security, a parallel thread of policy work resulted in the emergence of usable privacy as a research discipline. Control of personal information has long been recognized as an important part of privacy in the modern age [Westin, 1970]. Privacy had also long been associated with computer security, since security mechanisms provide the necessary data access controls through which privacy is technically implemented. Nevertheless, the driver that brought usable privacy research into the fold of usable security research may be the simple fact that both happened at the same time as a result of the commercialization of the World Wide Web.

The nature of the Web made it possible for retailers to capture tremendous amounts of information about consumers that had previously gone unrecorded—not just what consumers purchased, but every item that they looked at in an online store, which items were put into a basket, the order that the items were put in, which items were later taken out, and so on. A related concern was that the Web would be used to covertly collect information that would be used for marketing or price discrimination, and that children were especially vulnerable to these kinds of collection.

Surveys (e.g., Ackerman et al. [1999], Georgia Tech Graphic, Visualization, and Usability Center [1998]) found that consumers were generally ambivalent about the potential for data collection, with some willing to allow for collection in return for improved services and others not willing to make the trade. Specific concerns about the collection of information on children, and the potential of using children to collect information about their parents, led directly to the passage in the U.S. of the Children's Online Privacy Protect Act. But the nascent Internet industry successfully fought back against broader attempts at data policy regulation, arguing that it would be unwieldy, would stifle innovation, and would be largely ineffectual due to the international nature of the Internet.

Instead, the Internet settled upon a market-based approach to privacy regulation in which websites would tell users of their practices involving data collection and use and users would then be free to use the website services or go elsewhere. The World Wide Web Consortium developed the Platform for Privacy Preferences (P3P) [Hochheiser, 2002] as a tool by which websites could present their data use policies to users in an machine-readable format, with the goal that web browsers would then automatically digest this information and present it to users. This technical standard set the stage for more than a decade of research on P3P to see if the system, as developed and deployed, could actually be used by consumers to realize their privacy choices, and if it was properly being used by websites to document their actual practices.

2.3   CREATION OF THE UPS RESEARCH COMMUNITY (2000–2005)

At the start of 2000, it seemed quite possible that the interest in usable security would come largely from security researchers and practitioners. "Johnny" was presented at a premiere computer security research venue, while "Users" was published in one of the leading magazines of academic computer science. A popular metaphor for secure systems was that they were like a chain, only as strong as the weakest link. If humans were in fact the weakest link, the systems would only be securable if security researchers focused on building systems that were usable.

But UPS research remained a research specialty. In part this may be because only a few security researchers had the necessary background to perform user studies; and because only a few HCI researchers had the necessary security experience.

To solve this problem, a few academics that were predisposed to usable security issues created a series of opportunities for publishing research and meeting face-to-face. The first formal gathering took place at the Workshop on Human-Computer Interaction and Security Systems at the premiere conference in HCI, the ACM Conference on Human Factors in Computing Systems (CHI) [Patrick et al., 2003]. Organized by Patrick, Long, and Flinn, the workshop heralded the beginning of a field that would pair user studies with security analysis. Among the topics explored by the papers presented were the usability of ATM machines that featured biometric verification [Coventry et al., 2003]; a user study of the KaZaA P2P file-sharing interface, with the disturbing research conclusion that poor design choices in the interface and implementation encouraged people to share more information than they wished, and then hid this fact from users [Good and Krekelberg, 2003]; and an experiment evaluating the impact on consumer trust in websites when those sites are augmented with photos of attractive people [Riegelsberger et al., 2003]. (A relationship was discovered between attractiveness and trust, but it was not straightforward.)

Based on the success of the CHI workshop, Cranor, Ackerman, Monrose, Patrick and Sadeh organized a larger Workshop on Usable Privacy and Security Software (WUPSS), which was held at the DIMACS Center at Rutgers in July 2004. That two-day workshop featured 17 papers and five short talks chosen from submitted abstracts. Based on feedback from participants, Cranor organized the Symposium on Usable Privacy and Security software, first held at Carnegie Mellon University in July 2005 and held annually ever since. SOUPS combined refereed papers, topical speakers, discussion panels, and breakout sessions and quickly became the premiere publication venue for usable security research.

Concurrent with the first SOUPS, *IEEE Security & Privacy Magazine* featured a special issue on usable security [Cranor and Garfinkel, 2004]. Publishing restrictions allowed only a few articles to be published; the remainder were invited to submit chapters to a book on usable security that was published later that year [Cranor and Garfinkel, 2005].

2.4   MECHANICAL TURK

Another advance that has had significant impact on the research in UPS is Amazon's Mechanical Turk platform. Mechanical Turk (MTurk) is a crowd sourcing platform where people can post small jobs that users (referred to as Turkers) can complete in return for small payments.

Just as MTurk has become a valued platform for conducting user studies within HCI and the social sciences [Kittur et al., 2008], it has also been used by UPS researchers for investigating a broad range of topics, such as privacy configuration (e.g., Besmer et al. [2010]), CAPTCHAs (e.g., Bursztein et al. [2014]) and password chocies (e.g., Kelley et al. [2012]). Mechanical Turk has enabled researchers to conduct significantly larger studies, more quickly and cost effectively than was previously possible [Buhrmester et al., 2011]. For example, a recent study of password meters utilized 2,931 participants [Ur et al., 2012a], far more than could reasonably be brought into a university laboratory.

The use of MTurk has also raised questions of the validity of such studies and the bias of the users on this platform (see the discussion of Mazurek et al. [2013], p. 32). Indeed, the demographics of users on MTurk does differ from the general population, and even the general Internet population. Nevertheless, the diversity of MTurk is still better than many other viable recruiting techniques, such as using samples of college students [Buhrmester et al., 2011, Mason and Suri, 2012]. Additional concerns stem from whether "Turkers" take the tasks seriously, providing flawed or biased data. Studies can be constructed to detect and minimize the impact of such participants, such as through the use of screening questions [Downs et al., 2010] and questions regarding participants' understanding of instructions [Crump et al., 2013].

2.5   CURRENT UPS PUBLISHING VENUES

At the present time (Fall 2014) there exist both specialty venues for usable security work and a growing acceptance of usable security research at traditional venues that specialize in either usability or security.

The Symposium on Usable Privacy and Security (SOUPS) remains the only stand-alone conference devoted solely to the publishing of usable privacy and security research. SOUPS is organized annually by the Carnegie Mellon University's CyLab and is becoming an internationally hosted conference. In addition, the Workshop on Usable Security (USEC), started in 2007, has been co-located with several conferences, including the Workshop Information Security Economics (WISE) in 2012, the Financial Crypto and Data Security (FC) conference in 2013, and The Internet Society's Network and Distributed System Security Symposium (NDSS) in 2014.

Beyond SOUPS, there has been significant interest in usable security issues at other conferences that emphasize interdisciplinary approaches to security:

- **Financial Cryptography (FC)** is an annual conference organized by the International Financial Cryptography Association. The conference's emphasis on the practical aspects of securing financial transactions has a natural overlap with UPS topics such as authentication and phishing. In 2007, FC held a workshop on Usable Security [Dhamija, 2007] (USEC'07), which became the First Conference on Usability, Psychology, and Security in 2008 [UPSEC, 2008] (there was no second). FC continues to have occasional presentations on usable security and hosted USEC 2013.

- **New Security Paradigms Workshop (NSPW)** is an annual conference that explores limitations of current computer security paradigms and solicits papers (with a specific interest in position papers) that promote new ideas. The workshop is designed to provide attendees with significant opportunities for discussion and feedback. With regards to UPS, the conference is notable for having published one of the first significant articles calling for an alignment of usability and security [Zurko and Simon, 1996].

- **Privacy Enhancing Technologies Symposium (PETS)** is an annual conference that solicits "novel technical contributions" on both theoretical and practical aspects of technology that promotes privacy and anonymity. An unusual aspect of the symposium is that it solicits contributions from communities not typically inside of the computer science academy, including law, business, and governmental agencies.

There has also been a growing interest in usable security and privacy topics at some of the premiere security and usability conferences, including:

- **ACM SIGCHI Conference on Human Factors in Computing Systems (CHI)**, the premiere conference on HCI, has become a significant publication venue for research in usable privacy and security, with multiple paper sessions devoted to the topic.

- **ACM Conference on Computer Supported Cooperative Work (CSCW)** has interest in privacy issues related to social media and other collaborative applications.

- **ACM International Joint Conference on Pervasive and Ubiquitous Computing (Ubicomp)** has regularly published research on security and privacy issues related to mobile computing and location-based applications.

Finally, some of the very best UPS papers are now being published at the top-tier computer security conferences, including:

- **ACM Conference on Computer and Communications Security (CCS)**,

- **IEEE Symposium on Security and Privacy (IEEE S&P)**, and

- **USENIX Security Symposium**.

We see these lists as validation by the general security and usability communities that UPS research is important and has relevance beyond the community of UPS researchers.

CHAPTER 3

Major Themes in UPS Academic Research

Much of the UPS research of the past decade mirrors that of applied security work in general—tactical responses to specific problems of the day, rather than long-range strategic research. Tactical research is clearly important, as it addresses current needs and often results in immediate gains. However, literature reviews such as this are better suited to focusing on the longer-term strategic trends, as they represent the greatest opportunity for long-term payoff. Therefore we structure this section thematically, rather than chronologically, and some work that was only of tactical importance is left out. For the remainder we attempted to explain:

- What was the UPS problem, and how did it arise?

- Who was doing the research? In some cases themes were the result of intensive work by a single group that specialized in that area. In other cases, the theme was the result of a broad community effort. We believe that, in general, the most useful work has resulted from research performed at multiple institutions, although it is not clear whether multiple institutions attacked a problem because of its ripeness, or if a problem ripened as a result of multiple research efforts.

- Was the problem resolved? If not, why not?

In the following section we'll look at the few efforts to generalize from these various efforts to a general solution.

3.1 USER AUTHENTICATION

UPS research has been dominated by efforts to improve the ease, reliability, and security of end-user authentication. Researchers have explored ways to improve text passwords, to replace text with graphical passwords, or to supplement them with biometrics or multi-factor authentication. Despite these efforts, it appears that traditional text passwords will remain the dominant form of user authentication for the foreseeable future. We expect that the most successful uses of text passwords will combine them invisibly with anti-fraud measures that consider additional information such as the user's IP address, location, or browser cookies.

3.1.1 TEXT PASSWORDS

Identification by username and authentication by secret password is by far the most common technique for restricting the use of information systems to authorized users. Passwords have the advantages of being well understood and straightforward to implement. Passwords also provide for easy delegation through sharing. The primary weakness of passwords is that they can be learned by an attacker and used to access an account without authorization.

The challenge of using text passwords to secure an account has long been regarded as the prototypical UPS problem, with there being an obvious trade-off between the complexity of a password and the security that the password provides. Cognitive burden is further reduced when a single password is used to access many different computers, and when the password is rarely changed. Once again, strong security would seem to favor the opposite—a different password for each account, so that compromising one does not compromise others, and passwords expire between once a month and once a year, decreasing the window in which a compromised password can be used.

However, this straightforward tradeoff between usability and security is an oversimplification. Florêncio et al. [2014b] observe that there are essentially three attacks against passwords, each with very different requirements for password strength or complexity:

1. *Password stealing:* The attacker can obtain the password directly, using malware such as a keystroke logger or social engineering (including phishing). In these cases password strength does not matter, since the attacker does not need to brute force the password.

2. *Online attack:* The attacker attempts to log in as the user. Online password guessing attacks can be easily defeated with account lockouts when an incorrect password is presented multiple times in a row. With account lockouts even relatively weak passwords are sufficient to deny attackers access to specific accounts.

3. *Offline attack:* It may be possible for the attacker to obtain the system database in which passwords are stored (the "password file"). In general, there are three ways that passwords can be stored in databases: without encryption, with reversable encryption, and as one-way hashes. Password strength is irrelevant if passwords are stored without encryption or if the encryption can be reversed by the attacker. Password strength is only relevant if passwords are stored as one-way hashes. Florêncio et al. [2014b] estimate that passwords must be 10^8 stronger to resist an offline attack than an online attack, and that this "online-offline chasm" will only increase over time as computers get faster (as computer speed does not impact online attacks).

Meanwhile, Zhang et al. [2010] showed that password expiration policies are generally ineffective, as there is sufficient similarity between expired passwords and their user-chosen replacements as to make it straightforward to mount an offline attack against a new password if the expired password is known.

Thus, despite significant attention to password strength and the usability burdens of strong passwords, password strength is only relevant for protecting online accounts that do not employ a lockout system, or to protect accounts of systems where the password file is stolen and the password contains one-way hashes of user passwords. Florêncio et al. [2014b] discuss this issue at length and makes concrete recommendations on approaches for strengthening account security without the need to force users to adopt increasingly stringent passwords.

History of Passwords   Usernames and passwords appear to have been simultaneously invented at the Massachusetts Institute of Technolgy (MIT) as part of the Compatible Time Sharing System (CTSS) project, and at IBM for controlling access to the Sabre reservation system [Head, 2002, McMillan, 2012]. Many early multi-user systems allowed users to establish their own passwords without respect to external requirements.

Hoffman [1969] observed that many accounts on early systems could be compromised through a systematic password guessing attack, noting "in some systems the work factor, or cost, associated with trying different passwords until the right one is found is so small that it is worthwhile for an interested but unauthorized user to do just that."

Metcalfe [1973] also implied that systematic password guessing was a threat to networked systems, warning that: "Individual sites, used to physical limitations on machine access, have not yet taken sufficient precautions toward securing their systems against unauthorized remote use. For example, many people still use passwords which are easy to guess: their fist names, their initials, their host name spelled backwards, a string of characters which are easy to type in sequence (e.g., ZXCVBNM)."

Six years later, Morris and Thompson [1979]'s study of passwords found that 2,831 out of 3,289 of the passwords on the system they examined could be discovered through an offline dictionary attack.

In April 1985, the U.S. Department of Defense published it's "Green Book" *Password Management Guideline* [DOD, 1985]; the National Bureau of Standards (later renamed National Institute of Standards and Technology) followed with FIPS PUB 112, "Password Usage" [US Department of Commerce, 1985]. These documents established the direction of password requirements for the next three decades, setting lifetimes on password use (one year for most passwords, one month for systems requiring high protection); enshrining the concept that a maximum of three password attempts should be allowed before some kind of alarm is generated[1]; and proposing lengths of 6–8 characters, with longer lengths providing higher security. Over time, these rules have been extended to require mixed case, numbers, symbols, and significantly longer passwords—frequently resulting in user frustration. Cheswick [2013] traced many of today's rules that decrease password usability to these documents, and argued that many of the rules developed in the 1980s for password security and articulated in those documents are no longer relevant, as

---

[1] Brostoff and Sasse [2003] recommended that the number of allowable failed attempts could be raised from three to ten without negatively impacting security in a meaningful way, but this proposal seems to have been largely ignored.

complex passwords offer no defense against passwords captured by keystroke loggers, phishing attacks, or compromised system software.

Although early timesharing systems stored cleartext passwords, this approach was not secure, for a bug (or an attack) that revealed the contents of the file resulted in the compromise of every user account. Wilkes [1968] introduced the concept of storing not the passwords themselves, but an encryption of each password. To verify a password the system took the value entered by the user, encrypted it, and compared the encryption to the encryption on file. If the two values matched then, then password entered by the user must match the password originally supplied. Many readers, however, attribute the idea of storing encrypted passwords to Morris and Thompson [1979], who added the idea of further strengthening the stored password with a 12-bit random number (called a "salt"):

> "With this modification, it is likely that the bad guy can spend days of computer time trying to find a password on a system with hundreds of passwords, and find none at all. More important is the fact that it becomes impractical to prepare an encrypted dictionary in advance. Such an encrypted dictionary could be used to crack new passwords in milliseconds when they appear." [Morris and Thompson, 1979]

The Unix approach of storing password hashes in a file readable to all users led to the development of password "crackers," programs that perform dictionary attacks against encrypted passwords in an attempt to find the matching cleartext password. Password cracking became a tool for finding accounts with weak passwords and was used by both system administrators and attackers. Modern Unix systems attempt to limit the ability of attackers to crack passwords by hiding password hashes in "shadow" password files that are only readable by the system. Attackers that gain superuser status still have an incentive to copy the file and crack the passwords, however, as users frequently use the same password on multiple systems. Meanwhile, attackers have made good on Morris and Thompson's prediction and created "encrypted dictionar[ies] in advance" containing precomputed password hashes. Called "rainbow tables," these dictionaries have proven to be quite effective in cracking databases of passwords that are hashed without a salt.

Bishop and Klein [1995] reported on the results of cracking 5,525 passwords from a population of 13,892 users—roughly 2 in 5—and then evaluated the specific strategies employed both by users to create bad passwords and by crackers to guess them. Rather than allowing users to pick weak passwords, the authors advocated *proactive password checking* and introduced a new Unix password changing system called `passwd+` that checked passwords for weakness before allowing them to be set; password policy was determined by the site administration. This approach is now standard on many operating systems.

Passwords on Contemporary Systems   Today, billions of people world-wide access many password-protected systems that implement numerous password policies. Password policies are frequently the subject of public ridicule and there is an increasing realization that there is a disconnect between the goals of password policies and the effect that the policies actually have on

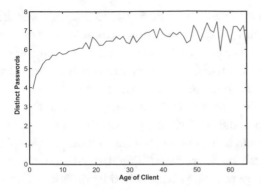

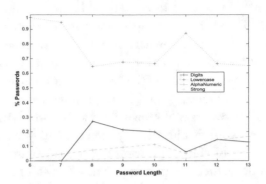

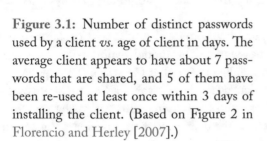

Figure 3.1: Number of distinct passwords used by a client *vs.* age of client in days. The average client appears to have about 7 passwords that are shared, and 5 of them have been re-used at least once within 3 days of installing the client. (Based on Figure 2 in Florencio and Herley [2007].)

Figure 3.2: Different types of passwords as a function of length averaged across all sites. Observe that a clear majority of passwords are lower case letters only. PIN's, or passwords that are purely numeric, account for about 20% of passwords (note that we did not record numeric passwords of length 7 or less). Alphanumeric passwords, consisting of upper case, lower case, and digits constitute a small portion. A tiny minority of passwords are strong, in the sense of containing upper case, lower case, digits, and special characters. (Based on Figure 7 in Florencio and Herley [2007].)

information security. Here, the literature is even less encouraging: problems with passwords have been evident for more than three decades, but the result of research and common sense reasoning has simply been the adoption of increased requirements for password length and character diversity. Long, complex passwords frequently seem to be a signal that organizations use to show their concern for security—the more onerous the password requirements, the greater the concern.

UPS research into passwords falls into roughly four categories:

1. studies of password policies,

2. retrospective studies of password databases that were stolen and publicly leaked,

3. laboratory and field studies of users who are tasked with picking and using passwords, and

4. field studies of actual password usage on operational systems.

Policy Studies   Florêncio and Herley [2010] evaluate password policies at 75 different websites and found that universities and government agencies generally had more stringent password requirements than financial institutions and retailers. The authors hypothesized that organizations that had to compete for users were required to balance usability and security, whereas organizations with websites with a captive user population did not need to balance the two factors.

Schechter et al. [2010] propose that a simple approach to preventing users from picking bad passwords is to keep a list of all passwords used to date and simply prevent users from picking a password that has already been chosen by more than a few people; the authors propose keeping the list of chosen passwords in a count-min sketch data structure. (Popularity-based schemes work best for companies such as Microsoft that have web properties visited by millions of users, although they can be adopted by small websites through the use of single-sign-on systems such as OpenID.)

Florêncio et al. [2014a] propose and analyze a mathematical model that explains in part why many users employ weak, easily guessable passwords. The model hypothesizes that users have a *finite* amount of effort that they can use to manage them; that the stronger the password, the more the mental effort to remember it; and that users do not value all of their password-protected accounts equally. Given these constraints, uniform requirements for strong passwords and prohibitions on password re-use have real costs to the user, in that they decrease the amount of effort available to protect accounts that matter the most. The model proposes three kinds of potential attacks: FULL attacks, in which all of a user's passwords are compromised (e.g., by malware); GROUP attacks, in which a single password is compromised that protects a group of systems; and SINGLE attacks, in which an account is compromised without compromising the password (e.g., by cross-site scripting). Taking into account these factors, the authors then examine the costs and security provided by a number of password management strategies and conclude in part [Florêncio et al., 2014a]:

- Remembering random and unique passwords is infeasible for other than very small portfolios.

- Realistic analysis of password effort allocation requires incorporating attack vectors affecting (1) all accounts, (2) accounts sharing a password, and (3) single accounts.

- While users are typically given advice that would minimize the loss for a specific site, it is in the best interest of users to minimize the expected loss of all of their sites plus the total effort required to achieve that level of expected loss.

- Users can minimize their overall expected loss by using stronger passwords on more important sites and weaker passwords on less important sites.

- Optimal password grouping tends to (i) group together accounts with high value and low probability of compromise and (ii) group together accounts of low value and high compromise probability.

Retrospective Studies   Much of what is known regarding user password choice today comes from the analysis of password databases that were stolen from popular websites and then published anonymously on the Internet. Companies that have been so victimized include Adobe, eHarmony, Gawker, LinkedIn, Sony, and Yahoo!

Surprisingly, in most of these high-profile cases the websites did not employ proper security measures. Some stored passwords in plaintext. Other websites encrypted the passwords with symmetric encryption algorithms using secret keys that were also recovered by the attackers, allowing all of the passwords to be decrypted. Some stored password hashes, but the hashes were not salted, significantly simplifying password cracking and allowing hashed passwords to be directly compared for equivalence. For example, the 32 million passwords stolen and released from RockYou in December 2009 were not encrypted. Florêncio et al. [2014b] provide an analysis of eight leaked password files with between 1.5 M and 150 M accounts, and show that password strength was only relevant for protecting the passwords in one of the data sets, as all of the others could be compromised as a result of the way that the passwords were stored.

Dell'Amico et al. [2010] surveyed three data sets of passwords, two of which had been illegally obtained and publicly posted, and performed both an empirical analysis and mathematical modeling of password strength. The authors concluded that, even though the majority of web passwords are weak, others are strong enough that "even extremely powerful attackers won't be able to guess a substantial percentage of passwords." (The findings are not contradicted by the fact that a sustained offline attack on a single password is likely to succeed.)

Kelley et al. [2012] presented a general critique of the problems inherent in using stolen encrypted passwords for research and provided a metric for measuring password strength of unencrypted passwords by simulating password-cracking algorithms. The authors found that the subset of passwords compliant with a particular composition policy exhibit different characteristics than passwords created by users required to comply with that policy. This implies that users who voluntarily create passwords stronger than the policy requires (and thus end up complying with a specific strong policy) exhibit different password creation behaviors than those who comply with the same strong policy because it is required.

Bonneau et al. [2012c] looked at the security of customer-chosen banking PINs, a special kind of password that can be 4–12 digits in length (but are typically 4 digits), are chosen by the user and typically never changed. Drawing from both databases of compromised accounts and mathematical models of user behavior, the authors show that certain PINs are dramatically more likely than others. Examples of likely PINs include 4-digit years (e.g., 1900 through 2020), simple patterns (e.g., 1234), and keypad patterns (e.g., 1937). The authors wrote that a primary risk of PIN guessbility is not that a specific user will be targeted, but that attackers will be able to compromise a significant fraction of accounts systematically guessing likely PINS—the optimal strategy being to guess 1234 followed by 1990, 1989, 1987, and 1986, after which the account will likely be locked out. (Bonneau and Preibusch [2010] found that 126 out of 150 of most popular identity, e-commerce, and content websites studied failed to implement any kind of account lockout to limit online password guessing, but the study did not consider ATM cards.) The authors propose a blacklist of 100 PINs (e.g., 0101, 0202, 1234, etc.), which, according to their model, reduces the chance of breaking into an account with 6 guess from 1.9% to 0.2%. Further improvements can be achieved with user-specific blacklists (for example, blacklisting the user's birthday in the form of DDMM or MMDD).

Laboratory Studies   Password laboratory studies can include both strict laboratory studies, in which users choose and demonstrate passwords in a controlled environment, and online studies, in which users are asked to access a website or service that was created for the experiment and that the users would not have otherwise accessed. Password creation can be a primary task, or it can appear incidental to another task—for example, establishing a password so that the user can return to an online service. Increasingly, online studies typically use Amazon's Mechanical Turk, although other services are emerging as well.

Komanduri et al. [2011] conducted a user study with more than 5,000 participants and found that 16-character passwords with no other requirements were generally as strong as 8-character passwords that required the use of 4-character classes and a dictionary check. The findings disproved the hope among many password researchers that password length requirements by themselves would cause users to pick passwords that were both easy to remember and hard to guess.

Ur et al. [2012a] assessed the impact of password meters (Figure 3.3) in a laboratory study with 2,931 subjects. The study found that password meters do in fact cause users to change their behavior, and that better passwords come from showing users more stringent meters—i.e., the meters that require characters from many different character classes. "Unfortunately, the scoring systems of meters that we observed in the wild were most similar to our non-stringent meters. This result suggests that meters currently in use on popular websites are not aggressive enough in encouraging users to create strong passwords. However, if all meters a user encountered were stringent, he or she might habituate to receiving low scores and ignore the meter, negating any potential security benefits."

One of the great values in conducting laboratory studies is that they make it possible to test popular notions of ways to improve password security without risking compromise of actual production systems. For example, after the popular XKCD comic recommended that users create strong passwords by combining multiple words to form a passphrase (Figure 3.4), Bonneau and Shutova [2012] found that passphrases created in this manner had significantly less randomness than had been expected, because many users chose the same strings of characters. Surprisingly, long passwords were also more error prone to type: Shay et al. [2012] tested passwords composed from a sequence of three or four English words against random character passwords generated by a computer. The 1,476-participant online study found that long passwords created from English words were not more memorable, took longer to enter, and that users made more entry mistakes than random system-assigned passwords that were shorter but had similar entropy. Shay et al. [2014] presented a follow-up study with 8,143 participants and a cracking algorithm modified

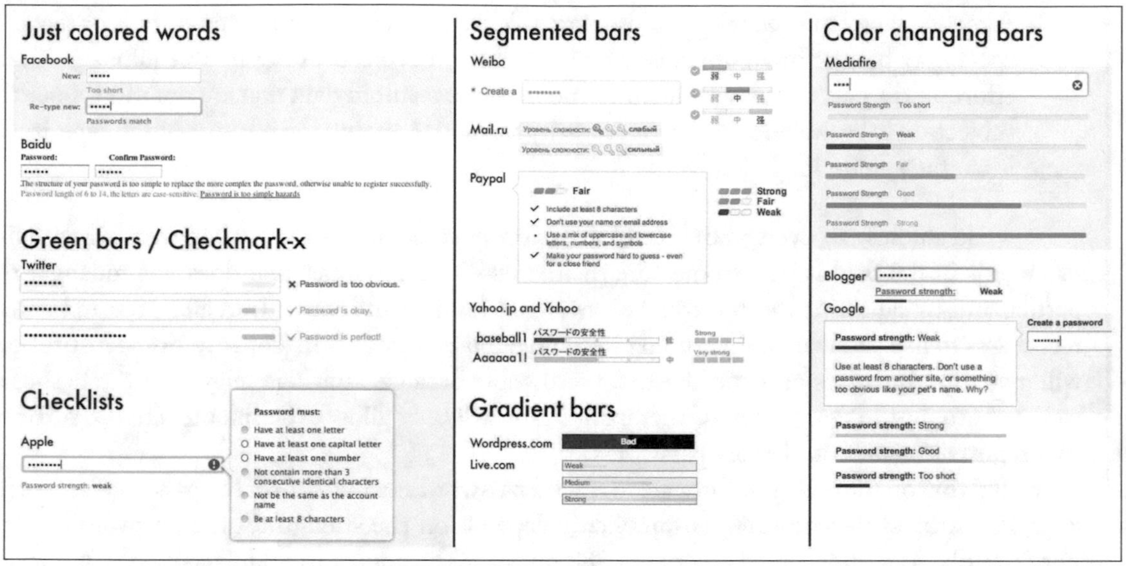

Figure 3.3: A categorized assortment of the 46 unique indicators found across Alexa's 100 most visited global sites [Ur et al., 2012a].

for longer passwords. Unlike the previous study, the 2014 study allowed users to create their own passwords. Among the findings were that common substrings such as "1234" and "password" are present within 1.2% to 4.2% of all passwords. Passwords that included these substrings were more easily cracked than those without them. For example, 43.6% of passwords containing "1234" were cracked while only 13.9% of passwords that did not contain "1234" were cracked.

However, Shay et al. [2012] also found that the majority of users in the online study used some kind of password manager or password storage scheme, eliminating the need for a memorable, easy-to-type password in the first place.

Field Studies   A common criticism of laboratory and online studies is that they may lack *ecological validaity*—that is, the studies may not accurately replicate actual user behavior.

1. Subjects may be less invested in their laboratory passwords than in other passwords (e.g., banking passwords), because they may have little incentive to pick and protect a strong password. This is especially true of studies conducted using Mechanical Turk.

2. Alternatively, users may pick passwords that are stronger than they would normally pick becuase they may be trying to please the investigators or because the users know that they will not need to continue using the strong passwords after the study concludes.

3. A related concern is *priming*—if users are told that the study is about passwords or security, users may behave in an unrealistic manner. But, to avoid priming may require significant effort on the part of the experimenter and may also result in data that are not valid, since the subjects may be unconcerned about security as they think that the purpose of the experiment is to study something else.

Field studies can overcome some of these concerns, but a challenge when working with live passwords in the field is how to measure their strength in a manner that does not endanger the participants by capturing their cleartext passwords. Most institutions will not allow researchers direct access to live passwords, since doing so could put user accounts in jeopardy. Some institutions will give experimenters password hashes, presumably because attackers might get the hashes as well and attempt to crack them. Other institutions will only allow experimenters to use software that reports statistics on the raw passwords.

Relying on the ability of software to crack a password as a measure of the password's strength is problematic, as the measurement implicitly depends on the strength of the password cracker. For example, Yan et al. [2004] recruited 288 out of 300 students in a University of Cambridge first-year science survey course; 95 students assigned to a control group were given "traditional" password advice, 96 students were told to pick a random password consisting of letters and numbers, and 97 were instructed to pick a *passphrase* based on a mnemonic. The passwords were used to access the school's central computing facility. One month later, the experimenters made a copy of the password file and attempted to crack the encrypted passwords and found that they could crack roughly 32% of the passwords in the control group, 8% in the random password group, and 6% of those in the passphrase group. Kuo et al. [2006] critiqued Yan et al. [2004], noting that the strength of the passwords was determined using a password cracker that did not attempt to crack mnemonic passwords. Hypothesizing that users select their mnemonic passwords using phrases that can be readily found on the Internet, the researchers created a 400,000-entry dictionary based on common phrases and found that they could crack a significant number of mnemonic passwords, calling into question Yan et al. [2004]'s conclusions.

The conflict between Yan et al. [2004] and Kuo et al. [2006] also demonstrate one of the inherent difficulties in doing UPS research: it's hard to have an ecologically valid model of the adversary, in part because the adversary adapts when users are given new recommendations.

In addition to its retrospective study, Kelley et al. [2012] also conducted a laboratory study of 12,000 user-generated passwords using Amazon's Mechanical Turk. Users were invited to create passwords according to seven different password-composition policies; the study then evaluated the strength of the passwords using several different password guessing algorithms (including Weir et al. [2009a], which had been previously shown to be able to crack 28%–129% more passwords than John the Ripper, a standard password cracking program). The primary contribution is the demonstration that a requirement for long passwords alone, "with no other restrictions," provided "excellent resistance to guessing" with the tools of the time. The paper also found that entropy alone is not an effective measure of password guessbility.

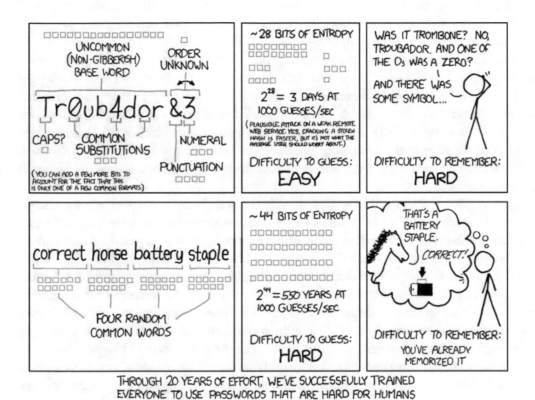

THROUGH 20 YEARS OF EFFORT, WE'VE SUCCESSFULLY TRAINED
EVERYONE TO USE PASSWORDS THAT ARE HARD FOR HUMANS
TO REMEMBER, BUT EASY FOR COMPUTERS TO GUESS.

Figure 3.4: Randall Munroe's XKCD 936 provided guidance on choosing a password. The idea of using cartoons for computer security education was also suggested by Srikwan and Jakobsson [2008]; some results of their efforts can be seen at http://securitycartoon.com/. Cartoons used as part of an embedded training are presented in Kumaraguru et al. [2007]; the study found that training materials with cartoons were more effective than those that did not use cartoons. Each XKCD contains hidden "mouse-over" text. For this cartoon the text states: "To anyone who understands information theory and security and is in an infuriating argument with someone who does not (possibly involving mixed case), I sincerely apologize." In fact, Munroe's advice was tested by Bonneau and Shutova [2012], Shay et al. [2012], and Kelley et al. [2012]. Surprisingly, long, multi-word passwords appear to offer no more security than short passwords drawn from multiple character sets, and appear to be no more secure once password crackers are adopted for this kind of advice. Used with permission. http://xkcd.com/936/

Mazurek et al. [2013] employed Mechanical Turk users to create password for the purpose of calibrating the strength of an ensemble-password guessing approach that was used in a study of CMU's operational system (see below). The researchers invited subjects to create passwords according to a variety of password composition rules and then attempted to crack the passwords. Unlike other studies in which researchers were only provided with password hashes, in this case, researchers benefited by knowing the ground truth. Not surprisingly, the study found that longer passwords drawn from multiple character sets are significantly harder to crack than passwords that are shorter or drawn from less complex character sets. Using a variety of statistical techniques, the researchers where then able to argue that passwords created with Mechanical Turk, by users instructed to create strong passwords, bore greater statistical similarity to high-value passwords used in production systems than to the low-value passwords that had been released as the result of consumer website attacks.

Fahl et al. [2013] attempted to address directly the question of ecological validity of laboratory password studies. "The main question we wanted to answer was: Do passwords generated by participants asked to role-play a scenario in which they have to create a password for fictitious accounts resemble their real passwords?"

The authors use an expansive definition of "resemble," examining the strength, whether groups of passwords are created according to a system (which can have the result of making weak passwords pass for strong ones), and specifically whether the passwords provided in the study were the same as those that are actually used. The authors could answer their question because they had access to ground truth—working in collaboration with their university's IT department, they were able to compare the passwords provided by study subjects *with the actual passwords that the same subjects used for their University information systems.* The between-group study evaluated both online and lab password construction and considered both primed and unprimed subjects, for a total of four conditions. In total the researchers analyzed passwords from 583 online participants (with 66% being primed) and another 63 (53% primed) in the lab.

For each subject, three researchers manually scored the subject's actual passwords and the passwords created for the study to determine if the passwords were similar in strength and in composition to the actual passwords. By performing a manual review, the researchers were able to detect many password generation schemes that would have passed by automated tests. The researchers also scored "derogatory" passwords that included "references to the study indicating that the participant did not show normal behavior." This includes passwords such as "studiesSuck123" and "IamSoBored!!!" The experimenters also evaluated the entropy of the passwords using both the Shannon and NIST methods, and determined crackability using the popular *John the Ripper* password cracker.

After this extensive analysis, Fahl et al. [2013] found that 46.1% of participants created passwords that were similar in a laboratory study to the passwords that they created for their university account, and 24.0% offered somewhat comparable passwords, while 29.9% did not behave in the study as they do in the wild.[2] The researchers also found that the laboratory study generated significantly more realistic results than the online study—that is, the passwords that subjects in the lab study picked were much more representative of their actual passwords than those in the online study. Priming subjects did not make any meaningful difference. (Of course, priming in 2012 may be less significant than priming in 2006, given the near constant attention to cybersecurity issues in the popular media.)

For those conducting password studies, one of the most significant findings was that 26.5% of the study participants used at least one of their real passwords in the study. "Consequently, passwords gathered during a study should be treated with the same level of protection as real passwords." To protect the study data, the researchers kept their data in encrypted volumes on computers that were disconnected from their campus network, and placed all study data in an encrypted drive in a university safe at the completion of the project. "We will adopt this procedure for all future password studies, due to the considerable number of participants who used their real passwords during the study."

Studies of Operational Systems   The text password studies that carry the highest validity are those based on the study of actual systems. Challenges that the researchers face include gaining access to this information that does not compromise the security of the systems and people being studied, and the difficulty of drawing succinct, relevant conclusions from such large and diverse data sets.

Florencio and Herley [2007] evaluated passwords of 544,960 web browser users using an agent that they added to the Windows Live Toolbar between July 24, 2006 and October 1, 2006. The toolbar provided de-identified statistics regarding password length, strength, and the number of sites sharing the password—the first study to measure password behavior over such a large population, over a period of time, and to be able to perform correlation between multiple websites. The authors were also able to measure the frequency that users forgot their passwords by observing the use of URLs involved with password resetting (Figures 3.1 and 3.2). The study found that the average client had roughly 7 distinct passwords that were shared between websites and found that the vast majority of passwords were all lowercase or all numeric. The study also confirmed that passwords were generally poor, frequently re-used, and frequently forgotten.

Zhang et al. [2010] studied the security provided by password expiration policies and found that expiring passwords does not, in general, improve the security of systems. The primary reason for password expiration is so that a stolen password will stop working at some point in the future. However, using a dataset of password hashes from actual accounts used by UNC students, faculty, and staff members, the authors show that it is relatively straightforward to guess new passwords given an expired password. The study was based on MD5 password hashes of 10,374 university accounts used between 2004 and 2009, with 4–15 password hashes per account. Dictionary-

---

[2]These findings somewhat contradict Schechter et al. [2007], who found that "role-playing participants behaved significantly less securely than those using their own passwords." However, there are key differences between these two studies, including a different task and a significantly different sample population.

based cracking was effective at cracking many passwords, especially when combined with Weir et al. [2009a]'s word-list generating method. Using only two quad-core computers with 76 GB of RAM, the researchers were able to crack 31,075 passwords for 7,936 accounts within a few months, cracking all of the passwords for 54% of the accounts, and half of the passwords for 90% of accounts. They determined that "at least 41% of passwords can be broken offline from previous paswords for the same accounts in a matter of seconds, and five online password guesses in expectation suffices to break 17% of accounts."

Bonneau [2012] analyzed roughly 70 M passwords belonging to Yahoo! users and estimate that passwords provided fewer than 10 bits of security "against an online, trawling attack, and only about 20 bits of security against an optimal offline dictionary attack." With 10 bits of security, an attacker will, on average, compromise an account roughly once every thousand tries.

Mazurek et al. [2013] partnered with the IT group at Carnegie Mellon University while the school was transitioning to a new authentication infrastructure and managed to capture statistical information regarding the plaintext passwords and authentication events for 25,000 faculty, students, and staff. The paper describes in considerable detail the technical measures that the group employed, including two-person code verification, to assure that actual passwords would never be seen by members of the research team. Also described are novel statistics developed for evaluating the strength of passwords while preserving privacy of the user base. The researchers found that there are significant differences between low-value passwords (such as those revealed from online attacks against major consumer websites) and high-value passwords (such as those used to access services at one's employer or university).

Other important findings were that men had stronger passwords than women, computer science users had the strongest passwords (and users in the school of business had the weakest), but that these effects are generally weak. The study also found that "users who had expressed annoyance with CMU's complex password policy were associated with weaker passwords," and suggested that education might be useful to address the issue. Finally, the researchers found that passwords created by Mechnical Turk users specifically for experimental use, while not a "perfect substitute for high-value passwords," could be used in many kinds of experiments that required genuine passwords. "These results indicate that passwords gathered from carefully controlled experimental studies may be an acceptable approximation of real-world, high-value passwords, while being much easier to collect." [Mazurek et al., 2013]

Passwords in Summary   Despite their failings, passwords persist. Bonneau et al. [2012b] evaluated dozens of proposals to replace text passwords with another authentication system. The paper (and Bonneau et al. [2012a], the expanded technical report) creates an evaluation framework with 8 "usability benefits," 6 "deployability benefits" and 11 "security benefits." In a master stroke of data reduction, the authors then reduce two decades of authentication research to a single table (Figure 3.5) that explains that the longevity of password-based authentication is their ease of deployability—passwords have the advantage of incumbency:

"In closing, we observe that, looking at the green (vertical) and red (horizontal) patterns in Table 1, most schemes do better than passwords on security—as expected, given that inventors of alternatives to passwords tend to come from the security community. Some schemes do better and some worse on usability—suggesting that the community needs to work harder there. But *every* scheme does worse than passwords on deployability. This was to be expected given that the first four deployability benefits are defined with explicit reference to what passwords achieve and the remaining two are natural benefits of a long-term incumbent, but this uneven playing field reflects the reality of a decentralized system like the Internet. Marginal gains are often not sufficient to reach the activation energy necessary to overcome significant transition costs, which may provide the best explanation of why we are likely to live considerably longer before seeing the funeral procession for passwords arrive at the cemetery." [Bonneau et al., 2012a]

One can argue with the rankings and classifications presented in the paper, of course. For example, OpenID [Recordon and Reed, 2006] is criticized for deployability because it may not be "Server-Compatible" even though there is broad support for it. In fact, it may be easier on many platforms to implement OpenID authentication than to operate and maintain a password-based authentication system, since OpenID outsources identification to an identity provider. Of course, in so doing, OpenID creates new risks as well, since a compromised identity provider may now result in a large number of compromised accounts.

It seems that text passwords will be present for a long time to come. Herley and van Oorschot [2012] suggest that we acknowledge this and propose that a systematic research program—combined with a willingness to use the results—could result in simultaneously increasing the usability and security of passwords. The first step, the authors argue, is to focus on the actual security requirements. Returning to the actual security provided by strong passwords—defense against offline attacks when an attacker manages to obtain a copy of a hashed password database—the analysis shows that in many cases anti-fraud techniques such as account-lockout and host reputation may be more effective at protecting user accounts than requiring complex passwords.

3.1.2 PASSWORD MANAGERS

Password managers are a commonly proposed solution to the password problem—storing the password for each website (or other service) in an encrypted database. Password managers have been available commercially since the 1990s, and there are a number of such managers readily available. However, the design and implementation of password managers poses challenges of its own. Password managers must store high-value credentials in a manner that is secure. People who use password managers typically don't know their passwords, so password managers need to have some way to access the encrypted database from multiple systems. Another challenge is simply

				Usability							Deployability					Security									
Category	Scheme	Described in section	Reference	Memorywise-Effortless	Scalable-for-Users	Nothing-to-Carry	Physically-Effortless	Easy-to-Learn	Efficient-to-Use	Infrequent-Errors	Easy-Recovery-from-Loss	Accessible	Negligible-Cost-per-User	Server-Compatible	Browser-Compatible	Mature	Non-Proprietary	Resilient-to-Physical-Observation	Resilient-to-Targeted-Impersonation	Resilient-to-Throttled-Guessing	Resilient-to-Unthrottled-Guessing	Resilient-to-Internal-Observation	Resilient-to-Leaks-from-Other-Verifiers	Resilient-to-Theft	Resilient-to-Phishing	No-Trusted-Third-Party	Requiring-Explicit-Consent · Unlinkable
(Incumbent)	Web passwords	III	[13]																									
Password managers	Firefox	IV-A	[22]																									
	LastPass		[42]																									
Proxy	URRSA	IV-B	[5]																									
	Impostor		[23]																									
Federated	OpenID	IV-C	[27]																									
	MIcrosoft Passport		[43]																									
	Facebook Connect		[44]																									
	Browser ID		[45]																									
	OTP over email		[46]																									
Graphical	PCCP	IV-D	[7]																									
	PassGo		[47]																									
Cognitive	GrIDsure (original)	IV-E	[30]																									
	Weinshall		[48]																									
	Hopper Blum		[49]																									
	Word Association		[50]																									
Paper tokens	OTPW	IV-F	[33]																									
	S/KEY		[32]																									
	PIN+TAN		[51]																									
Visual crypto	Pass WIdnow		[52]																									
Hardware tokens	RSA SecurID	IV-G	[34]																									
	YubiKey		[53]																									
	IronKey		[54]																									
	CAP reader		[55]																									
	Pico		[8]																									
Phone-based	Phoolproof	IV-H	[35]																									
	Cronto		[56]																									
	MP-Auth		[6]																									
	OTP over SMS																										
	Google 2-Step		[57]																									
Biometric	Fingerprint	IV-I	[38]																									
	Iris		[39]																									
	Voice		[40]																									
Recovery	Personal knowledge		[58]																									
	Preference-based		[59]																									
	Social re-auth.		[60]																									

● = offers the benefit; O=almost offers the benefit; no circle = does not offer the benefit.
■ = better than password; ■ worse than passwords; no background pattern = no change.
We group related schemes into categories. For space reasons, in the present paper we describe at most one representative scheme per category; the companion technical report [1] discusses all schemes listed.

Figure 3.5: Based on Bonneau et al. [2012b, Table 1].

getting the system to work—properly identifying fields for usernames and passwords and filling in the correct values.

Password managers fall into several broad categories.

- *Client-based password managers* store passwords in an encrypted database on the client. Typically these are implemented as browser extensions that automatically fill in the username and password when asked. Some browsers include this functionality as a feature that remembers usernames and passwords in encrypted storage. For maximum usability, there must be some way to synchronize the database so it can be accessed from different clients.

- *Mobile password managers* store passwords in an encrypted database on a cell phone or other mobile device. When the user wishes to log in to a website the user displays the site's username and password and then types it in.

- *Online password managers* store passwords in a central database. A browser extension typically fetches the password from the remote database, decrypts it, and enters it into the web page.

- *Hashing password managers* eliminate the need to store an encrypted database by deriving each site's password from the hash of the user's master password and the remote site's domain name before sending the password. Password hashing was broadly introduced by the Stanford PwdHash browser extension [Ross et al., 2005], although the first web-based password hashing system appears to be the Lucent Personal Web Assistant [Gabber et al., 1997] and a system from DEC SRC [Abadi et al., 1997].

Despite the availability of password managers, there has been little research of systems within the research community. The experience of PwdHash showed the importance of conducting usability studies when proposing new security mechanisms that require human input. The authors of the original PwdHash paper performed a limited usability evaluation of PwdHash with five users, but most of the article is devoted to how the extension works and the technical problems addressed in creating it. Ross et al. [2005] performed a more detailed usability evaluation with 26 users and found significant issues impacting both usability and security. More importantly, perhaps, the evaluation found that many users reported that tasks were completed and were "easy" even when they failed to complete the task with the proper security measures, an example of the "user evaluation challenge" (Section 1.2). Chiasson et al. [2006] performed a usability study with 26 users of both PwdHash and Password Multiplier [Halderman et al., 2005], another password manager, and found that both had usability problems that resulted in security exposures.

Tapas [McCarney et al., 2012] is a system that seems to overcome many security and usability problems associated with password manager systems. The system is based on a password-manager browser extension, a smartphone "wallet" that contains passwords, and a Rendezvous server that is part of the Tapas infrastructure that allows the manager and the wallet to communicate with each other. The Wallet application is bound to the manager by scanning a QR code, which results in a self-signed TLS certificate being transferred from the Manager to the Wallet (an example of *device pairing*, further discussed below). To log in to a website, the user takes out the mobile phone and taps the desired account. This sends the encrypted password from the Wallet to the Manager, where it is decrypted and provided to the remote website. In the event of a phishing attempt, the Tapas browser extension notifies the user that the password sent was for the wrong website. A user study with 30 participants found no significant usability problems with Tapas. Users reported that Tapas was significantly more enjoyable to use than the built-in Firefox password manager. A follow-up study based on usability feedback resulted in improved user comprehension regarding where passwords were stored and the overall security model.

3.1.3   GRAPHICAL AUTHENTICATION

Graphical authentication is a knowledge-based authentication method that utilizes images and the computer's graphical input (mouse, touch screen) in the formation of the password instead of text and keyboard. [Monrose and Reiter, 2005]

Graphical authentication has received a large amount of attention in the UPS research community for a variety of reasons. Like authentication research in general, graphical authentication attempts to find a solution to one of the most visible and clear problems in usable security—the problem of authenticating users. The established principle that humans remember visual information more readily than other information also provides strong motivation and appeal to this topic. The goals and metrics are clear and focused, clarifying experimental design and the resulting outcomes. There are also many different design possibilities and variations that can be examined, making the problem a good fit to academic research. Biddle et al. [2012] presented the most recent comprehensive survey. Rather than replicate that survey here, we instead summarize the research to show how it fits into the broader UPS research agenda.

Graphical authentication was first proposed with a scheme by Blonder in 1996 in a U.S. patent [Blonder, 1996], with the first academic research reported in the classic 1999 "Draw-A-Secret" paper at USENIX Security [Jermyn et al., 1999]. Figure 2.1 summarizes the proposed approach.

Graphical authentication schemes fall into three main categories [Biddle et al., 2012]. One class of schemes has users create their own simple drawing or visual pattern, related to the original "Draw-A-Secret" scheme, a simplified mechanism of which Android phones now offer. A second class of schemes requires users to remember a set of images as a password. Variations utilize different kinds of images, such as the users' own photos [Pering et al., 2003], faces [Davis et al., 2004], or random art [Dhamija and Perrig, 2000]. This scheme has the advantage of relying on users recognizing a set of images, which humans are particularly good at doing. The final class of schemes, expanding on Blonder's initial patent, is cued-recall, where the password is composed of a set of points on an image. The cues provided by the image aid in remembering the password.

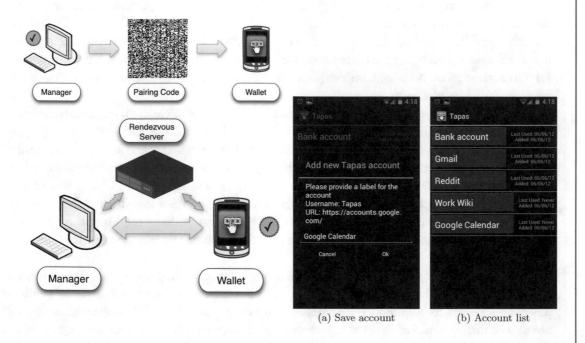

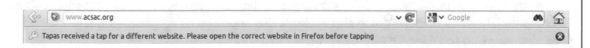

Figure 3.6: (top) Tapas setting up an out-of-band communication channel (initiated by the manager), and (bottom) setting up a two-way network communication channel, initiated by the wallet. From McCarney et al. [2012].

(a) Save account (b) Account list

Figure 3.7: Screenshots of the Tapas Wallet.

Figure 3.8: The notification the Tapas extension displays for mismatched user intent [McCarney et al., 2012].

In the most commonly investigated version of this, called PassPoints, users click on 5 locations on an image to form their passwords [Wiedenbeck et al., 2005].

As the research on graphical authentication has advanced, many of the originally proposed schemes have been evaluated by multiple groups. There has been significant focus on some of the security shortcomings, such as shoulder surfing and hotspots (e.g., Tari et al. [2006], van Oorschot and Thorpe [2011]); researchers have attempted to design new graphical authentication mechanisms that overcome these issues. Graphical authentication remains especially relevant for authentication on handheld devices [Schaub et al., 2013], as graphical authentication is particularly suited for platforms where keyboards are lacking.

Yet, despite these advantages and the breadth and depth of research on graphical passwords, the impact of this research is mixed. Several commercial systems did follow the research (e.g., Passfaces[3] and grIDSure[4]). Yet, until only very recently, few users had ever come across a graphical password. Research results have not proven that graphical schemes are better or preferable in many cases, often still suffering from some of the same problems as text-based passwords [Biddle et al., 2012]. Studies comparing schemes lacked consistency and few investigated the long-term implications, such as interference [Biddle et al., 2012]. And perhaps the biggest drawback to graphical authentication is that authenticating with them frequently takes longer than with text-based passwords.

Despite these shortcomings, the research in graphical authentication has contributed to the wider understanding of authentication. Cueing is a method utilized by one set of graphical password schemes to help reduce the burden of recalling passwords. This notion of cued recall can also be further explored in other knowledge-based schemes. For example, challenge questions use cues (the question) to help users remember the shared secret (the answer). Research on hot spots within graphical passwords has further demonstrated that knowledge-based authentication schemes are likely to suffer from predictable patterns. Users attempt to choose passwords that are easy to remember, resulting in common patterns of behavior. This allows dictionaries and algorithms to be constructed to guess such passwords [Oorschot and Thorpe, 2008, van Oorschot and Thorpe, 2011]. However, persuasion mechanisms can reduce this predictability. Persuasive Cued Click-Points (PCCP) provided a small viewport randomly positioned on an image, within which users would choose the next point for their passwords [Chiasson et al., 2012]. Studies demonstrated that usability of PCCP was similar to the non-persuasive version, yet with reduced hot spots. The same research group also explored this notion to using persuasion for introducing randomness into text-based passwords [Forget et al., 2008].

Even more encouraging, the lack of commercial use of graphical passwords is changing with mobile devices. The Android Pattern Lock system provides one graphical authentication method, albeit much simpler than most of the researched schemes, where users draw a pattern on a 3x3 grid. Even more recently, Windows 8 devices have a wider variety of graphical authentication

---

[3]http://www.passfaces.com/
[4]http://www.gridsure-security.co.uk/

with little published research yet on the use and outcomes of those. The ubiquity of mobile and touch devices, with limited keyboards, may finally lead to mainstream graphical authentication, as the time to type in a text-based or PIN-based password is not a significant improvement over graphical passwords (for one example, see von Zezschwitz et al. [2013]).

Many of the security concerns with graphical authentication highlighted in the previous research exist in today's commercial uses. In the case of the Android Pattern Lock, for example, smudges on a screen can make it easy to figure out passwords [Aviv et al., 2010a], there is no protection against shoulder surfing, passwords are frequently weak, likely to contain hotspots, and are easily shared. Yet, the overwhelming user need in this context is speed and simplicity, which perhaps outweigh the possibilities of password stealing and hacking just to unlock a phone. In retrospect, the concerns of shoulder surfing and hotspots may not be critical for this use case.

These recent commercial developments point to a possible future for graphical authentication research—to more deeply examine the context and trade-offs presented in mobile computing, and other domains where graphical mechanisms are comparable to traditional passwords, or where the negative issues such as hotspots and shoulder surfing are perhaps less important in reality. For example, Schaub et al. [2013] describe the design space for graphical authentication on mobile devices. There is still a need to understand the applicability, trade-offs, and usability on different devices, factors that lead to success or adoption, and the impact of variations of graphical authentication on the usability and security on mobile or other touch-screen platforms.

3.1.4   BIOMETRICS

Biometrics is the comparison of live anatomical, physiological, or behavior characteristics to the stored template of a person [Coventry, 2005]. Biometrics is a user identification technology that is frequently treated as if it were an authentication technology. There are a large variety of biometrics available, including fingerprints, finger and hand geometry, retina or iris scans, facial and voice recognition, and keyboard and touch dynamics.

Biometric identification is inherently a computer-recognition task: the user's biometric is measured and reduced to a template or a signature that is stored. At some later point in time, the biometric is measured again and the new measurement compared to the stored value. If the two templates match to within a predetermined threshold, the templates are deemed to belong to the same individual. Thus, there are four possible conditions for any biometric match.

- The two templates are from the same person, and the system declares a match ("true positive").

- The two templates are from different people, and the system declares a non-match ("true negative").

- The two templates are from the same person, and the system declares a non-match ("false negative").

- The two templates are from different people, and the system declares a match ("false positive").

Most biometrics research has focused on accuracy (the stability of the biometric over time), performance (the ability to perform a one-to-many identification with a large database), and the ease with which a biometric can be subverted.

Biometric systems are typically evaluated according to their ability to match properly—for example, by reporting the True Acceptance Rate (TAR), the False Acceptance Rate (FAR), the True Rejection Rate (TRR) and the False Rejection Rate (FRR). Because these measures are determined by the matching threshold, researchers sometimes prefer to report the Equal Error Rate (EER) (the value for which the FAR equals the FRR) or simply to plot the TAR against the FAR as a Receiver Operating Characteristic (ROC) curve.

But, whereas the security of a biometric may be determined by having a high TAR and a low FAR, the usability of a biometric depends on other factors that are less frequently discussed.

Biometric systems are not democratic—different people have different success rates with the same biometric. Some people may be utterly unable to use a biometric—they may be missing a finger or unable to speak. The prevalence of such individuals determines a biometric system's Failure to Enroll Rate (FER). Another consideration is that enrolled individuals may be unable to use a biometric at a given instance—for example, a voice recognition system may be unusable if an airplane is passing overhead or during a thunderstorm, or the person's voice may sound different with a bad cold.

Another consideration is the ease with which the biometric is captured [Jain et al., 2006]. This may depend in part on whether the biometric is measured in a supervised context (such as at an airport) or in an unsupervised context (for example, over the Internet, or using a mobile phone). A system that tests well for usability and security when users are being closely monitored and assisted may have poor usability when users are unsupervised. Worse, attackers may discover ways to present a device with false data for the purpose of impersonation or to avoid a match.

Unlike most other technologies discussed in this book, biometric systems have additional acceptance hurdles that may be unrelated to security or usability. For example, privacy activists have long expressed concerns regarding the use of fingerprints as a universal identification system. More recently, concern has been raised in using fingerprints for computer identification because fingerprints cannot be changed if the database is compromised.

Coventry et al. [2003] reported that individuals were hesitant to use fingerprint-based ATMs for fear that the fingerprint readers were not hygienic. Users may be unwilling to enroll or use fingerprint systems because of the association between fingerprints and criminality, or because they fear that using their fingerprint as an authenticator may put them at risk for having a finger cut off by a criminal [Patrick, 2008]. For example, a 2005 BBC report claimed that a group of hi-tech car thieves had cut the finger off an accountant in Malaysia when they wanted to steal a car that was secured by a fingerprint reader [Kent, 2005].

Like other authentication systems, there seems to be confusion and misinformation in the general population regarding the mechanism, implementation, and usefulness of biometrics [Moody, 2004]. This confusion may create general apprehension regarding their use. For example, Heckle et al. [2007] conducted a laboratory study in which 24 participants role-played the use of a fingerprint biometric identification system to make a purchase at an online bookstore and found reaction to biometrics was highly dependent upon the kind of information being protected and the use to which that information was being put. Nearly half of the participants in the study expressed second thoughts regarding the use of biometrics as the study progressed. Pons and Polak [2008] surveyed 86 undergraduates and graduates in Computer Information Systems at a major southeastern U.S. university and found that they generally had little familiarity or interest regarding biometrics. This surprised the authors: they expected that their students would be familiar with "cutting-edge technologies."

> "Given the low levels of general familiarity and experience with biometrics, it appears that the subjects could not clearly assess the security benefits that such system would provide, nor the potential privacy concerns that are inherent in use of the technology. The overall level of familiarity was so minimal that most students lacked the necessary knowledge to see what privacy issues could arise from the system's implementation." [Pons and Polak, 2008]

Although the typical use of biometrics is to provide identification when a resource is first accessed, behavioral biometrics can also be used in the background to keep verifying or re-authenticating the computer's user. The most common use is to utilize the patterns of behavior with the computer's input device, such as keyboard dynamics. Although there have been many studies of keystroke dynamics approaches, different methodologies and testing regimes makes it difficult to compare the different techniques. A primary challenge appears to be maintaining multiple templates for each user (since typing patterns may depend upon context), and updating that template over time. Peacock et al. [2004] surveyed the literature a decade ago, while Crawford [2010] provides a more recent review. More recently, researchers are examining the dynamics of gestures on a touch screen to provide multi-factor or continuous authentication [Burgbacher and Hinrichs, 2014, Sae-Bae et al., 2012].

The future of biometrics as a general use authentication technology remains unclear. For many years biometrics were the subject of curiosity, appearing in movies but not readily available to consumers or businesses. In the late 1990s low-cost fingerprint readers allowed some vendors to include biometrics on some laptops. Nevertheless, the devices do not seem to have been widely used. In recent years governments have adopted biometrics as part of border control systems: it is now routine for travelers to be fingerprinted or have their faces or irises captured as part of entering a country. Meanwhile Apple has included a thumbprint reader on the iPhone 5s. It remains unclear if this increased exposure to biometrics will result in broader consumer understanding, interest, and demand for biometric technology. If so, there are sure to be increased efforts in making these systems both reliable and usable.

3.1.5   TOKEN-BASED AUTHENTICATION

Another authentication approach is to provide users with a device or *hardware token*. Services typically authenticate these devices through some kind of secret (S). The secret is either shared between the service and the device, or it is a private key that is validated with a certificate.

In general, hardware tokens rely on two approaches:

- **Time-Based One-Time Passwords:** The device contains both a secret (S) and a clock (T). The device periodically computes a function $f(S, T)$ and displays a portion of the result on a display. The authentication system also knows f, S and T and can therefore calculate what the device is showing at any given time. The original time-based system was the SecureID, developed by Security Dynamics[5]

- **Challenge-Response Authentication:** These systems are similar to time-based systems, except that the function combines a challenge provided by the report server with its internal secret. Examples of this kind of authentication are today's smart card systems in which the card contains a public/private key pair. The remote server provides a challenge to the card, which the card signs and returns with a copy of the card's public key certificate. The remote server is thus able to verify that the card actually contains the private key, and that the public key has been signed by an appropriate Certificate Authority.

Token-based systems are frequently combined with passwords, creating a *multi-factor authentication* system.

Token-based systems have existed since the 1980s but use was limited due to significant deployability and usability problems. Deployability of these systems is difficult because they require that both tokens be distributed and servers be upgraded before they can be used. This is sometimes called a *bootstrap problem*. For example, SecureID required that an organization purchase tokens, purchase a server, and distribute the correct cards to the correct users. By design, users cannot log in if they lose their tokens, if they leave them at home, or if the token breaks. Smart cards have the additional usability problem of requiring that users have both a smart-card reader and the necessary drivers available on every computer that they wish. Some hardware vendors attempted to get around this problem by including both the smart card chip and the reader chip in a single USB package, although this did not solve the driver problem. Other vendors have deployed tokens that appear as USB human interface devices (USB HID) and then transmit information as if they were keyboards.

Despite their prevelance, relatively little research has examined the usability of these systems. Piazzalunga et al. [2005] performed a small study comparing smart cards and USB tokens, finding that users had difficulty properly inserting the smart card. Weir et al. [2009b] compared several one-time password tokens as a 2-factor authentication for eBanking and found that participant's felt that all of the devices offered the same level of security, and based their preference on

---

[5]Security Dynamics purchased RSA Security and changed its name to that of the acquired company in 2006.

convenience and usability. (This is another example of the User Evaluation Challenge discussed in Section 4.)

As cell phones, and smart phones in particular, have become ubiquitous, they have been widely adopted for two-factor authentication. Two popular authentication techniques are sending a text message to the users's phone with an authentication code, and having the user run an authentication application on the phone itself. Although it might seem easier to make use of an individual's cell phone, again there is a bootstrapping problem: there needs to be some way to register the user's cell phone number or to establish some kind of shared secret between the user's phone and the authentication server—a topic discussed in "Device Pairing" below (Section 3.5), and current systems need to be modified to make use of the second factor. Again, there has been little research within UPS on the use of these techniques.

3.1.6   MENTAL COMPUTATION AND ONE-TIME PASSWORDS

One of the complaints with two-factor authentication systems is that, by design, they prevent users from logging in with only a password. That is the point of these systems, of course, since passwords can be trivially stolen using a variety of means (e.g., keystroke loggers or phishing attacks). An alternative paradigm proposed and tested by several researchers is for the user to play the role of a token and perform a challenge-response interaction with the remote server.

Brostoff et al. [2010] presented an evaluation of GrIDsure, a commercial system in which the user picks a sequence of cells on a 5x5 grid as their password. Once enrolled, users attempting to authenticate are shown another grid, this one filled with numbers, and the user enters the numbers in the square that correspond to their chosen square. The system defied eavesdropping because the chosen grid positions cannot be learned by observing a single PIN use (Figure 3.9). The authors evaluated 83 participants and found that 91% could log in after 3–4 days and 97% after 9-10 days. An important part of this study was a two-year follow-up during which 25 participants were retested: 27% could recall their patterns. The authors concluded that GrIDsure "is usable if people have one pass-pattern," but that security is decreased if the attacker can observe multiple interactions. Usability might also be significantly impacted by "interference," if users must use the GrIDsure system to log in to multiple systems using multiple patterns.

Kelley et al. [2013b] implemented a system similar to GrIDsure called PassGrids. The research system uses a larger grid with color-coded areas (for improved localization and memorability) and allowed the researchers to test variants that required mental arithmetic. A two-part study with 1,600 participants using Mechanical Turk found that between 92%–96% of the participants could complete problems involving some math operation, although 83 participants (5%) got nine or more problems wrong. Mean completion time was between 5–8 seconds, allowing the authors to conclude that the math did not pose a significant authentication barrier for the Mechanical Turk workers, although it might for others. Most of the participants found that using PassGrids was fun. Unfortunately, a problem with the study is that the statistics include only those who successfully completed the task, and a dropout rate of 16–45% was observed—with high dropouts being associated with more complex PassGrids variants. It is possible that those who did not understand PassGrids, or found the mental arithmetic too complex, were dropping out, although the authors note that the demographics of those dropping out were the same as those who had completed.

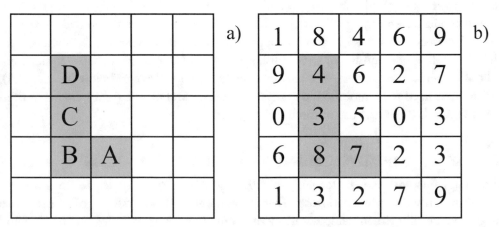

Figure 3.9: The GrIDsure system. a) Users enroll by picking four cells (in this case, A, B, C and D). b) users authenticate by typing the numbers shown in the chosen cells (in this case, 7834). (Based on Brostoff et al. [2010].)

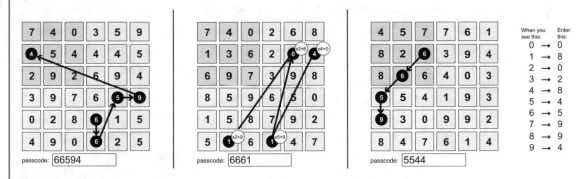

Figure 3.10: Kelley et al. [2013b] increase the security of the GrIDsure system by adding mental arithmetic that the user must perform before entering their passcode.

3.1.7   CAPTCHAS

The final means of authentication we discuss are interactive tests to determine that it is a human being that is interacting with a computer system and not some kind of automated process. Such tests are called CAPTCHAs (Completely Automated Public Turing Test To Tell Computers and Humans Apart) [Ahn et al., 2003]. The usability challenge of CAPTCHAs is to have a task that is so hard that it cannot be performed by a computer, but easy enough that it can be performed by any person. As previously noted, Hidalgo and Alvarez [2011] presented a 70-page analysis of CAPTCHAs.

Yan and El Ahmad [2008] are two of the first to discuss the design and usability issues of text-based CAPTCHA schemes, including the issues surrounding the distortion of text characters, the content of the text, and how it is presented. Others have explored audio and video CAPTCHAs [Kluever and Zanibbi, 2009]. Today one of the most popular CAPTCHAs is re-CAPTCHA, which uses pairs of smeared type scanned from old books as the CAPTCHA target [von Ahn et al, 2008], attempting to put the time users must spend on authenticating for a societal benefit.

However, the existence of such tasks that meet the CAPTCHA requirement should not be assumed! That is, there may be no tests that are easy for people, hard for computers, and easily delivered over the Web. In part, this is because those attempting to "break" CAPTCHAs can submit an unlimited number of attempts against a CAPTCHA server and they can continually improve their techniques. Another issue is success rate: a human attempting to pass a CAPTCHA must be able to pass it reliably on the first or second attempt, whereas an attack that lets a computer pass the CAPTCHA one in a thousand attempts may be quite significant.

Bursztein et al. [2010] conducted a study on both Amazon's Mechanical Turk and an "underground captcha-breaking service" and found success rates ranging from 93% on eBay CAPTCHAs (compared to eBay's reported success rate of 98.5%) down to 35% for CAPTCHAs from *mail.ru*. Bursztein et al. [2011] studied 15 CAPTCHA schemes currently in use and found that 13 were vulnerable to automated attacks that they developed for the paper. Even more recently, Bursztein et al. [2014] performed an extensive evaluation of the usability of common text-based CAPTCHA schemes, finding that different feature combinations, such as the character sets used and the amount of rotation of characters, impacted usability in complex ways. They demonstrate the usefulness of such systematic evaluation, using their results to modify Google's CAPTCHA scheme, resulting in 20% fewer incorrect CAPTCHAs being submitted.

Whereas academics typically attack CAPTCHAs with software, actual criminals may attack CAPTCHAs with low-paid workers. As a result the future of CAPTCHAs is unclear. Motoyama et al. [2011] surveyed the web service abuse marketplace and found that the going rate for freelance CAPTCHA-solving is $1 per 1,000 solved. "Thus today, CAPTCHAs are neither more nor less than a small economic impediment to the abuser" of many web services. Li et al. [2010] surveyed 41 schemes used by financial institutions to protect e-banking transactions and found that it was possible to break *all of them* using automated means. Xu et al. [2013] found that a state-of-the-art moving-image CAPTCHA that was hard for people to solve was relatively straightforward to break using existing computer vision algorithms.

Today there is great variation in the use of CAPTCHAs. Some websites use them consistently, others only use them when there is an incorrectly entered password or two. Some websites only show CAPTCHAs when the user is attempting to log in from an IP address that was previously unseen. Other approaches are discussed in Van Oorschot and Stubblebine [2006] and Alsaleh et al. [2012].

Overall it seems that CAPTCHAs are technology that decreases usability without providing any significant increase in security. In the end, the real value of CAPTCHAs may be to deter only the relatively unsophisticated attacks and attackers.

3.1.8 FALLBACK AND BACKUP AUTHENTICATION

Fallback and backup authentication provide means for a user to access an account after the primary authentication has failed. Fallback authentication mechanisms have different usability challenges, as their use is intended to be rare, with little to no practice [Reeder and Schechter, 2011]. As a result, fallback and backup authentication systems may be easier to bypass than primary authentication.

A common technique for fallback authentication is the *challenge question* answers to which can be requested in advance from users (e.g., "what is your favorite color?"), determined from publicly available information (e.g., "Have you ever lived on North Main Street?"), or based on private information available to the challenging organization (e.g., "What was the amount of your last bank deposit?"). Just [2005] provided design criteria for creating challenge questions: answers to questions should be hard to guess and attackers should not be able to infer the answers by consulting public records. To be usable, designers must consider *applicability* of the questions to the entire population (don't ask the name of a person's favorite aunt, because people may not have aunts); *memorability* so that users remember what they provided; and *repeatability* so that the typed response is matched—for example, discouraging users from typing "St." instead of "Street" and refraining from asking about a user's "favorite" since favorites are subject to change. Although it would seem that a reasonable alternative would be to allow users to pick their own challenge question, follow-up work [Just and Aspinall, 2009] found that this was not the case: given the choice, users frequently pick challenge questions that have low entropy answers.

Schechter et al. [2009] performed a user study of the challenge questions used by the four most popular webmail providers with 130 individuals and 13% could be guessed within five attempts by guessing the most popular answers of other participants, 17% of the answers could be reliably guessed by acquaintances with whom the participants were unwilling to share their passwords, and 20% of the participants forgot their own challenge question answers within six months.

Other approaches of backup authentication include email-based authentication and two-factor approaches (e.g., SMS messages). Schechter and Reeder [2009] argue that all of these methods are subject to spoofing—indeed, they have been spoofed in very high-profile incidents—and presented results of a small survey (N=18) indicating that users may be willing to answer a large number of questions to reset their account password. If anything, the paucity of research on backup authentication indicates that this is an area ripe for additional research.

3.2   EMAIL SECURITY AND PKI

Secure messaging has been a perennial target for UPS researchers, starting with Whitten and Tygar [1999]. After all, email is a daily task for most computer users, but the vast majority of messaging systems offer no end-to-end message security. The obvious way to provide security is by using a digital signature to protect the message from malicious tampering and to use encryption to prevent unauthorized parties from gaining access. Indeed, the very first paper on public key cryptography [Diffie and Hellman, 1976] identified sending and receiving signed, encrypted messages as the motivating use case for the new technology, as did the first academic publication introducing the RSA encryption algorithm [Rivest et al., 1977]. Digital certificates and the basis of today's Public Key Infrastructure (PKI) were invented by Loren Kohnfelder as part of his MIT undergraduate thesis [Kohnfelder, 1978] as an efficient and scalable system for distributing public keys. With these building blocks, there was widespread expectation among security researchers that developing a secure email system merely required standardizing on formats for representing keys and messages, and the creation of software to perform the encryption and decryption. Much of the 1980s and 1990s were spent doing just that. But, while there were many technical successes, nearly four decades later the vast majority of email sent over the Internet is neither signed nor encrypted, as each part of the problem proved to be dramatically more complicated than originally thought.

By the late 1990s three incompatible secure email systems were available for businesses to use. Lotus Notes implemented secure messaging with proprietary technologies. S/MIME was widely implemented in consumer and business software including Microsoft Outlook, Netscape Communicator, and eventually Apple Mail, but was failing to gain traction. PGP, available as both free and commercial products, was used by some academics and software developers, and was generally regarded as difficult to use.

Key management is the fundamental usability challenge of secure email. To send a person an encrypted email, it is first necessary to obtain the recipient's public key. It's important that the sender have the *correct* key—otherwise an active adversary might be able to perform a man-in-the-middle attack.

Lotus Notes solves the key management problem by creating keys centrally, providing them to users through the systems' proprietary client, and automatically encrypting and decrypting email messages as necessary [Zurko, 2005]. Despite having more than 144 million licensed mailboxes in 2005, the success of Notes has been largely ignored by academics, presumably because many of them do not have access to the platform.

S/MIME solves one aspect of key management by attaching the sender's public key certificate to every outbound email that is digitally signed. The public key certificate can be used both to verify the signature and to send an encrypted response [Ramsdell and Turner, 2010]. The challenge for users is obtaining the S/MIME digital certificates. The initial public/private key pair must be created in a different application and then sent to a third-party Certificate Authority for signing. This process is largely automated by modern web browsers, which incorporate the certificate creation in a larger "ceremony" [Ellison, 2007] that can include exchanging email messages and the providing of payment information.

Garfinkel et al. [2005] found that the need to involve a third party in order to send and receive an encrypted email message significantly hampered S/MIME adoption by consumers and small businesses. However, it was not a barrier to *receiving* S/MIME messages that were digitally signed but not encrypted.

PGP takes a different approach to solving key management: users create their own private and public keys and provide them directly to the individuals with whom they wish to communicate. PGP also implements a "web of trust" concept in which users can sign each other's keys and choose to trust the signatures of their friends. The web of trust is critical for the proper functioning of the PGP key servers: without it, there is no way for a key server user to determine the correct key for the intended recipient, since attackers can upload any number of keys, with any identity that they choose, to the key servers.

Whitten and Tygar [1999] performed a cognitive walkthrough and a laboratory user study of a version of PGP for the Mac and concluded that, even though the software was "usable" by conventional standards, the software required that the user have a clear understanding of the underlying concepts of public key technology—something that most users did not have and that the software didn't teach. Whitten's solution was to have software selectively reveal new features as the user was ready for them [Whitten, 2004], effectively applying Carroll's "training wheels" [Carroll and Carrithers, 1984] to the security domain.

"Key Continuity Management," also called Trust on First Use (TOFU), is yet another approach to public key management for systems that present a public key to a client each time a service is used. With this approach, public keys (digital certificates) are assumed to be valid the first time they are encountered. A copy of the key is stored. On subsequent uses the keys are compared against the stored key and the user is warned if the key has changed. This is the security model used by the popular SSH remote access service [Ylonen, 1996].

Garfinkel and Miller [2005] performed a laboratory test of KCM against an active attacker using a modified version of Whitten and Tygar's scenario. They found that KCM was useful in allowing some subjects to avoid attack, but only if they had been given a briefing explaining the on-screen KCM indicators.

Ellison and Schneier [2000] explore other possible reasons for the failure of PKI-based systems, arguing that there is a poor match between the user requirements and the requirements imposed by PKI technology and business models. For example, PKI requires unlimited trust in certificate authorities and there is no way for users to know if their private key has been compromised and used without their permission. As a result, users had little incentive to adopt PKI, and such adoption was required for S/MIME to be effective. Wilson [2008] argued that PKI nevertheless gained use as the "[t]he naïve early vision of a single all-purpose identity system" was replaced by application-specific uses of PKI that used individual certificates to certify relationships rather than identities. That is, PKI was more like a credit card than a driver's license.

3.2.1   AUTOMATIC, TRANSPARENT ENCRYPTION

Another approach to solving the key management problem is to make it entirely transparent, or "opportunistic." That is, protocols and implementing software can distribute public keys at every opportunity and enable encryption whenever possible.

Wood [1984] presented a visionary paper at the 1984 ACM Annual Conference describing the so-called "fifth generation computers" of the 1990s that would use the public key encryption technology to solve the persistent security issues of computer networks. Message authentication codes and digital signatures would protect the contents of messages from modification, and sophisticated key management systems for "changing keys, procedures for backing-up and archiving encrypted keys, recovery procedures, and the like" would put users in control of their security.

> "Ideally, all this will be entirely transparent to the end user. He will of course, through application system or local operating system facilities, have the ability to specify what part(s) of his data he wishes to encrypt/decrypt, apply a MAC to, or sign with a digital signature. And he will additionally have some responsibility for maintaining the secrecy of his personal keys, perhaps via his own memory or that in a small plastic card." [Wood, 1984]

Transparent encryption has generally been more successful at securing network communications and data stored in mass storage systems. For example, transparent encryption is the basis of the SSL encryption used for secure web browsing. For email, the main use of transparent encryption is provided between mail transfer agents (MTAs), as provided by the SMTP STARTTLS command [Hoffman, 2002, Newman, 1999], although Garfinkel [2003] implemented a transparent encryption proxy for use with PGP that implemented opportunistic key generation, key distribution (by attaching public keys to sent messages), encryption (by encrypting messages when the public key of the recipient was in the key chain), and decryption (by decrypting incoming mail messages). However, no user test was performed. Bobba et al. [2009] extend the idea to mailing lists with a proxy that automatically performs encryption, decryption and key management for the users running on top of the Mailman mailing list system. Once again, no user test was performed, but the system was deployed into a production environment for a pilot test.

Surprisingly, when user tests were actually performed of automatic, transparent encryption systems, the results were not what was expected. Ruoti et al. [2013] describe both the implementation *and a user study* of Pwm (Private WebMail, pronounced "Poem"), a system that provides transparent end-to-end encryption to existing webmail systems (Gmail, HotMail, and Yahoo! Mail). The researchers tried to build a system that was totally automatic, requiring very little user interaction. Pwm managed most aspects of the message security, including key generation and management, and message encryption/decryption. Significant effort was spent to integrate with existing systems. The researchers then conducted two user studies: a first with 25 users that evaluated specific email security tasks, and a second with 32 users that compared Pwm to the Voltage SecureMail Cloud system, a commercial secure webmail system that is based on identity-based cryptography. In each study, a small but significant number of users sent messages without enabling encryption. Follow-up interviews revealed that some users felt that anyone who installed Pwm could decrypt messages encrypted with the system—that is, the keys had become so invisible that some users no longer knew that the keys existed or understood their use.

The researchers then built another user interface that made the encryption process dramatically more manual. Called MP, the system relied on having the user copy unencrypted text into a window, click a button to "encrypt," and then paste the encrypted message back into the email client. In post-test questioning, the researchers learned, not surprisingly, that MP users had a better understanding of the underlying encryption and data protection mechanisms than did the Pwm users. But they were surprised to discover that MP's System Usability Scale score was just as high as the fully transparent system. "Contrary to our initial thinking, users are not opposed to manual encryption. Users preferred manual encryption because they felt it helped them understand, and thereby trust, the system… [P]articipants felt that MP was more secure based on its manual encryption."

The researchers concluded:

"We were surprised that users were accepting of the extra effort that manual encryption requires in MP compared to the transparent encryption in Pwm. Even more significant was the feeling of trust fostered by manual encryption in MP.

"Our experience demonstrates that automatic encryption hides so many details that users are confused about what precisely is occurring and can sometimes lead users to mistakenly disclose plaintext when the encryption option is too similar to no encryption.…" [Ruoti et al., 2013, p.11]

However, contradictory findings were reported by Fahl et al. [2012], who reported on a transparent encryption facility developed and deployed for protecting Facebook communications. An initial study with 514 participants demonstrated that many Facebook users want a means for protecting their communications. A laboratory study with 96 participants found that automatic encryption and key management was an important requirement from the intended user base. A final study with 15 participants found that all were able to encrypt Facebook conversations successfully without error. It may be that the final study was so small that the confusion found by Ruoti et al. [2013] didn't emerge, or it may be that managing secure communications on Facebook with Fahl et al. [2012]'s plug-in was easier than managing secure email with Ruoti et al. [2013]'s system.

3.2.2   FUTURE OF SECURE MESSAGING

After four decades of research and development, many consumers now have access to easy-to-use secure messaging. These systems are generally integrated with commercial applications, such as Lotus Notes, Skype and Google Chat, that handle all aspects of user registration, key generation, and communications. Despite these advances, relatively few users still choose to encrypt many of their messages. A study by Gaw et al. [2006] reveals possible reasons why. The researchers interviewed members of an activist organization, where employees had real needs and reasons for ecrypting messages. They describe that social perceptions around encryption may also hinder its adoption. Encrypting email was seen as important for protecting secrets, and helps to flag such messages as secret, but going beyond that was considered paranoid. Again, one method for overcoming this issue is to automatically encrypt all messages, removing the decision from the user, and the subsequent social implications of that decision.

Although easy integration and automation unquestionably increases usability, it is unclear if security is compromised— Edwards et al. [2008] note that automation makes users more susceptible to invisible failures that may compromise security, as well as to intentional attacks. Edwards et al. [2008] also note that automation makes users more vulnerable to attacks by technology providers (for example, surveillance), and that a provider's power can be both easily and invisibly abused. This is especially true of encryption software, which fails invisibly.

3.3 ANTI-PHISHING EFFORTS

"Phishing" is a form of computer-mediated social engineering in which the attacker attempts to coax information (typically authentication credentials) out of an unsuspecting victim by impersonating a legitimate service. Although the phrase "phishing" has been used to describe many different kinds of attacks, this section focuses on attacks that have these characteristics:

- The attack is automated and typically directed against many people. For example, the phishing attack might begin with an email campaign.

- The attack involves impersonation. For example, the email message might appear to be a message from a financial institution telling the victim that there has been suspicious activity on their account.

- The attack usually involves direction to a website. For example, the email might contain a link that appears to be a link to `http://www.wellknownbank.com/` when in fact it is a link to `http://129.1.2.3/`.

- The linked website prompts the user for authentication credentials or other kinds of sensitive information.

There are many variants to the basic phishing attack. "Spear phishing" is a variant in which an attacker uses knowledge of a specific victim to craft personally compelling email messages. In other variants, the website may exploit web browser vulnerabilities to download and implant malware on the victim's computer, without the need for the victim to log in.

Instead of being initiated by email, the user can be directed to the fraudulent website by malicious browser plug-ins or DNS cache poisoning [Weaver et al., 2003]. While this is not strictly phishing, similar approaches need to be employed to detect the spoof sites.

3.3.1 A BRIEF HISTORY OF PHISHING

The term "phishing" appears to have originated in 1995 as "fishing" in conjunction with a program called AOHell that allowed automated attacks on users of America Online [Garfinkel, 1995]. AOL responded by terminating the accounts of the attackers, but they simply returned using new (sometimes stolen) accounts. Eventually AOL modified its service to distinguish user-generated mail from "Official AOL Mail," as indicated by a blue envelope icon in the user's mailbox (Figure 3.11). The word "fishing," morphed to the word "phishing," the "f" to "ph" transformation being popular with the computer underground since 1971 [Lapsey, 2013].

Phishing moved from AOL to Internet email, which lacked a mechanism for email authentication. Academic publications describing phishing as a "new" attack appeared in 2003 [Mann, 2003, McLaughlin, 2003]. A year later, security experts were claiming that phishing attacks "against significant financial institutions have led to six-figure losses" and were recommending that users "be careful opening attachments on e-mail, or about clicking on hyperlinks and URLs included in a mail message." [Treese, 2004]

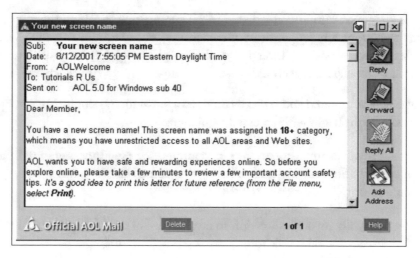

Figure 3.11: America Online responded to phishing attacks by modifying its user interface so that official AOL mail looked different than mail sent by other users. As a result, official messages could not be spoofed by outsiders or other AOL members [Garfinkel, 2005, p.199].

Phishing is pervasive because it is cheap to conduct on a massive scale, it is rare for attackers to get caught, and successful attacks yield credentials that can be used for both financial theft and unauthorized system access.

In phishing, the attacker's fundamental challenge is to mislead the victim into thinking that they are communicating with a legitimate website when in fact they are not. Attackers can fool users with homographic domain names that leverage domains with identical visual appearance but different Unicode representations [Fu et al., 2006], *cousin-name attacks* (e.g., "paypal-secure-login.com" instead of "paypal.com"), or simply domains that are visually similar (e.g., "bankofthevvest.com" masquerading as "bankofthewest.com"). Dhamija et al. [2006] analyzed 200 distinct phishing websites, identified specific tactics used by attackers, and then performed a limited use study testing the effectiveness of each. They found that the best phishing sites could fool more than 90% of participants in their laboratory story.

Jakobsson and Ratkiewicz [2006] presented techniques for conducting a phishing attack for a study that the researchers claim are both *ethical* and *accurate*. The researchers sent spoof emails to approximately 100 subjects and observed response rates between 7% and 19% depending on the nature of the attack email. The authors also presented a model that explains the exponential growth of phishing emails with even very modest spoofing rates, since one of the primary uses of a compromised e-mail account or end-user computer is to send more phishing messages.

Jakobsson and Myers [2006] presented a comprehensive although unfortunately dated collection of expanded articles and original contributions describing phishing attacks and countermeasures. Herley and Florêncio [2008] presented an economic analysis that surprisingly revealed that, while phishing is effective, the amount of money that is actually being stolen may be quite low, and, as a result, the scourge of phishing is being perpetrated by relatively few individuals. This is important, as it implies that enforcement actions against attackers are not likely to be effective in addressing the problem. Sheng et al. [2010] conducted an online study of 1,001 respondents and found that women were more susceptible than men, and that participants aged 18–25 were more susceptible than those who were older. Hong [2012] provides a brief overview of the current state of phishing attacks and anti-phishing mitigation.

In many ways phishing mitigation is the perfect UPS research problem, in that the goal of phishing attacks is to trick users into giving up security-critical information. Many defenses have been systematically analyzed and overcome by the attackers, making phishing mitigation both an exciting two-sided game and a potent source of research funding.

Because it is generally not possible to stop attackers from sending fraudulent email or from registering fraudulent websites, efforts to combat phishing are largely based on four approaches.

1. Filters to prevent users from receiving the phishing messages in the first place, or from blocking their browsers when there is an attempt to access a fraudulent site,

2. Indicators to help users to distinguish legitimate from fraudulent content,

3. Training to help users to detect phishing attempts, and

4. Improved techniques for protecting passwords.

Of these, the first approach is best—prevent users from falling for phishing messages by blocking the messages in the first place. Good filters are also a clear application of Cranor's "Human in the Loop" model (Section 5.1—whenever it is possible to remove a human interaction from a security problem, it is best to do so [Cranor, 2008]). The other approaches exist for when filtering fails. All of these techniques are discussed below.

3.3.2   PASSIVE SECURITY INDICATORS

Early phishing websites had great variation, some with many typographical errors or looks that differ significantly from their targets, while others strongly resembled the sites they were attempting to mimic.

In the first wave of anti-phishing research, researchers and developers created browser enhancements that they hoped would make it easier for users (especially naïve users) to distinguish legitimate from fraudulent websites. For example, eBay created a browser plug-in that would tell users when they were on the eBay or PayPal website, while SpoofGuard and Spoofstick were toolbars that reported to the user that they were on a web page that was likely fraudulent.

Laboratory testing found passive indicators to be generally ineffective. Wu et al. [2006a] performed a "Wizard of Oz" laboratory study with three simulated toolbars that reliably reported when a website was likely to be a phishing site. The study put users in a realistic shopping scenario in which they were accessing websites on behalf of their manager, using a machine that had security software installed because, the manager was worried about phishing attacks. Three toolbars were tested.

- *A neutral information toolbar* reliably indicated the domain name, registration date, and hosting country of the domain; 45% of subjects using it were spoofed.

- *A SSL-verification toolbar* prominently displayed if a site used SSL and provided the site's logo and Certificate Authority; 38% of subjects were spoofed.

- *A system-decision toolbar* displayed a red light if a site was potentially fraudulent; 33% of the users were spoofed.

Even with primed users, Wu et al. [2006a] found that the toolbars were either ignored or disregarded by a significant fraction of users. When asked why they did so, subjects said that they thought the toolbar was wrong and gave explanations as to why. For example, subjects rationalized that the spoof Yahoo! website in Brazil might be legitimate on the grounds that Yahoo had probably opened a new branch office in South America.

Of all the various data sources available for making a phishing or spoofing determination, researchers have devoted the majority of their efforts to leveraging the information available in SSL certificates, since the trusted channel provided by SSL is essential to any kind of web security and since the data in the SSL certificate was presumably verified by a trusted third party for the very purpose of preventing spoofing.

Herzberg and Jbara [2008] criticized Wu et al. [2006a]'s finding that the SSL-verification toolbar did not provide sufficient information to prevent spoofing. The criticism was based in part on the fact that Wu et al. [2006a] based its design on earlier versions of TrustBar that placed the warning "WARNING: THIS PAGE IS NOT PROTECTED" at the top of every web page that was sent without encryption, even when the pages were on legitimate websites.

The researchers revised TrustBar to take into account both identity information from SSL certificates and a logo or name provided by the user during a customization process. The new tool

Figure 3.12: The trusted password window displays the visual hash that matches the website background. (Figure 6 from Dhamija and Tygar [2005]).

Figure 3.13: The website displays the visual hash as a background of a form element (Figure 8 from Dhamija and Tygar [2005]).

generated its own private signature key that is used to sign logos and other information, so that this information could be securely shared between multiple TrustBar installations belonging to the same user. The revised tool also allowed users to report suspicious sites. Finally, the tool could detect so-called "picture-in-picture" attacks, in which the attacking website displays a second browser inside the first, with the goal of convincing the user that the inner browser is legitimate. A laboratory study found that TrustBar provided protection against some phishing attacks, but the study was limited to 23 undergraduate computer science (19 male) students at an Israeli college, not a representative population.

Dhamija and Tygar [2005] proposed a generalizable solution ("dynamic security skins") that gave each website a unique look-and-feel that would be generated by the browser and thus not spoofable by attackers. Essentially, the "skin" is a dedicated area on the web browser where the username and password are entered (Figure 3.12). The skin is dynamically generated based on the website and may be with a visual hash based on the remote site. The visual hash can also be used as a background to a form—for example, a form that requests a user's credit card number (Figure 3.13). The theory was that users would be alerted if the background or security image associated with their bank's website changed and would not enter their username and password.

To be effective, each user needed their own authentication image for each website that they visited. Otherwise, the authentication image could be spoofed as well. Petnames is a similar approach, although each user assigns a name to the website, rather than an image [Stiegler, 2005, Yee and Sitaker, 2006].

Dhamija and Tygar [2005] did not user test security skins, but a similar system called SiteKey was developed by a company called PassMark Software and deployed by Bank of America and other large financial institutions. Schechter et al. [2007] performed a direct test of the security offered by systems such as SiteKey in a potentially adversarial situation using real financial passwords: test subjects were recruited from the street and asked to check their bank balance on a computer provided by the experimenters. A total of 67 people were tested and subjected to a variety of attacks, including removal of the "https" SSL indicator (with an SSL-stripping proxy), removal of the SiteKey-like site-authentication image (it was replaced with a message that the security system was being upgraded and, as such, was not available), and the presentation of an SSL certificate warning. Users were divided into three groups—19 who role-played (they used credentials provided by the experimenters), 20 who role-played but were primed to "behave securely," and 28 who were required to use their own username and password. The authors found that subjects using their own credentials were significantly less likely to log in, but only if they received the SSL warning page. Meanwhile, users who had SSL disabled did not notice (and, by virtue of having SSL disabled, did not receive any SSL warnings). The lack of the SiteKey site-authentication image was only acted upon by two out of 22 users in the study.

A criticism of the study is that the experimenters did not determine if the users did not notice that the security features were absent, or if they noticed and simply chose not to change their behavior.

Table 3.1: Results from a user study by Schechter et al. [2007] reporting the number of participants who correctly chose not to provide a password in response to several simulated attacks.

First chose not to enter password...	Group 1 Role playing	Group 2 Sec. primed	Group 3 Pers. accnt.	Groups 1 ∪ 2	Total
upon noticing HTTPS absent	0 0%	0 0%	0 0%	0 0%	0 0%
after site-authentication image removed	0 0%	0 0%	2 9%	0 0%	2 4%
after warning page	8 47%	5 29%	12 55%	13 37%	25 44%
never (always logged in)	10 53%	12 71%	8 36%	22 63%	30 53%
Total	18	17	22	35	57

Poor website design also contributes to the susceptibility of many users to phishing websites by making users more forgiving of the very design mistakes that phishing websites are likely to exhibit. In a study of 125 popular websites, Stebila [2010] found that 53 websites had complicated URLs; 29 had lock icons in the body of the page or as a favicon, where they are spoofable, rather than relying on the browser to show the lock icon in the browser's chrome), 19 had HTTP login pages with HTTPS form submission, giving users the impression that their credentials would not be submitted with encryption; and 16 had a domain name that did not match the organization.

The result of these design errors may be that users are habituated to ignoring security indicators that might otherwise help them to be more secure.

Passive security indicators nevertheless survive in most modern browsers.

- **Extended Validation (EV) Certificates:** In response to the declining cost and ease of obtaining SSL certificates without providing any business information, industry created EV certificates. Unlike traditional SSL certificates, EV certificates can contain a company's legal name, contact information, and even a logo. The higher-priced TLS certificates also require site administrators to provide legal information about the corporation obtaining the certificate. All of this is designed to act as a deterrent to the procurement of EV certificates by criminals.

  Biddle et al. [2009] tested the ability of 40 laboratory subjects to use EV certificates to learn important information about the credibility of an e-commerce website; the experimenters found that participants were in general confused about the content of EV certificates and that the interface of Internet Explorer 7 contributed to the confusion. The experimenters found specific problems with the language used by alert windows and the information that they conveyed. By redesigning the interface, laboratory subjects tested with higher rates of understanding in an amount that was statistically significant but not substantial.

- **Domain Highlighting:** Many modern browsers use typography to visually distinguish the Internet domain from the remainder of the URL, a practice called *domain highlighting*. Lin et al. [2011b] tested domain highlighting combined with training on 22 participants, and found that it allowed some but not all participants to avoid phishing attacks successfully.

- **Key Continuity Management (KCM) / Trust On First Use (TOFU):** Another way to avoid spoofing is to assume that the first use of the key is correct and generate an error if the public key changes in the future. This use of uncertified public keys to stop spoofing was introduced by Ylonen [1996]; the phrase "Key Continuity Management" was coined by Gutmann [2004] to describe the practice. Today the term "Trust on First Use" appears to be more widely accepted.

  Garfinkel and Miller [2005] tested an email interface that implemented KCM/TOFU for keys used to digitally signed email messages in a 43 user between-subjects study. They found that subjects who were provided with both KCM/TOFU information and an explanatory briefing were significantly more resistant to spoofing attacks than those who did not receive the information.

  Today, Mozilla Firefox allows users to trust explicitly an untrusted certificate, but only after a warning message is seen. Unfortunately, this conditions users to expect warnings and click through them [Sunshine et al., 2009], rather than reserving the warnings for circumstances that might be more likely to represent a man-in-the-middle attack—for example, when a certificate changes.

3.3.3   ACTIVE SECURITY WARNINGS

Active warnings interrupt the user's activity and demand a response. Active warnings must somehow convince users to take the warning seriously, rather than simply "swat" it away by clicking a button, but they must also allow users to disregard the warning because the warning might be wrong. Additionally, users that are unable to bypass warnings may disable the security software entirely or switch to a competing program that allows warnings to be disabled, even if the warning is correctly displayed and the user is in fact wrong.

Egelman et al. [2008a] compared passive and active warnings and found that the active warnings that take over the entire screen were far more effective than passive warnings in the toolbar. The within-group study found that its user population was highly susceptible—97% of 60 participants in the laboratory study fell for at least one of the simulated phishing attacks. Nevertheless, 79% of the users heeded the active warnings that they experienced and did not proceed to the phishing website, compared to only 1 of 10 users who heeded the passive warning.

While active warnings may be heeded more often, many users still ignore such warnings and "click through" to the site rather than navigate away. For example, studying 25 million warning impressions *in situ*, Akhawe and Felt [2013] found browser click-through rates of 7%–25% for malware warnings, and 9%–35% for phishing warnings (lower numbers are better), with significant dependencies on the platform, browser, specific week of the study, and release channel through which the user obtained the software (e.g., Stable, Beta, Dev, or Nightly), with uses of the Nightly release consistently exhibiting among the most risky behavior.

Design choices, sometimes subtle, have been shown to have impact on the click-through rates of active warnings. Early work proposed that active warnings should be *polymorphic*, displayed differently each time to reduce habituation, and *audited*, holding users accountable for their choices [Brustoloni and Villamarín-Salomón, 2007]. However, these concepts were only tested in small laboratory studies.

Sunshine et al. [2009] redesigned SSL warnings based on warnings-science principles and lessons learned from a survey of 409 Internet users. Their redesigned warning first asked users a question regarding the kind of site they are attempting to visit, and then presented a scary-looking warning for bank and eCommerce sites. Fewer participants in a 100-person between-subjects laboratory study ignored this new warning in a banking scenario.

Bravo-Lillo et al. [2011] redesigned two warnings based on a set of design guidelines compiled from the previous research:

- follow a visually consistent layout,

- comprehensively describe the risk,

- be concise, accurate, and encouraging,

- offer meaningful options, and

- present relevant contextual and auditing information.

The researchers also designed a set of warnings based upon literature of mental models of security risks. They then evaluated these warnings, comparing against existing browser warnings, in an online Mechanical Turk study of 733 participants. The redesigned warnings did lead to safer behavior in many of their high-risk conditions, but did not contribute to increased understanding of warnings.

Felt et al. [2014] further studied variations in Chrome's SSL warning, examining the impact of icons of people watching, the number of steps to proceed past the warning, page style, and coloring, as well as comparing against Firefox's design, which contains different layout, text, and buttons. In a large-scale field trial, they found significant differences between the Chrome and Firefox designs, but little impact from any other factor. Additional work needs to be done to isolate the aspects of Firefox's design that impact this difference. For example, Firefox makes it relatively easy for a user to trust a website's certificate after an initial SSL warning, whereas Chrome does not. This feature may result in lower warning rates for Firefox if users frequently return to the same sites.

Despite the improvements to active browser warnings, many users are still ignoring them. There is evidence of warning fatigue, where users are more likely to click through warnings they see frequently [Akhawe and Felt, 2013]. Thus, browser developers should limit the number of warnings that users encounter. This leads to the question of whether detection of suspicious sites is sufficiently accurate that it may be better simply to block users altogether [Sunshine et al., 2009], rather than continuing to try and get users to heed warnings about unsafe websites. Of course, users could always respond by using a different browser to get to the website that they are convinced they need to access. This may be the primary reason that browser vendors still allow users to circumvent the warnings and proceed to the danger.

3.3.4 TRAINING

While passive browser indicators by themselves do not prevent phishing, there is some evidence that their usefulness can be improved through user training—especially user training that is continuous and integrated into realistic attack scenarios. However, it is unclear if the training has only a short-term impact and requires repetition, or if it results in long-term substantive changes in the trained population.

In order to train users to avoid phishing attacks it is necessary to first understand why people are falling for them. Downs et al. [2006] reported on a preliminary interview study with 20 non-expert computer users and found that users generally did not understand the risks or the attacks. The researchers identified specific strategies that people use to evaluate the legitimacy of email messages and to make sense of web-browser warnings. One of the key findings was that users frequently misinterpret security cues. For example, while 85% of the participants understood that the "secure site lock icon" signified that the site was somehow secure, only 40% knew that the lock had to be displayed in the browser's chrome. The study also found that security information was contextualized: participants who knew not to provide their social security number in response to faux Citibank e-mails were not similarly protective of their Amazon password. Training can correct these misconceptions.

There are a variety of anti-phishing training materials freely available online, such as OnGuard Phishing Education[6] and PayPal[7]. Sheng et al. [2010] found a 40% reduction in dangerous behavior when users were trained with effective material. However, that requires users to actually read and attend to such material.

The CyLab Usable Privacy and Security Lab (CUPS) at Carnegie Mellon University utilized principles from learning sciences to design two alternative training methods. Anti-phishing Phil is a game that teaches people how to detect potential phishing URLs to avoid fraudulent websites [Sheng et al., 2007]. A between-subjects laboratory study found that participants who played the game performed better at determining phishing sites than those using just a tutorial of training messages based upon the game [Sheng et al., 2007]. A larger field study of over 4,000 participants confirmed these findings, and found that users retained their knowledge for at least a week [Kumaraguru et al., 2010].

Another approach is "embedded training," in which participants are sent phishing-like emails, except that the embedded links bring the users to websites that inform them that they fell for a phishing attack and provide the users with additional training. Kumaraguru et al. [2009] tested PhishGuru, a system that sends real users simulated phishing emails: clicking on the link results not in being attacked, but in receiving training. In developing their training materials for PhishGuru, researchers examined the use of text and graphics as well as using comics. Early laboratory studies found the comics performed better than the text/graphics messages [Kumaraguru et al., 2010]. In a real-world 515-participant study, the researchers found significant retention of training information, even after 28 days [Kumaraguru et al., 2009]. Further, a second training message appeared to further improve performance. Unlike a previous study at Indiana university [Jagatic et al., 2007], which generated negative response from a significant number of participants, the authors of Kumaraguru study [2009] report positive comments in the post-study survey, such as "I really liked the idea of sending CMU students fake phishing emails and then saying to them, essentially, HEY! You could've just gotten scammed! You should be more careful—here's how...." One key difference between the two studies was that subjects of the Jagatic et al. [2007] study enrolled without their consent, whereas the Kumaraguru et al. [2009] was an opt-in study. The CMU study also found that participants who click on phishing links tend to do so within 8 h after the email was sent, emphasizing the importance for institutions to update URL and domain blacklists as quickly as possible when they experience a phishing attack.

However, another study failed to replicate these findings. Caputo et al. [2014] aimed to replicate the previous PhishGuru field study, but, in an industrial setting and with a controlled sampling technique. The study differed by examining retention over a longer 90-day period, and did not utilize comic-style training materials "because senior members of the corporation didn't

---

[6]http://www.onguardonline.gov/phishing
[7]https://www.paypal.com/webapps/mpp/security/antiphishing-protectyourself

feel that a comic strip was the appropriate format for corporate employee training."[Caputo et al., 2014]. Researchers recruited 1,359 participants chosen from different job strata. Their results did not show any improvement for those receiving training. In further exploring why, follow-up interviews revealed that many participants merely skimmed or barely read the training materials. Some also questioned the legitimacy of the material, worried that it was part of a phishing attack. Thus, there is still a challenge in embedding training that users will pay attention to and retain.

3.3.5   PASSWORD MANAGERS

With the advent of phishing, researchers sought to use the password managers' trusted position to address the phishing problem. The idea was that even if the user thought the remote site was legitimate, the password manager would know that the site was not and would not provide the correct password. Thus, password managers are well-placed to solve the twin problems of password proliferation and phishing. However, password managers are under-utilized, possibly due to usability factors.

Wu et al. [2006b] found that password managers can effectively prevent phishing because it is hard to trick them into submitting a legitimate password to a spoof website (the mechanisms used to spoof humans generally do not spoof password managers). But that, even with strong wallets, other techniques remain by which users can be tricked into bypassing the manager and revealing their password.

3.4   STORAGE

The primary security issues specific to storage are *assured deletion* and *durability*. Assured deletion means that information intentionally deleted by the user should by unrecoverable, while durability provides for the ability to retrieve information that has not been intentionally deleted.

It has long been recognized that when applications and operating systems delete data in response to a user command, the data is simply unlinked but still resides on the media. There exist many specialized tools, both commercial and open source, for recovering deleted information. For many years, computer users or administrators were told that it was their responsibility to remove sensitive information from a computer system before it was decommissioned or re-purposed. This guidance was enshrined in standards such as Kissel et al. [2006] and DoD [1995].

Garfinkel and Shelat [2003] showed that a significant number of computers and storage media purchased on the secondary market contained sensitive data that could be readily recovered. In some cases sensitive information was plainly visible, as if a computer had simply been turned off and sold with no attention to the data it contained. In other cases user files had been deleted (but were still recoverable), although application files had been left intact. This was deemed to be a failed attempt to remove sensitive information. Finally, in some cases the media had apparently been "formatted" with the Windows FORMAT command, which, at the time, wrote new file system structures but did not actually overwrite the disk contents.

The authors held that requiring users to use specialty programs to erase files or sanitize media was a usability failure, and that, instead, this behavior should be built into the basic operating system. Microsoft addressed this in Windows 7 by modifying the FORMAT command to overwrite data, and the Macintosh operating system offers a "secure empty trash" (which unfortunately has a high performance cost associated with excessive overwriting of the storage media [Garfinkel, 2005]). Nevertheless, other systems still require specialty software.

The tendency of computer systems to hide rather than overwrite deleted information is a longstanding problem that has been observed in memory allocation strategies [Chow et al., 2005] and documents [Byers, 2003]. Information disclosure can also result when the information displayed by a word processor or production tool does not match the information stored in the document file [Garfinkel, 2014].

However, many users do not seem to be significantly concerned about the inadvertent leakage of private data in documents or discarded systems. Ion et al. [2011] conducted 36 in-depth interviews in Switzerland and India in an attempt to gauge attitudes about cloud storage systems and found that users minimized these risks for data that they stored at home, but felt that unauthorized access was a significant risk of data stored in the cloud. The survey also found that users would be willing to pay for services that provide strong privacy guarantees.

3.5 DEVICE PAIRING

The term "device pairing" describes a process by which two devices are associated so that they can work together. Pairing is more than simply connecting devices—for example, connecting two computers with a cable. Pairing creates a persistent relationship so that the devices may mutually authenticate in the future and securely transfer data over an open network (e.g., the public Internet or an open wireless network). Today, pairing is commonly used for establishing trust relationships between wireless devices—for example, pairing a mobile phone with a Bluetooth headset. Pairing is also used for binding authentication tokens with identity providers, and for pairing secure applications to servers (e.g., PGPfone or Zfone). Pairing protocols are complicated by the limited I/O facilities of some devices.

There are many possible threats to device pairing.

- Some pairing protocols have inherent cryptographic weaknesses. For example, some pairing protocols rely on passphrases to encrypt keying material; if the pairing protocol can be observed by an attacker, it is possible to perform a dictionary attack on the encrypted data to recover the keys.

- Instead of pairing device A with B, the user may inadvertently pair A with an attacker's device (e.g., E), which then pairs with B. This is called a *Man-in-the-Middle* or *Evil Twin* attack.

- The attacker may convince the paired devices to renegotiate a key or even repair in such a way that the man-in-the-middle attack can be initiated.

- The pairing protocol may be so complicated or error-prone that users avoid it.

Early Pairing Protocols   Early authentication tokens, such as the Security Dynamics' SecureID token (later renamed RSA Security), relied on shared secrets that were established during manufacturing, prior to distribution of the device to the customer. Stajano and Anderson [2000] introduced the *Resurrecting-Duckling* model of device pairing in which a master device (the "mother") establishes a shared secret with each new client device (the "duckling") through a process called *imprinting*. The authors wrote that the most satisfactory way to transmit the secret is in plaintext over a physical connection. These secrets must be protected with some kind of tamper-proof hardware to prevent cloning. If the client needs to be re-used, its memory is wiped (it is killed) and then paired again (the "resurrection") with a new mother.

The advantage of the resurrecting-duckling model is that it is easy to understand: the pairing is initiated by a physical connection, and any client can be reset to a factory-fresh mode.

Wireless Pairing with Out-Of-Band Information   Technologies such as infrared data and Bluetooth were created to allow portable devices to communicate without the need for cables. Users of such devices also need ways to establish shared secrets and (by design) do not have cables that they can fall back upon. An obvious way is for a human to simply type the shared secret into both devices—for example, by typing a 128-bit wireless encryption key into both a router and a client. This was the approach used by early wireless LAN systems. Encryption keys proved difficult to distribute; typing them proved error prone. As a result, many early wireless systems used no encryption at all due to usability concerns.

Modern wireless network protocols rely instead on the typing of so-called short authentication strings (colloquially "passwords" or "PINs") that are used to create or validate cryptographic keys. The typed string can be thought of as being sent over a secure out-of-band (OOB) channel involving the user's eyes, brain, and fingers. The idea of using short authentication strings to authenticate encryption channels was introduced by Vaudenay [2005].

Pairing without typing   An alternative to typing a short authentication string is to use some other channel to transmit the out-of-band information.

Early work in this area includes "Talking to Strangers" [Smetters et al., 2002] and "Network-in-a-box" [Balfanz et al., 2004], which employed so-called "location-limited channels" (e.g., infrared data and high-frequency audio) to bootstrap the transfer of security credentials necessary to establish a secure wireless network. Saxena et al. [2011] demonstrate secure pairing over a unidirectional visual channel—for example, a phone pairing to a laptop by monitoring a flashing LED, or pairing two phones together. Mutual authentication is provided through an unauthenticated back channel. The scheme was user tested in a laboratory with 20 users, who took an average of 47 seconds to pair the first time, and 39 seconds to pair the second.

Soriente et al. [2008] explore communicating the OOB information over an audio channel. While the use of audio-based pairing is largely unexplored in the marketplace, these kinds of schemes might have considerable use for individuals with vision impairment, or for devices that lack displays but have a speaker and/or a microphone. Such schemes could provide considerably more security than the current Bluetooth approach of putting devices into a "pairing mode" and then having them promiscuously pair with any other device that knows the pre-set PIN of "0000" or "1234." Likewise, schemes that rely on vibration or button pressing are applicable for devices that are so simple that they cannot even have an audio interface but have a button.

Other approaches for sharing a secret include tapping a rhythmic sequence on each device [Lin et al., 2011a], or even shaking two devices together and using built-in accelerometers for key agreement [Mayrhofer and Gellersen, 2009]. Gallego et al. [2011] turns pairing into an enjoyable game, a process called gamification, although no user test is provided.

Pairing by Comparing Hashes   Instead of transferring a shared secret by OOB, another approach is for both machines being paired to agree on a shared secret—for example, using a Diffie-Hellman protocol—after which each device displays a hash of the key and the user confirms that the two are the same. Each bit of the hash confirmed by the user reliably reduces the chance of a Man-in-the-Middle attack by $\frac{1}{2}$.

Perrig and Song [1999] displayed a piece of random art based on the hash of an encryption key on two devices and the user verifies that they are the same, while Roth et al. [2008] transform the hash into a sequence of color that is displayed simultaneously on the wireless access point and on the user's screen. The user proves the absence of a hostile middle-man by watching both flashing displays at the same time and verifying that the sequences are the same. Alternatively, the public keys can be authenticated using information that is provided over the OOB channel to both authentic devices (presumably bypassing the evil twin). For example, a user can type the same 6-digit PIN on both devices, or type a PIN that one device displays on a second.

HAPADEP is a pure audio pairing system that uses a high-speed acoustic modem to share one or two public keys between two systems. Once shared, the verification hash is transformed into either a pleasant melody or (with a voice synthesizer) a Madlibs-style sentence that both systems play at the same time (Figure 3.5). The system was tested with a laboratory test of 20 subjects, with 95% finding the sentence verification easy or very easy, while only 50% found the melody verification to be similarly easy or very easy.

Pairing for Authentication   Many modern token-based authentication systems that use mobile phones accomplish pairing by having one device photograph a 2D bar code that is displayed on a second, providing an out-of-band channel for the exchange of secret information. Clarke et al. [2002] appear to present the earliest of these systems; they proposed a system in which a cell phone with a camera takes a photograph of a computer's screen to record a 2D barcode; the handheld device can then be used to authenticate at a public terminal to a remote computer. McCune et al. [2005][8] realized the approach on a Nokia 6620 feature phone and proposed a variety of useful applications. Google Authenticator is a modern implementation of this system; Google authen-

---

[8] McCune et al. [2004] provide additional details not in McCune et al. [2009].

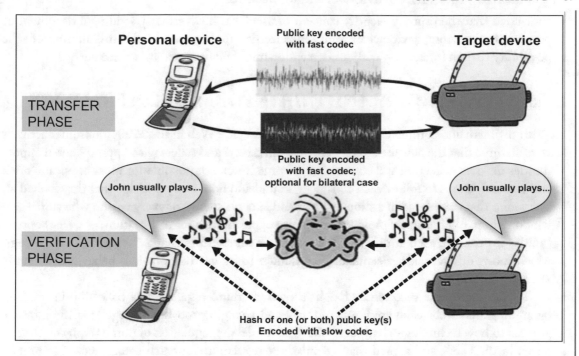

Figure 3.14: HAPADEP: Human-Assisted Pure Audio Device Pairing. (Based on Soriente et al. [2008].)

ticator is based on the RFC 4226 Time-based One Time Password (TOPT); the 2D barcode is a QR code that contains a URI with a label and the RFC 4226 secret parameters [Google, 2012].

Multi-modality Evaluations   Kumar et al. [2009] and Kobsa et al. [2009] report on two separate usability studies of pairing protocols. Each study evaluated 13 prototype pairing methods that were implemented in Java on two Nokia smart phones, with each study having approximately 20 participants. The studies found that comparing two sequences of numbers on two devices was both faster and more accurate than all of the other methods tested. The primary risk of the method is that users might approve the pairing without actually checking the numbers; this risk can be avoided by forcing the user to type a number displayed on one device into another, at a cost of increasing the rate of false rejection as a result of human error.

Ion et al. [2010] evaluated four pairing methods (typing digits, taking a photograph of a barcode, verifying a melody and pressing a button). The researchers made an effort to recruit non-technical users and examined how pairing preferences were impacted by a security briefing and by different kinds of tasks requiring pairing (printing a document, making a payment, and sending a business card). With a laboratory user study and interviews of the 25 subjects, the researchers concluded that the primary security concern of users was inadvertently sending a document or payment to the wrong device: users were *not* concerned about a man-in-the-middle attack or the possibility that an interaction without encryption might be observed by a third party.

3.6 WEB PRIVACY AND FAIR INFORMATION PRACTICE

With the birth and commercialization of the World Wide Web in the 1990s, consumer activists were alarmed that the new technology provided marketers and sellers with unprecedented opportunities for data collection and control. At the time it was not possible for most physical ("brick and mortar") stores to follow each consumer around and note every package that they looked at, every item that was placed in a shopping cart and later taken out, or every person who stopped to window shop. Online stores provided these very opportunities for observation, as well as opportunities for control, such as different prices to different consumers and "behavioral advertising," which shows different advertisements to consumers based on their previous behaviors [Ur et al., 2012c].

Web merchants successfully fought several efforts to regulate data collection in the U.S. by arguing that web technology was too new and changing too fast to regulate. The industry pointed to how technologies had successfully prevented the regulation of pornography on the Internet in the U.S.[9], and argued that a similar self-regulation approach could be used to protect consumer privacy through "notice and choice" [Cranor, 1999]. Essentially, marketers would provide consumers with notice regarding their data collection practices and consumers could then choose whether or not to provide personal information, shop, or take their business elsewhere. In the U.S., "notice and choice" was largely implemented by the publishing of "privacy policies" that disclosed corporate practices. Enforcement was ultimately the job of the U.S. Federal Trade Commission, which could take action against organizations that did not follow their posted policies as an unfair trade practice. Such privacy policies were similar in spirit to the "click-wrap" license agreements for software that emerged in the 1990s, which required that users accept a legal agreement before the software would run properly.

3.6.1 PRIVACY POLICIES

The lack of usability of website privacy policy notices is one of the earliest problems identified by the UPS community. Because privacy policies in the U.S. are voluntary, there are no restrictions as to the format and content of such policies. As a result, privacy policies can be unstructured and jargon-filled documents that are difficult to read and comprehend, rendering them useless to many consumers [Grossklags and Good, 2007, Hochhauser, 2001, Jensen and Potts, 2004].

---

[9]In Reno v. ACLU (521 U.S. 844), the U.S. Supreme Court's held that provisions in the Communication Decency Act prohibiting the "indecent transmission" and "patently offensive display" of pornography over the Internet violated the First Amendment of the U.S. Constitution, in part because of the existence of the Platform for Internet Content Selection (PICS) provided a less restrictive means for parents to shield their children from Internet porn [Resnick and Miller, 1996].

Similar to end-user license agreements [Good et al., 2005], a number of studies have demonstrated that users rarely read online privacy policies [Jensen and Potts, 2004, Jensen et al., 2005]. However, "if all American Internet users were to annually read the online privacy policies word-for-word each time they visited a new site, the nation would spend about 54 billion hours reading privacy policies" [McDonald and Cranor, 2008]. Thus, even if privacy policies contained notices that conflicted with users' privacy preferences, users would not realize those conflicts and behave counter to their preferences [Good et al., 2005].

The UPS research community has examined improved methods for viewing privacy policies. For example, Kelley et al. proposed the use of a table format, inspired by the successful nutrition label on most U.S. packaged foods, to convey a site's privacy policy [Kelley, 2009, Kelley et al., 2009, 2010]. The final design, shown in Figure 3.15 was iteratively improved through a series of focus groups and laboratory studies. They then compared this approach to a standardized text format and a full text policy in a Mechanical Turk study with 794 participants [Kelley et al., 2010]. Users performed better with both the standardized text and table formats, although the more visual table format may be easier to scan and scale.

Kay and Terry [2010] investigated using graphical design principles to draw attention to the content of policies, incorporating factoids, vignettes, and iconic symbols into a license agreement, increasing the time users spent reading the policy as well as retention of the content. Despite users' lack of attention to existing privacy policy documents, if that information is made more salient, users will utilize that privacy information in their decision making. Tsai et al. implemented the PrivacyFinder, which displayed a simple privacy meter alongside the list of webpages of a search [Egelman et al., 2009, Tsai et al., 2011]. The researchers performed a series of experiments examining users' choices in purchasing products from websites. Participants were invited to a laboratory study for an online shopping experiment, where they were tasked with purchasing real products from real vendors (chosen by the researchers) with their own credit cards. The products were both privacy insensitive (batteries) as well as privacy sensitive (a sex toy). Participants were more likely to purchase products from the sites with higher privacy scores, even when the products were more expensive. Participants also paid more attention to indicators when purchasing the privacy sensitive items [Egelman et al., 2009].

3.6.2   P3P

The Platform for Privacy Preferences (P3P) was proposed as a platform for machine-readable privacy policies, aimed at reducing the time required by people to read natural language policies [Note, 2006]. P3P allows sites to specify a policy that can be interpreted by the browser, giving users the ability to specify their general preferences and be notified when websites do not conform [Hunker, 2008].

Rather than reading textual policy documents, users then interact with privacy agents for specifying their policies. Cranor et al. investigated the design of a usable P3P user agent, called Privacy Bird, as a plug-in for Internet Explorer through iterative designs and evaluations [Cranor

The Acme Policy

types of information	how we use your information					who we share your information with	
	provide service & maintain site	research & development	marketing	telemarketing	profiling	other companies	public forums
contact information	!	!	OUT	OUT	▬	IN	▬
cookies	!	!	OUT	OUT		IN	
demographic information	▬	▬	▬	▬	▬	▬	▬
financial information	▬	▬	▬	▬	▬	▬	▬
health information	▬	▬	▬	▬	▬	▬	▬
preferences	!	!	OUT	OUT	▬	IN	!
purchasing information	!	!	OUT	OUT	▬	IN	▬
social security number & govt ID	!	▬		▬	▬	▬	▬
your activity on this site	!	!	OUT	OUT		IN	!
your location	▬	▬	▬	▬	▬	▬	▬

Understanding this privacy policy

!	we **will** use your information in this way
▬	we **will not** collect or we **will not** use your information in this way
OUT	we **will** use your information in this way unless you opt-out
IN	we **will not** use your information in this way unless you opt-in

contact us   call 1 888-888-8888
www.acme.com

Figure 3.15: A privacy label. (Based on Kelley et al. [2010].)

et al., 2006]. Privacy Bird used icons to provide immediate feedback as to whether the site matched a user's privacy preferences. Internet Explorer is the most widely-used agent, where users choose between "Low" to "High" privacy preferences.

However, in order to work properly, P3P policies need to represent the website's written policy accurately, they need to be understandable by browsers, and users need to specify their general preferences with a P3P policy interface [Cranor et al., 2006]. Early experience with P3P indicated privacy policies were "derived and specified in a somewhat ad-hoc manner, leading to policies that are of limited use to the consumers they are intended to serve" [Stufflebeam et al., 2004]. Later studies confirmed this. For example, Cranor et al. [2008] found that deployment of P3P was inconsistent across industry and generally poor: conducting typical searches, they found that only 10% of the top-20 results of their web searches had P3P policies; restricting the results to e-commerce sites, the number rose to 21%. They found that 470 new P3P policies created over a 2-month period in Fall 2007 contained syntax errors that might prevent automated processing. Most concerning, they found that most P3P policies had discrepancies with their natural language counterparts—in some cases, discrepancies that resulted in significantly different meanings. Reay et al. [2009] surveyed the 100,000 most popular websites on the planet and found roughly 3,000 P3P policies and another 30,000 compact policies. Performing an automated analysis of the policies, they found that "Websites generally do not even claim to follow all the privacy-protection mandates in their legal jurisdiction," but note that they did not examine the actual practice of the websites, only the posted policies. "Furthermore, this general statement appears to be true for every jurisdiction with privacy laws and any significant number of P3P policies, including European Union nations, Canada, Australia, and Websites in the U.S. Safe Harbor program," the authors wrote.

3.6.3   BEHAVIORAL ADVERTISING

A more recent issue in Web privacy has focused on the practice of behavioral advertising—advertising that is customized based upon a user's previous browsing activity. Advertising networks utilize cookies to track users across multiple sites on which they operate, enabling them to deliver ads based upon the set of sites and pages users have previously visited. Similar to the P3P initiative, advertisers have argued for a self-regulatory approach to providing users with information about the practices and "opt-out" methods for limiting the tracking and use of their browsing behavior. A W3C working group has been formed to standardize a "Do Not Track" mechanism to allow users to opt out of this tracking, which is already built into several browsers (http://www.w3.org/2011/tracking-protection/).

Several studies have investigated users' perceptions of behavioral advertising. In a 48-participant interview study, Ur et al. [2012c] found that American Internet users find the concept of behavioral advertising to be both potentially useful, but also privacy invasive ("creepy"). There is also significant confusion about the practice of behavioral advertising. Users do not understand the mechanisms through which advertising can be targeted to them (i.e., cookies), and thus, are also confused about how to prevent such tracking, such as by deleting cookies, using the "Do Not Track" private browsing mechanism in a browser, or using an opt-out cookie [McDonald and Cranor, 2010]. Thus, while consumers did indicate an understanding that some behavioral advertising is occurring, current practices are misunderstood and violating users' expectations. Agarwal et al. [2013] asked similar questions about the perceptions of users in India, identifying an additional concern of being shown ads that were embarrassing or sensitive—that others would make inferences (often incorrectly) about the users' browsing activity. This implies that selective ad blocking would also be a useful privacy tool.

Leon et al. [2013] further examined the factors of the organizational policies and uses of personal information that impacted users' willingness to allow the collection of information for online behavioral advertising. Nearly half of the 2,912 Mechanical Turk participants indicated that they would not like to share personal information for behavioral advertising under any circumstances. The scope of use and data retention period impacted the willingness of the remaining participants' to share their personal information.

Leon et al. [2012] evaluated the usability of existing privacy tools for limiting behavioral advertising in a between-subjects laboratory study with 45 participants. Tools included those that set opt-out cookies for different advertising networks, settings within the web browser to block selective cookies or use privacy browsing, and browser plug-ins that selectively block cookies based on various rules. The study identified serious usability flaws with every available tool. Many tools require or allow users to block based on the names of the advertising networks, which are unfamiliar to consumers. Additionally, existing tools have weak defaults and poor communication to the user about problems that arise due to the tool usage.

3.6.4 SUMMARY

Cranor [2012] argued that "notice and choice" mechanisms for protecting consumer privacy are not working. Current solutions are not providing users with an accurate understanding that can be used to inform privacy decisions, and methods for opting-out suffer from serious usability issues.When faced with a conflict between long-term policy goals and immediate needs or wants, the immediate often wins out.

In addition, organizations may not be able (or willing) to present their data collection policies to consumers in a manner that can be understood. There is also insufficient enforcement that the practices reported by organizations are even accurate in the first place. "P3P is an example of a technical mechanism designed to support, but not enforce, the privacy-by-policy approach. Since there has been no external enforcement that P3P policies are accurate, P3P has become a useless standard" [Cranor, 2012].

Overall, it seems that the primary success of P3P and other technical measures was in preventing the early adoption of significant regulations and laws governing online privacy and data collection. Thus, Cate [2010] stated that the challenge is identifying the cases in which "notice and choice" works and identifying alternative data protection methods for when it does not.

3.7 POLICY SPECIFICATION AND INTERACTION

Beyond website privacy policies, there are many different systems requiring users to view and author security and privacy policies, from administrators responsible for organizational privacy policies, to co-workers configuring who can access shared files, to consumers modifying settings for who can view their online photos. Thus, another research theme is understanding how users interact with, make decisions about, and author such policies, in order to improve how security and privacy policies can be represented to users.

Many of these policies can be considered access control—determining who has access to systems and information. Access control mechanisms for end users fall into the category of discretionary access control, where users determine the policies for their own information.

Within the UPS community, researchers acknowledge that the act of determining access to information is part of the larger goal of sharing information. Thus, studies of access control are often part of a more general study about the sharing habits and behaviors of users. Research on file sharing demonstrates the importance of studying sharing behaviors more broadly, in order to understand the policy implications.

Several studies have surveyed and interviewed users within a corporate setting. For example, Dalal et al. [2008] conducted a small interview study to identify a variety of file-sharing requirements and problems, including the needs of providing access to information for short periods of time, or to new or unplanned groups of people, as well as the tendency to overshare information when it is too difficult to limit it appropriately. In addition, users often need to share information with themselves, in order to move files between various devices. Voida et al. [2006] also conducted an interview and survey study of file sharing, where users reported that they had difficulties in choosing a technology in which to share files, and tended to forget who they shared files with. Additionally users report that they may have to modify policies regularly, as work teams evolve, or to grant temporary access [Whalen et al., 2006].

Mazurek et al. [2010] conducted interviews with 33 participants across 15 households, examining participants' needs and attitudes toward sharing information at home, as opposed to the workplace. Participants expressed detailed and nuanced access control needs for their personal information, with dimensions including not just who could access information, but also for what purpose, and whether they were present in the home. Participants also reported that protecting files is not simply about unauthorized access, but that there is a need to distinguish between read and write permissions [Mazurek et al., 2010].

Despite a wealth of file-sharing technologies, the most common way for people to share files with other people is through email, because of the simplicity and immediacy of sharing [Smetters and Good, 2009, Whalen et al., 2006]. One implication is that email lists may become de facto access control lists, determining which groups of users can see files [Smetters and Good, 2009].

Johnson et al. [2009] further examined why individuals share files by email, even when they are given a range of file-sharing solutions. They concluded that email gives "individuals at the end-points" direct control over the sharing of their information and compare the success of email over other file sharing techniques to be similar to the success of free market economies over centrally managed economies.

However, email can also lead to sharing information unintentionally, as users accidentally reply to too many people or do not realize the reach of an email list. Facemail attempts to combat this (Figures 3.16 and 3.17), using photographs of email recipients as a passive indicator to remind the sender how many people (and who) would be receiving an email message. In testing, users were found to be able to determine rapidly (in less than 1 s) if messages would go to a small or large number of users; in one case Facemail prevented one of the paper's authors from inadvertently sending an email message to the wrong person.

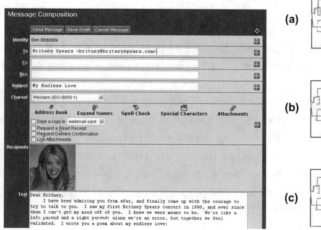

Figure 3.16: Facemail composition window. (Figure 1 from Lieberman and Miller, 2007)

Figure 3.17: Progressive scaling grid showing (a) 10 faces, (b) 100 faces, and (c) 1,000 faces. (Figure 3 from Lieberman and Miller, 2007)

Given the long history of shared file systems, there are relatively few user studies of them specifically. One exception is the work by Smetters and Good [2009] that mined the access control policies for a shared file system within a medium sized technology organization. They found that the policies could be quite complex, but one reason appears to be user error as repeated or overlapping access was granted. Thus simplifying the access control patterns provided to the user may reduce redundancy and user mistakes. Users create a large number of groups, and actively modify them over time. Yet, there is evidence that users rarely "clean up" access, removing people from email lists or from file access who no longer require it. Most files inherited access rights from their containing folders, so that users rarely set policies on individual files.

Beyond just setting file permissions, users report a need for and use of a variety of techniques to protect files. For example, users reported "locking" files so that content could not be modified [Whalen et al., 2006] as well as relying on social conventions to help limit who accesses information [Mazurek et al., 2010, Whalen et al., 2006].

Common guidelines for creating more usable access control mechanisms across each of these studies include:

- make access control more visible, by incorporating policies alongside the context of use,

- simplify access control patterns and interfaces,

- support ad-hoc and temporary sharing,

- support real-time policy updates, and

- support and reflect social conventions.

There have been a limited number of prototype systems designed and evaluated that encompass these guidelines. For example, Voida et al. [2006] proposed the "Sharing Palette" to provide a simple and visual view of who content is shared with. Vaniea et al. [2012] created a prototype interface for photo sharing to demonstrate that users were more likely to notice and fix access control permission errors when the permissions were displayed in closer proximity to the content they were sharing. Bauer et al. [2008] investigated the benefits of a smartphone system called Grey, in place of keys in an office environment. They found that the ability of users to provide real-time policy updates resulted in better matches to users' ideal policies. Mazurek et al. [2010] also found that, for content in a home setting, users expressed a desire to match the social conventions of being asked permission for access to personal information. Such a mechanism would potentially add burden, as users must be notified whenever a request is made and make decisions based upon each of those requests. However, a study simulating such a system found positive evidence that real-time requests would be useful [Mazurek et al., 2011].

Beyond access control, a number of projects have explored different representations of security and privacy policies that would be more usable than existing interface mechanisms. For example, the SPARCLE project [Bauer et al., 2009, Brodie et al., 2005, 2006, Johnson et al., 2010, Sasse et al., 2009, Vaniea et al., 2008] explored using natural language for an organizational privacy policy specification that then gets automatically translated into a formal policy language. They demonstrated that the natural language was easier for end users, yet could still be made just as powerful. Another approach is to use visualization, such as the expandable grid, which visualizes policy rules in a grid format [Reeder et al., 2008a]. The visualization enables users to view and express the policy in terms of categories of data and people, rather than sets of rules that could be combined in unintuitive ways. In an empirical study with 36 participants, users were significantly more accurate and faster at understanding and modifying permissions policies with the expandable grid as compared to the native Windows XP file permissions interface. This approach was also evaluated with Facebook privacy policies [Lipford et al., 2010] and P3P policies [Reeder et al., 2008b], inspiring the initial versions of the Nutrition label, as discussed above [Kelley et al., 2009].

Security and privacy policies can be complex, making design of intuitive and fast interfaces that are different on every site and platform challenging. Yet the complexities of these policies, and the challenges that users currently face in correctly and quickly modifying them, strongly motivate continued focus on this topic. Reeder [2008] discusses this issue at length.

3.8   MOBILE SECURITY AND PRIVACY

While in 2008, smart phones were only used by 10% of the population of the U.S., that quickly grew to 48% in 2012, with even higher penetration in younger age groups[10]. The same trend has been seen worldwide. Users of smart phones are surfing the web, maintaining personal information and contacts, and interacting with a variety of applications. This new computing platform presents several additional security and privacy challenges that we highlight in this section, including the ability of phones to access the sensors of the phone and the personal information stored on the phone.

3.8.1   LOCATION PRIVACY

One of the key features of mobile computing is the use of a user's location to customize an application or enable additional forms of personal interaction. Thus, location privacy is a heavily researched domain of privacy.

Location sharing services (LSS) involve the sharing of one's location with sets of friends or contacts. One of the first such systems was ActiveBadge, prototyped by Xerox Parc researchers in an office environment [Want et al., 1992]. Subsequent similar prototypes highlighted that the decision to share location was based upon not just who wanted to know, but also, why a person requested location information [Consolvo et al., 2005, Lederer et al., 2003]. Participants desire the ability to control the granularity of their location [Iachello et al., 2005], not just for privacy reasons and plausible deniability, but also to provide a level of detail that is more useful to the requester [Consolvo et al., 2005]. Users report using location sharing for a variety of reasons, including reporting approval or promotion of places and events, recording and sharing visits and travel, and shaping appearance by indicating interesting activities [Patil et al., 2012].

While much of the early work in location privacy had to utilize scenario-based or prototype systems to examine users' perceptions and behaviors around sharing location with other people, the widespread use of smart phones with GPS has enabled researchers to now examine these

---

[10]http://www.nielsen.com/us/en/newswire/2012/survey-new-u-s-smartphone-growth-by-age-and-income.html

questions with deployed systems. One of the most studied experimental location-based systems is "Loccacino," where users' locations are automatically shared with friends [Sadeh et al., 2009]. Users can create rules for sharing based on groups, time of day, and specific locations. Important privacy features include plausible deniability, audit logs, and real-time feedback [Tsai et al., 2009]. Studies found that users became more comfortable sharing location over time, and also evolved more complex privacy settings involving not just who, but also, times of day and locations [Benisch et al., 2011, Toch et al., 2010]. Machine-learning algorithms were also able to learn privacy profiles and improve rule accuracy, potentially reducing user burden [Ravichandran et al., 2009, Wilson et al., 2013].

In contrast, as of this writing, one of the most popular commercial location-based systems is Four-square, an application where users explicitly "check in" to a particular place [Lindqvist et al., 2011], and that location is shared with a group of friends (often integrated with Facebook or Twitter). There is little configuration and access control, privacy is primarily managed by refraining from checking in to a location. As such, users have few stated privacy concerns over sharing their locations in this mode [Patil et al., 2012]. Thus, many of the early research results regarding the expression and management of privacy policies for location information are simply not needed in such similar applications. In addition to dedicated location-sharing services, location is now more tightly integrated into other platforms, such as Facebook, which can automatically geotag posts that users make. While this is also an explicit form of location sharing, the automatic tagging can cause location to be overlooked and shared when not intended [Patil et al., 2012].

A different class of applications is Location-Based Services (LBS), applications customized based upon a user's location—such as localized coupons or advertising, navigation services, and tour guides. There has been significantly less study of these types of services, despite their current availability and popularity on mobile phone platforms. For example, one study of 273 iPhone users found that they granted location acess to at least two-thirds of the apps that requested them [Fisher et al., 2012]. Kelley et al. [2011] found that users do have serious privacy concerns for their location being shared with advertisers, one example of a location-based service, and that their preferences can be complex based upon not just who is granted access, but also, the time of day and location.

3.8.2   APPLICATION PLATFORMS

Current smartphones provide a platform on which users can install applications from external vendors, which can in turn access data on the phone and utilize the phone's resources. In addition to location data, this can include access to a users' contacts, photos, and other personal information, as well as use of the camera and microphone to record personal information.

While platforms differ on the mechanism, generally users grant any apps they install on their smartphones a set of permissions to access information or use phone resources upon installation. Yet, similar to consent and end-user license agreement dialogs [Good et al., 2005], users pay little attention and have limited understanding as to what they are consenting to. Through a survey and interview study, Felt et al. [2012b] found that 83% do not pay attention to the permissions dialogs during app installation, while only 3% correctly answered multiple questions on what those permissions meant. As a result, users are more likely to pay attention to app reviews and recommendations than to the privacy permissions [Chin et al., 2012]. One reason is that these warnings contain language that most users do not understand [Kelley et al., 2012]. Another is that these warnings do not correspond to user concerns or risks. Felt et al. [2012a] surveyed 3,115 Android users about a variety of potential privacy risks of app usage. Participants indicated that they were most concerned with risks that would cost money or delete important information, and least concerned with simple uses of phone resources. Yet, the same one-page dialog contains permissions as benign as making the phone vibrate and as concerning as sending text messages that could charge the user money [Felt et al., 2012a]. The approach that Android uses to ask for such permissions is also limiting, generally providing an all-or-nothing consent dialog prior to any interaction with the application. Users are thus unable to determine when apps access their information and for what purpose. When presented with views of data leakage, users were surprised by the frequency as well as the destination of their data, particularly to advertising organizations [Balebako et al., 2013, Jung et al., 2012]. Despite this confusion, another study demonstrates that users would choose or pay more for apps with fewer permissions when that information is salient [Egelman et al., 2012, Kelley et al., 2013a].

Research for improvements to these permissions dialogs is still young. Kelley et al. [2013a] redesigned the interface of the Google marketplace where users acquire apps, making summaries of the privacy permissions more visible and available prior to installation. While the new Privacy Facts interface did impact which apps were chosen in both a laboratory and online Mechanical Turk study, participants still reported that privacy information was not very important in their decisions to download new applications. Beyond redesigning just the interface, Lin et al. [2012] proposed using crowdsourcing to first identify permissions that would be of most concern or most unexpected to users. A complementary approach is to provide notifications or visualizations of actual data access while applications are running [Balebako et al., 2013, Jung et al., 2012]. Thompson et al. [2013] utilized laboratory experiments to investigate how users could perform attribution of app behaviors, finding that participants could better understand what applications were doing with such attribution mechanisms. A key challenge to these real-time approaches is how to provide useful information about data access and leakage, as well as the ability to control information flows, without overwhelming users with unwanted notifications.

3.8.3   MOBILE AUTHENTICATION

There are two types of mobile authentication to be investigated. Authentication to the phone itself can protect personal data if the phone is lost or stolen. This is often currently performed upon each access, or phone unlock. A different type of authentication is logging in to sensitive sites or applications, such as a bank site, where attackers could target those passwords or data.

Mobile authentication is more challenging than typing a password on a laptop or desktop, as the small screen size and lack of keyboard make it difficult to type in long and complex passwords. Today, all mobile operating systems allow users to lock the devices with PINs or passphrases, with various kinds of account lockout if the wrong password is provided too many times in a row. There is widespread acknowledgement that PINs and passphrases are frustrating on the mobile device and that many users do not take advantage of the opportunity afforded to secure their devices. (See the discussion of Kurkovsky and Syta [2010] on p. 2.) Indeed, the "Draw a Secret" (DAS) graphical password [Jermyn et al., 1999] was created specifically for the purpose of securing mobile devices, with the belief that users would want an easy-to-use alternative to PINs and passwords. Yet, users often use their devices in public, increasing the concerns of shoulder surfing.

Chin et al. [2012] found that users are more concerned about accessing sensitive information, such as banking information, on their phones than on traditional computers, due to security concerns. Yet, the context captured by a mobile phone could also be utilized to strengthen authentication. Das et al. [2013] explored whether the information captured automatically by a phone could be used for autobiographical authentication. Hayashi et al. proposed Context Aware Scalable Authentication (CASA), which selected the method of active authentication based on a user's location [Hayashi et al., 2013], requiring stronger authentication when the user was not at work or home. Similar to keyboard biometrics, researchers are also demonstrating that the biometrics of graphical gestures can also be used as a means for implicit, continuous authentication on mobile devices [Burgbacher and Hinrichs, 2014, Sae-Bae et al., 2012].

3.9   SOCIAL MEDIA PRIVACY

The rise of social media applications has brought a new focus on privacy, and many opportunities for research in multiple disciplines. Sites such as Facebook and Twitter grew rapidly in the mid 2000's. Most of the growth was among young college-aged users, and a common sentiment expressed by people and the press at the time was that users were posting so much personal information online that they must not care very much about their privacy. Early studies on Facebook demonstrated that users' privacy attitudes did not impact their decisions to disclose private information [Barnes, 2006, Tufekci, 2008], and the majority of users did not alter the site's default, and open, privacy settings [Acquisti and Gross, 2006].

The strong desire for online social interaction and communication certainly led to significantly more personal information being placed online, but also created constant and challenging privacy issues and decisions, which interfaces and applications have not been able to keep up with. Studies showed that users did have significant privacy concerns and problems [Besmer and Richter Lipford, 2010, Krasnova et al., 0009, Skeels and Grudin, 2009, Wang et al., 2011a]. For example, participants in a study on photo sharing expressed a sense of helplessness of ending up in photos posted on Facebook that they did not like [Besmer and Richter Lipford, 2010]. Wang et al. [2011a] studied a variety of regrets users reported from posting on Facebook, often because they misjudged the audience or others' reactions to what they posted.

Over time, users have also taken various actions to protect themselves as they were able. For example, there is evidence that contemporary users are making more use of privacy settings on Facebook and other sites [Johnson et al., 2012] than was demonstrated in earlier work. Greater privacy concerns have also been shown to correlate with lower engagement with social media sites [Staddon et al., 2012]. Yet, while users have increased their efforts to hide from strangers over time, they also appear to be disclosing more information to friends, increasing the risks of data privacy issues as social media organizations and 3rd-party application developers are also granted access to that information [Stutzman et al., 2013]

A number of researchers have investigated the needs and behaviors surrounding information disclosures on social media platforms, particularly on the current most popular Facebook. For example, studies have demonstrated that users do consider the audience and appropriateness of the information they share on their profiles and through status updates [Boyd and Heer, 2006, Strater and Lipford, 2008]. These imagined audiences have evolved over time as social media site and use has grown[Litt, 2012], although users tend to underestimate the scope of that audience [Bernstein et al., 2013]. The existing mechanisms and interfaces for controlling the access to social media content can be complex and confusing [Egelman et al., 2011], and users take a variety of other strategies, such as self-censuring, creating multiple profiles, and carefully managing their friend lists, to control their privacy [Lampinen et al., 2011, Stutzman and Hartzog, 2012, Stutzman and Kramer-Duffield, 2010, Wisniewski et al., 2012]. A survey conducted by Johnson and Egelman recently found that, while controls on Facebook seemed to address adequately user's concerns over strangers accessing content, settings were not sufficient at managing the threat of "insiders," friends accessing content the user would not like them to see [Johnson et al., 2012]. Indeed, one of the challenges of social media is that users interact and share information with multiple and overlapping social circles, which often have different social norms and expectations [Tufekci, 2008].

There have been several interfaces proposed to improve privacy settings on social media sites. For example, AudienceView provides a more concrete representation of the policy by visualizing the outcome on the profile of the policies for different groups of users [Watson et al., 2009]. Lipford et al. [2010] also compared AudienceView against a Facebook version of the expandable grid interface, and found that both were reasonable alternatives to the standard Facebook interface, with users having a preference for one or the other [Lipford et al., 2010]. Egelman et al. proposed a Venn diagram approach to highlight overlapping groups [Egelman et al., 2011]. These efforts in designing privacy interfaces have demonstrated that more structured, visual, and concrete interfaces improve user understanding and performance. Other efforts have focused on providing users a better understanding of the impact of their privacy settings. The PViz tool also allows for exploration of the entire privacy policy as a more abstract visualization [Mazzia et al.,

2012]. Schlegel et al. [2011] investigated an ambient visualization using an "eye" metaphor to provide users with quick feedback as to the personal information being queried by others.

One common solution to privacy on social media is customizing the sharing of information based on social groups, a form of access control. Facebook and Google+ both offer functionality for grouping friends and sharing based on those customized groups. Johnson et al. [2012] found that over 50% of their 260 participants had created such a group. Kairam et al. [2012] analyzed the most common circle names on Google+ and found that a large percentage fell into work or school categories. However, while users may state a desire for separating sharing based on such social spheres such as work colleagues and close friends and family [Skeels and Grudin, 2009], in practice this appears to be problematic for users. Current interfaces make it difficult to understand and deal with overlapping and conflicting social spheres [Egelman et al., 2011]. Setting up groups also takes time and thought, which may be too burdensome or complicated [Watson et al., 2012]. To help reduce this burden, researchers are investigating automated techniques for grouping friends and determining access rights for them [Jones and O'Neill, 2010]. Yet, proposed methods have not been shown to be sufficiently accurate for use.

Customizing the sharing to groups of friends may not turn out to be a viable and scalable solution after all. Watson et al. [2012] performed an interview study of 27 Google+ early adopters, and highlighted that, while users like the friend-grouping circles functionality of Google+, few used it for privacy reasons, but instead, to direct content at those who will be most interested. This reduces the risks of mismanaging group membership. Kelley et al. [2011] also demonstrate a key challenge with group-based controls, in that even when carefully constructed there can be many exceptions. Users may just not be able to fit all of their friends into neat and memorable categories. Thus, even if the burden of forming groups was reduced through automated grouping mechanisms, this form of access control may still not match users privacy needs. Providing mechanisms to allow users to flexibly control access to content within their social networks remains a significant research challenge.

Another privacy challenge on social media sites is that information is not just shared by a user, but also by others—friends can post messages on a user's Wall or Timeline, or tag users in posts and photos. Thus, existing settings need to also reflect this kind of collective privacy. For example, Besmer and Richter Lipford [2010] describe the problems related to photo sharing on Facebook, where users have little control as to photos uploaded by friends, which are attached to their profiles through tags. Yet, users did not want to be equal co-owners of those photos with matching privacy controls, but instead, desired mechanisms that both reflected the rights of photo owners as well as the social obligations between friends to respect each others' privacy. Lampinen et al. [2011] discuss additional collaborative privacy strategies, such as asking others for approval or deleting tags. All note that few mechanisms exist within the social media sites for the collaboration and negotiation between users around sharing and privacy.

While much of the work in social media privacy has been focused on information disclosures, returning to the social definitions of privacy presented a broader perspective. For example, Wisniewski et al. [2012] defined a framework of boundary mechanisms and coping mechanisms for users of social network sites, based upon the original privacy-as-boundary regulation definition put forth by Altman [1974]. In addition to just information disclosure, they highlight aspects such as who to friend, how to manage communication and interaction with friends and between social circles, and how to control incoming information as aspects of the privacy decisions users are faced with. Thus, maintaining and controlling privacy on social media sites is not just about access control to pieces of information, but can include a wide range of settings and mechanisms that regulate a user's interactions with others. Yet many of the coping strategies adopted by users can be maladaptive, such as changing one's offline behavior to reduce online privacy violations [Wisniewski et al., 2012], increasing stress and possibly decreasing the positive benefits of online social interaction. These signal a clear need for greater or more flexible support for privacy needs in social media.

While much of the research has examined the privacy needs and behaviors of users interacting with other users, significant data privacy issues have also been uncovered. One heavily researched example is applications, such as on Facebook, which are developed by 3rd parties and have access to a user's profile information. These issues have been similarly examined in the context of mobile phone applications, which also provide 3rd party application platforms. Within the context of Facebook, Besmer and Lipford [2010] demonstrated that users had little understanding of what of their information was accessible to 3rd parties, yet desired significantly less than was available. In a survey study of 516 participants, King et al. [2011] further demonstrated a lack of understanding of apps, yet also that increased knowledge of application platforms did not correlate with privacy concerns. Others have highlighted the risks of the data shared on Facebook, such as the ability to answer challenge questions [Rabkin, 2008] or use the information to infer other sensitive data [Acquisti and Gross, 2009]. Yet, these risks and uses of information are significantly less transparent than the interaction with other users, resulting in users being unable to make informed privacy decisions regarding their information and behavior.

Interface issues are again similar to the mobile phone app installation results. Users generally must accept all requested persmission prior to ever using an application. Wang et al. [2011b] proposed a more fine-grained interface, with additional cues highlighting when the policy would violate a user's general Facebook privacy settings. Besmer et al. [2009] proposed filling in the requested permissions with the real information that will be shared from the user's profile, making the privacy decision more contextual and concrete. Still, as Besmer et al. [2009] notes, users may be unable to make informed privacy decisions if they are required to create such a policy at installation time, prior to ever interacting with the application.

3.10   SECURITY ADMINISTRATORS

Many of the mechanisms and tools researched by the information security community address the needs of professional security administrators and cyber analysts—those who configure network and communication infrastructures and software, determine and implement organization-wide security and privacy policies, investigate and mitigate attacks, and so on. While consumer-side users have increasingly complex responsibility for securing their own devices and information, significant responsibility still falls to technology professionals for maintaining the security of the underlying infrastructures and devices that end users rely upon, as well as the wealth of information and technology within industrial, educational, and government organizations. While security administrators and cyber analysts are a significantly smaller user population than consumers, improving the usability of their tools to improve their decision-making abilities in reduced time could have an incredibly large impact.

Within the UPS community, the most significant research studying security administrators has been performed by two different groups. Haber, Kandogan, and collaborators conducted 5 years of ethnographic studies of system administrators, and published several papers focusing specifically on security administration [Haber and Bailey, 2007, Haber and Kandogan, 2007, Kandogan and Haber, 2005]. Similarly, researchers at the University of British Columbia conducted 34 interviews of security administrators in 16 different organizations as part of the HOT-Admin project (Human Organization and Technology Centered Improvement of IT Security Administration) [Botta et al., 2011, 2007b, Hawkey et al., 2008, Werlinger et al., 2008, 2009].

Together, their research uncovers a general understanding of security administrators and guidelines for tools supporting their work. Security administration work involves research into emerging threats, situational awareness, and integrating and processing huge amounts of data from a variety of tools and sources. Thus, the key skills that security administrators utilize are inferential analysis, pattern recognition, and bricolage [Botta et al., 2007b]. The organizational environment within which administrators work is complex, with heterogeneous tools and infrastructure. Thus, security administration work often requires collaboration and coordination with other stakeholders across the organization—communication breakdowns can lead to security vulnerabilities or errors [Lu and Bao, 2012]. Design guidelines for tools for security administrators include providing flexible reporting, knowledge sharing and coordination for those multiple stakeholders, facilitating archiving and task prioritization, and providing data correlation and filtering functionality [Jaferian et al., 2008].

Despite the previous work, relatively little research has looked at more specific tools and tasks that are part of security administration work. Werlinger et al. [2008] examined intrusion detection systems, identifying a number of usability issues and design guidelines. Jaferian et al. [2009] present a case study of an organization adopting an identity management system. Both of these examples were also conducted by the HOT-Admin research group, contributing to a set of more general design guidelines for IT security management tools [Jaferian et al., 2008].

Given the heterogeneity of systems, the tools used by security administrators need to be tailorable to the specific environment of the organizations. Thus, administrators often use text-based tools, preferring their power, familiarity, and flexibility over visual tools. They also often create their own tools, such as customized scripts. To address the limitations of text-based tools, a research community has grown around exploring the use of visualization for security-related information, nicknamed VizSec, and has held a yearly symposium since 2004. For example, the IDS RainStorm visualizes intrusion detection alarms for a 24-hour period across an entire organization's set of IP addresses [Conti et al., 2006]. NVisionIP visualizes traffic flows to/from every machine on a large computer network [Lakkaraju et al., 2004, Yurcik, 2006].

Visualizations have been proposed, both commercially and in research, for a variety of specific types of data, such as IDS alerts, network flows, attack graphs, and others. However, visualization is still not widely used in commercial tools. Fink et al. interviewed eight cyber-analysts, uncovering a number of reasons why they do not use or trust visualization tools [Fink et al., 2009]. First, current visualization tools are not interoperable and sufficiently flexible, whereas text-based tools allow for more easy sharing and integration of data across tools. Many visual tools can simply not handle the needed volume of data efficiently. In addition, analysts do not trust any tools that hide or smooth underlying data, preferring detailed text views. For example, a study comparing a command line tool to a visualization for intrusion-detection tasks demonstrated that participants were faster and more confidant using the text-based tools, but explored more tangential information and got a better overview of the data from the visualization [Thompson et al., 2007]. Thus, while visualization may help to address information overload with one specific data source, security experts have a great need for tools that improve integration of information across data sources, to support information foraging and correlation, as well as facilitate communication amongst the varied stakeholders. Visualization may also be a source of vulnerability as it may cause important information to be overlooked [Conti et al., 2005]. Research in visual analytics systems, which emphasizes supporting human reasoning and analysis of data in addition to visual representations of information, may help advance the use of more visual tools that better support the overall workflow needs of security experts.

CHAPTER 4

Lessons Learned

The academic quest to align usability and security started in the 1990s with a few key observations:

- **Security is a Secondary Task:** Users are not focused on securing their systems, they want to use their systems for accomplishing other goals.

- **Humans are Frequently a Weak Link:** Humans are inherently part of the system that provides for information security. Having spent decades hardening the technical infrastructure, vulnerabilities resulting from poor usability are now the cause of many incidents.

- **The "Barn Door Properly":** Once information is released, it can't be recovered. While many interactive systems make it possible to recover from errors, recovering from security incidents is fundamentally different.

In the intervening two decades, adversaries have learned to exploit UPS problems. Users now have dramatically more systems under their control, and services such as e-commerce, e-banking, and online social networks have increased the consequences of poor security choices. Nevertheless, UPS is generally better today than it was two decades ago, because researchers and developers have a more advanced understanding of when humans need to make decisions, what information they need to make those decisions, and how that information should be presented. The remainder of this chapter attempts to briefly summarize what's been learned.

4.1 REDUCE DECISIONS

There is a natural tendency of programmers to defer choices to the user. Early on we learned that software should not default to low levels of security and privacy and require that users voluntarily set the levels higher. At the same time, systems that start with unreasonably high security thresholds, but allow users to lower the levels, can also result in lower overall security as the settings are lowered so that users can get their work done. Ideally, users should only be given the ability to change security and privacy defaults when it is absolutely necessary that they be able to do so for normal operations. Otherwise, unsophisticated users can fall victim to social engineering attacks that try to trick them into lowering their security settings.

In some cases, configurability can even cause problems for moderately sophisticated users: TOR provides anonymity for TCP connections by sending them through three relays. The system explicitly does not allow users to configure additional number of hops: doing so would provide no additional anonymity, and would, in fact, make users stand out, since the non-standard configuration would act as an identifier [Dingledine and Mathewson, 2005]. A systematic examination of Tor usability problems [Clark et al., 2007] concluded that usability could be further improved with an all-in-one installer that delivered the Tor client with a pre-configured browser. The result of this research was the "Tor Browser Bundle," which addressed many usability problems and is widely believed to have contributed increase in Tor's adoption. However, even the integrated system suffers from several "stop-points" that impact both adoption and secure operation [Norcie et al., 2012].

Thus, in keeping with Cranor's "Human in the Loop" model [Cranor, 2008], humans should be removed from the loop as much as possible and only involved in security decisions when no automated choice is feasible.

However, fully automating security decisions can still have drawbacks and cause confusion during occasional exceptions [Edwards et al., 2008]. For example, Ruoti et al. [2013] studied a case in which nearly invisible encryption resulted in usability problems. If users are unfamiliar with the settings to begin with, determining the cause of a problem and the needed changes may be difficult, causing users to bypass the security technology altogether.

4.2   SAFE AND SECURE DEFAULTS

When users are given configuration options, in order to reduce decisions, defaults must be safe and secure. This is especially critical because most users accept defaults as they are. This is not a new idea: Saltzer and Schroeder [1975] identified the need for "Fail-safe defaults" as one of their guiding design principles for building secure systems. Modern systems do a better job of having safe and secure defaults than those of a decade ago, although many systems still default to "open" privacy setting rather ones that are more restrictive.

4.3   PROVIDE USERS WITH BETTER INFORMATION, NOT MORE INFORMATION

To make security-critical decisions, users need the correct information presented in a manner that they can understand, at the time they need to make the decision.

For example, users of online services frequently do not understand how their information can be accessed or shared. The first attempted solution was for websites to post "privacy policies" describing their practices in detail. Such policies may have been occasionally read by lawyers, but were largely ignored by users. Privacy policies were distilled to machine-readable forms and displayed by toolbars, but they were still found to be not useful for end-user decision making. What did work was displaying privacy information next to search results, so that users could incorporate that information in their decision about which site to visit, and displaying the information at the top of a web page when the site was first visited—that is, presenting compact but useful information to the user when the information was needed.

Likewise, early work on anti-phishing indicators (such as toolbars) provided users with details regarding the use of SSL, highlighting of domain names and locations, in a much more compact form. But, users who tried these toolbars discovered that this information required them to reason about very technical aspects of web pages. In the end, toolbar technologies and other kinds of passive indicators (Section 3.3.2) were found to be largely ineffective to prevent phishing. On the other hand, passive indicators did help users to understand inadvertent information disclosure when private messages were sent to large distribution mailing lists (Figure 3.17) [Lieberman and Miller, 2007]. Passive warnings that appear closer to their context, such as right next to sensitive data entry, may also be successful [Maurer et al., 2011], since they provide the information to the user where it will be seen and when it is needed.

In the mobile space, Android permissions dialogs at app installation are both difficult to understand and time-consuming to read. While both provide accurate information (generally), users have not been able to use them to make informed decisions or to audit the capabilities that their app request [Felt et al., 2012b]. Thus, neither are accomplishing the goal of providing users with sufficient notice so they can provide informed consent. What appears to work better is for mobile app to request permission to use privacy-sensitive information when they are about to use it.

We have also discovered a paradox of granularity. When information is too abstract, users have little understanding of the specifics. When simple controls are provided, there are many exceptions and corner cases that users are unable to express. Yet, often, adding additional granularity adds complexity, decreasing usability. Thus, we need to balance the correct level of granularity in various domains. The best solutions are likely to be where users can combine multiple simple controls together to achieve flexibility.

4.4 USERS REQUIRE CLEAR CONTEXT TO MAKE GOOD DECISIONS

The context of a user's decision has elements of both *time* and *purpose*.

Early efforts simply gave users lots of information up front and asked users to make decisions with long-lasting consequences. But, provided with such information in advance, users were rarely able to make informed decisions that were consistent with their intentions at a later point in time.

Decisions that users make about security and privacy are inherently contextual. The decision to open a port on a firewall is rarely done when a firewall is installed: instead the decision is made when someone needs to use a service and it is blocked. With respect to privacy, a user who wishes to protect the privacy of their location may feel differently when an application needs that information to help them find a nearby restaurant. Decisions made in advance frequently lack the necessary context.

Purpose is another aspect of context that is frequently shielded from users. Users that provide their location to an application so that they can find a restaurant may not realize that the information is also shared with advertisers to provide targeted advertisements.

We have also learned that, in the heat of the moment, users will frequently choose lower levels of protection in order to accomplish a specific goal: the short-term motivation to complete the task overpowers the long-term goal of maintaining an abstract privacy or security policy. Typically, these short-term decisions have very real long-term consequences, in that a combination of single or special cases causes overall policy to degrade over time. For example, a user may lower the security of a system to accomplish a particular task, but forget to raise it back up afterwards. This implies that interfaces for expressing one-time or limited-time exceptions are probably useful, as they mirror the way that people think about privacy and security.

4.5   INFORMATION PRESENTATION IS CRITICAL

In order to reach a broad audience, information must be presented in a manner that is clear, graphically engaging, and lacking in jargon.

When given the choice, even experts prefer plain language to technical language. Whether users are specifying policies (Section 3.7) or reading them (e.g., privacy policies or app permissions), we have learned that users frequently do not read or understand highly detailed descriptions about what is actually being done. Overall, it seems preferable to use simple language and graphics that may be less precise than detailed language, but are read. Experience has also shown that tabular presentations are more inviting than blocks of text.

The past decade has seen an evolution towards more understandable warnings and privacy policies. At the same time, "control panels" on desktop computers and mobile devices have grown visibly more complex, although the research community has not documented these trends over time or attempted to isolate causes and impacts.

4.6   EDUCATION WORKS, BUT HAS LIMITS

Research has shown that people who receive good anti-phishing education are indeed less likely to fall for phishing attacks. But education has its limits—in some phishing attacks, the attack message is truly indistinguishable from a legitimate message, so there is no way for a user to make use of their education.

Education can be improved with metaphors that link an application's functionality to related concepts in the world. Information security is most frequently related to physical security, with notions of protecting one's belongings with locks and doors. Other security concepts have been related to medicine (e.g., viruses), crime (e.g., hackers), and warfare [Camp, 2009]. Choosing good metaphors can help users better understand security risks and behave more securely [Raja et al., 2011]. The metaphors do not have to be entirely accurate, but can be chosen to influence the desired behaviors. For example, users who think that hackers are primarily motivated by mischief still find it important to protect themselves by being careful which sites they visit [Wash, 2010].

At the same time, we have learned that the power of education and training is limited by other economic factors. Research has shown that individuals have a limited effort budget to protect their security and privacy. Few individuals will expend more effort than their perceived benefit.

CHAPTER 5

Research Challenges

This chapter explores challenges facing UPS researchers. We use the word "challenges" to describe the research problems that remain, and are likely to remain, problems. We also focus on challenges specific to UPS, rather than challenges that UPS shares with security or usability in general.

A fundamental challenge of UPS remains one that was identified by Whitten and Tygar [1999]: security is a secondary task. Any UPS solution, other than reducing configuration and increasing delegation, requires a user's time and thought—things that come at the expense of the user's primary task. As Herley [2009] points out, users frequently do not see the payoff. Research on phishing education and persuasion shows that some people can be taught or nudged to act in a manner that is more secure, at least for a period of time. Nevertheless, such education and the resulting behavior changes may not be worth the effort if the risk is low or if the ability to recover is high.

Just as users are hard pressed to evaluate the risk and benefit of a security measure, researchers have a similar challenge. As a result, researchers that propose new security mechanisms must establish that they are worth the increased cost. Frequently the justification is missing—even if the precept is true.

The speed of technological development also poses a specific challenge for UPS researchers: it is remarkably difficult to replicate studies based on web technology. For example, Sotirakopoulos et al. [2011] attempted to replicate a similar study [Egelman et al., 2008a], *conducted just three years before,* with a slightly adjusted methodology to overcome some of the prior problems. The researchers found that they largely could not, since the underlying web infrastructure of browsers had changed.

With this background in mind, we present specific *subject challenges* in performing areas of UPS research, as well as domain challenges that we believe impact all aspects of UPS work.

5.1   SUBJECT CHALLENGE: AUTHENTICATION

Authentication was one of the first UPS research areas and it remains an area of great operational difficulty. The majority of authentication actions are performed with fixed passwords and this seems unlikely to change in the future. Passwords aren't just used for user accounts—they are stored in email clients that periodically check for mail, they are in routers to control administrative access, and they are used to unlock mobile phones and override parental controls.

Two positive developments are the current trend towards the use of single-sign-on systems such as OpenID (and others), and the increased use of two-factor systems such as Google

Authenticator and the U.S. Government's HSPD-12 cards. We lack statistics as to how popular these systems actually are. However, such centralized authentication systems may also have undesirable social issues, such as the centralization of power. Users locked out of their Google accounts may be locked out of a lot, and a compromised Google account can give the attacker access to substantial resources.

Biometrics remain a challenge because they cannot be changed, fears of privacy, tracking, and the fact that they are not democratic—for every biometric, there is a group of people who can't use it, and another group who are not reliably distinguished by it [Doddington et al., 1998].

In the meantime, the intellectual and functional burden of passwords increases every year. Users have more passwords for more accounts, and the growing power of computers results in increasingly stringent password requirements.

We have a clear vision of what we want—we want to be able to sit down and use a computer or mobile phone without delay. Passwords seem to be the least bad authentication system available in most instances. Replacing them is one of the great challenges of UPS.

5.2   SUBJECT CHALLENGE: ADVERSARY MODELING

Modeling adversaries and incorporating attacks directly into study protocols remains a significant challenge in UPS research.

Security mechanisms are designed to defend against attacks by an adversary. However, UPS research has frequently focused solely on the usability of security mechanisms and evaluated whether or not the system can be used correctly—not on whether the mechanism accomplishes its goal of defending systems that are under attack

Security systems must be designed with a threat model, since it is impossible to protect against everything. But, in UPS, the threat model is frequently not well understood. For example, in graphical passwords, many researchers attempt to come up with schemes to defeat shoulder surfing. Yet, in practice, there are many other kinds of attacks against graphical systems that may be more likely—such as attackers that can guess hot spots or infer passwords from residue on a computer screen when a device is stolen.

Thus, it is necessary to test the usability of privacy and security mechanisms in the face of attacks. To do this, the experiment needs a model that describes what kinds of attacks adversaries might initiate. If the experiment focuses on "likely" attacks, then the experimenter needs to justify what it is that makes other attacks "unlikely" and what would prevent an attacker from choosing to attack with an unlikely attack instead of a likely one. Attackers can directly attack a system—attackers can pose as authorized users. Alternatively, attackers can attack users when they are attempting to use the system. Both of these conditions need to be considered when evaluating a security mechanism.

Likewise, it is important to test the usability of a system under both normal conditions and when the users of that system are under attack. However, it is conceptually challenging to design an experiment that tests operation under both normal and attack conditions. In part, this is because attack conditions are typically rare, so, many studies that attempt such tests typically subject users to much higher incidences of attack than is ecologically valid. This might make users succumb to attacks more frequently, or it might make users more vigilant and therefore more resistant to attack. For example, Garfinkel and Miller [2005] updated Whitten and Tygar [1999]'s "Why Johnny Can't Encrypt" study to include an active adversary that was attempting to steal a secret from the test subject. Adversaries have a great deal of options for this kind of theft, including the planting of malware on target machines and wiretapping communications lines. For "Johnny 2," the authors employed a "spear-phishing" (Section 3.3) style attack in which the mail server is unresponsive (possibly due to a related attack) and the campaign workers are forced to use their personal emails. In this case, users' who received additional indicators and briefings performed better, but a more subtle attack or weaker briefing might have resulted in an unobservable effect.

Another issue that arises when attacking users is the requirement for informed consent, as users may be less likely to be on the lookout for an attack in a safe laboratory environment than in a wild environment. Schechter et al. [2007] attempted to test this issue by having some of their subjects use a demo account to access a bank and having other subjects use their personal credentials. The second group was more security conscious than the first. Others papers that specifically address the issue of a simulated adversary include Egelman et al. [2008b] and Bravo-Lillo et al. [2013].

5.3   SUBJECT CHALLENGE: ADMINISTRATORS AND SYSTEM ADMINISTRATION

Most of the research we have discussed focuses on users who are not security experts, managing their personal devices and information. Yet, many of the reported security breaches involve organizations, where security and privacy work falls significantly on security experts. Thus, improving the ability of experts to perform their work potentially has the biggest return on investment. However, there are also significant challenges in doing research with experts and in improving the tools they use for their tasks.

As the existing research already demonstrates, security administrators are busy, highly paid professionals. Finding enough users who are willing and able to take the time to participate in research studies is challenging. Researchers from the HOT-Admin project [Botta et al., 2007a] describe recruiting participants for semi-structured interviews and observation as their biggest challenge. They found that establishing relationships and trust with such professionals may take time and personal contacts, as well as approval or endorsement from management in organizations.

Observing users in their real context often offers the best view on the needs and usability challenges of existing tools. Yet, those observations themselves present security risks, where professionals may be reluctant or even unable to allow outsiders to view their work. While usability studies in a lab may allow observation without such security risks, invariably the tasks will be simplified and less ecologically valid. Botta et al. [2007a] also discuss several potential strategies for conducting such research, such as partnering with tool vendors to study clients' behaviors and doing role playing design exercises with professionals.

Addressing the needs of security administrators is similar to addressing the needs of any expert and professional system: users need power and flexibility, help in finding and diagnosing problems, and support in data-driven decision making specific to their context. Security administration in particular involves many different tasks, with information from a variety of sources. On the one hand, this provides many opportunities for researchers to examine detailed tasks and needs, and investigate new interactions and interfaces to meet those needs. Very little of this research has been done currently.

On the other hand, this abundance of information and tools also presents a challenge in that any one tool may only have limited potential to improve the overall performance of users. The heterogeneity of the computing environments of organizations also leads to the need for customizable tools and techniques. Professionals' needs for power and flexibility drives their use of text-based tools, and that desire and familiarity with command-line tools may continue even if GUI-based tools are more usable. Still, tool vendors and open-source developers will benefit from additional research, both general and specific to particular tasks, that highlights usability flaws and design guidelines.

5.4   SUBJECT CHALLENGE: CONSUMER PRIVACY

With more and more information being digitized, shared, and accessible online, privacy is going to remain a big issue in the coming decade and will likely be a major driver for the use of security technologies by consumers and organizations alike. Evolving social norms towards various technologies will also cause privacy behaviors to evolve.

One key challenge that users are just starting to face is the time boundary problem [Palen and Dourish, 2003], where users will be faced with managing not just current content, but content that spans years and decades. Users may no longer want to share information that they were willing to share years prior. For example, users indicate less willingness to share posts as they get older [Ayalon and Toch, 2013]. What are the risks that users face with years of personal information available? Many of these risks may be difficult to convey to users—such as linking data across sites and inference of personal information from a variety of sources. In addition, few of these risks have yet been realized with actual negative consequences, or would be difficult to trace to the original source. There are interesting social implications as well. For example, what happens for kids who have their whole lives on sites such as Facebook in 20 years?

These challenges lead to a variety of research questions about how to protect and manage information over long periods of time. For example, how can systems help people clean up and clean out, to archive and save information in the case of problems, and to move data between platforms as site popularity waxes and wanes? How do social norms change as users adapt to managing their information over longer time periods and across multiple platforms? Research to understand these issues and guide design may continue to trail the development of commercial systems.

The proliferation of information also leads to key questions about content ownership. Who owns the content and has the rights to control it are legal and policy questions. Users have their expectations and perceptions, which are not always correct, and need to be able to understand what can happen with their information. For example, when a user deletes an account, the provider may retain the information to make it easier for the user to join again in the future. This apparent nod to usability may surprise many people who want to remove all of their information from the service. In addition, a large amount of content involves multiple people in some way—such as documents that are jointly authored and group photos. Additional research is needed to investigate how to allow groups of people to negotiate and coordinate the security and privacy of such information.

Privacy research has inherent challenges in measuring user attitudes and practices. Asking users about privacy is likely to influence stronger privacy-oriented attitudes than users would feel without such priming [Braunstein et al., 2011]. In addition, privacy behaviors are influenced by a range of concerns, benefits, and norms specific to the context of the user and system. Privacy metrics could be useful to understand users across systems, the relationship of privacy with other factors, enable comparisons between solutions, or be used within solutions to automate privacy settings. Yet, without sufficient context, general privacy metrics may not sufficiently predict or correlate with users' concerns and needs, as has been the case thus far. Thus, research needs to determine how to balance the contextual nature of privacy against the need for general privacy measures and solutions.

Finally, a number of researchers from a variety of domains are studying the privacy needs and behaviors of users on many different platforms, from many different perspectives. Yet, there is significantly less research into new mechanisms, interfaces, and interactions for managing privacy and solving many of the problems we already know about. We believe that the design and evaluation of privacy preserving mechanisms and interactions is a potentially rich area for research in the coming decade.

5.5   SUBJECT CHALLENGE: SOCIAL COMPUTING

Large-scale social media and social computing platforms are less than ten years old and, as we have described in the previous sections, pose profound research challenges that we as researchers still lack a clear, precise vocabulary to describe. One of the problems of transitioning from the physical world to the online world is that there are many more actors and opportunities for interaction. As a result, there are potentially many more adversaries:

1. the social media operator who may exploit a user's information in a way that is not aligned with the users' interests,

2. legitimate users who seek to access other users' information without authorization,

3. adversaries that obtain fraudulent accounts in an attempt to access the user's information,

4. adversaries that seek to plant or change information in the system to portray legitimate users in false light,

5. malicious applications that can access a user's information (or their friends' information) covertly and against the interests of the users,

6. criminals, organizations, and governments that gain unauthorized access to information stored in the social media infrastructure for the purpose of monitoring users or stealing their information, and

7. legitimate users with authorization, but who were not part of the intended audience of the information. This can include future users who were not able to access information at the time of disclosure.

For researchers, it is hard to design an experiment that measures the impact of these different adversaries on users, as users may not consciously distinguish between the different adversaries or even be aware of them. Likewise, it is difficult to design solutions that effectively protect against all of these threats.

Despite these challenge, we also believe that our goal as researchers should be to develop ways that social context information can benefit users and their security, rather than simply pose new threats. In the physical world, security occurs in a complex socio-technical environment, where social interactions are often as important as the policy or technical solutions. People are advised to walk in groups after dark for protection, pick up each other's mail when out of town, maintain neighborhood watches, and report suspicious packages or people. Recent research is also demonstrating how security information spreads informally among the stories that people hear from friends and acquaintances, rather than formal security education [Rader et al., 2012]. Outside of the security context, a variety of platforms are harnassing users' abilities to collaborate, influence each other, and collectively solve problems. One familiar and very successful example is Amazon, where suggestions for other products are presented, based upon what other users viewed or bought, reviews can be read and rated, and wishlists can be organized and shared among friends.

Thus we believe there exists an untapped opportunity for improving security by better utilizing this social environment within security mechanisms. Users already seek forums for answers to security configuration questions and virus problems, read application reviews prior to installation, and share advice on social media platforms. Such efforts could be made even easier. For example, one solution that has been proposed by several researchers is social navigation, providing views of the decisions of others, such as cookie or privacy settings, to help users make more informed or normative decisions [Besmer et al., 2009, Dieberger et al., 2000, Goecks and Mynatt, 2005]. There are still many unexplored questions in these proposed systems, such as: How do users interpret shared policy information; When do users pay attention to it; How much influence does it provide; How to prevent gaming or informational cascades; and What is the resulting impact on security or privacy outcomes on a large scale? Other "social" security systems have also been proposed. For example, Schechter et al. [2009] proposed a mechanism for fallback authentication by relying on trustees appointed by a user. Lipford and Zurko [2012] proposed using the social influence exerted in groups of users to provide community oversight of security behaviors, and discussed a variety of interesting possibilities and research ideas, but have yet to explore those issues.

5.6   DOMAIN CHALLENGE: ECOLOGICAL VALIDITY

Collecting data in a manner that has ecological validity remains a complex task for which there are no obvious right answers.

Laboratory studies of security face inherent problems. First, test subjects in the lab inherently face different threats and motivations than they do in the field. A person in a laboratory authentication study might exercise increased vigilance because they are attempting to please the investigator, or they might be less vigilant because their actual digital assets (money, friends, reputation) are not at risk of being compromised. The second, related problem is whether to conduct experiments with the subject's actual data and credentials or with fictitious ones. Presumably, a subject would be more vigilant about protecting a password used to secure their financial data than a password used to secure a test account created for the purpose of the experiment. Subjects that experience repeated attacks in the lab may be experiencing them at a significantly higher rate than they would in the field, further jeopardizing ecological validity. On the other hand, a subject might be less vigilant in protecting their true credentials in a laboratory environment, since the subject knows that the experiment is being overseen by an IRB or an ethics board that would not have approved the experiment if it might place the user's data at risk of being stolen. Thus, the context of a laboratory study may not be sufficiently similar to the real world to garner the same decisions from participants, or uncover the "true" problems that users face in the real world.

Although it may be relatively easy to find weaknesses of a new security scheme in the lab, there are many examples in which the weakness of a scheme was not discovered (or at least not publicized) until it was fielded to millions of users. For example, shortly after a simplified variant of Draw A Secret [Jermyn et al., 1999] was deployed by Google as a graphical authentication scheme for the Android platform, researchers discovered that finger smudges left on the smart phone's screen allowed an attacker with a bright light to rapidly determine the user's secret pattern [Aviv et al., 2010b].

Field studies of security face a different set of problems. Field studies lacking careful controls may provide deep understanding of participants' behaviors, but result in few metrics that can be used to compare systems and schemes across studies and settings. This lack of comparison is still a valid criticism of highly studied authentication schemes, let alone the systems in the many other areas we've discussed above. One solution is to replicate studies to extend findings to additional sets of users and settings leading to more general guidelines. Yet, a common criticism of HCI research as a whole is that replication studies are often not valued as sufficiently interesting or impactful by researchers or publication venues.

Another serious concern for field studies is the question of consent. The preferred approach for measuring susceptibility to a variety of attacks is to conduct a field experiment on individuals who have not given informed consent. The reason: informed consent primes the subjects and voids ecological validity. Jagatic et al. [2007] describe such an experiment—a large-scale phishing experiment performed on students at the University of Indiana. Even though the researchers obtained IRB approval, including a waiver of the requirement for informed consent as allowed under the U.S. "Common Rule" [US HHS, 2009], the experiment resulted in significant negative attention for both the university and the researchers because many of the experimental subjects resented being involved in the experiment without their permission and were alarmed that their university credentials had been compromised. (Ironically, the subjects learned that they had been tricked into revealing their passwords because the Indiana IRB required that the victims be informed and provided with training materials so that they would be less susceptible to phishing attacks in the future.) A similar study at the U.S. Military Academy at West Point elicited fewer complaints, possibly because of the nature of the institution [Coronges et al., 2012], or because enough time had passed that phishing studies are now considered ethically permissible.

5.7   DOMAIN CHALLENGE: TEACHING

Organizing knowledge is an essential part of research and education in the sciences. Unfortunately, UPS has grown up largely as a series of observations, experiments, and experiences with fielded software. Many attempts at organizing the UPS body of knowledge merely recount the careers of those that have been working in the field. A comprehensive UPS *framework* or *taxonomy* would allow new researchers to identify important areas that have not been explored. This book is a start, but it focuses on recounting research themes, and is not a principled model of the problem space and requirements. Such a framework could also provide guides for seeking out new research collaborators—especially important in UPS, given its interdisciplinary nature.

Conceptual models are useful for both explaining results to date and helping to predict the success (or failure) of technologies under development. Such models are especially important in UPS, as many exploitable usability problems only become apparent when technologies have been widely deployed, when they are used by individuals with less-than-average facility with computer technology, or when they are the subject of scrutiny by a sustained, engaged adversary.

Cranor's "Human in the Loop Model" [Cranor, 2008] is an approach for evaluating the kinds of security-critical tasks that should be automated and those that should require human participation. This is one of the few examples of UPS *methodology*, a sequence of steps that, when followed, help improve a UPS outcome. The model follows the flow of security-relevant information (a "communication") from the system to the human receiver, at which point, aspects of the human determine whether or not the communication will result in a behavior. For example, a user might encounter a warning that a website they are attempting to access contains malware: the human then has to decide whether to proceed to the website or do something else.

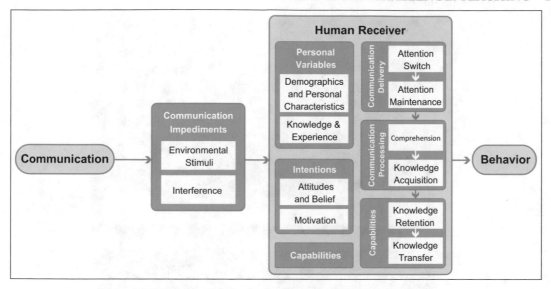

Figure 5.1: Cranor's human-in-the-loop security framework gives educators a way to teach students how to reason about security messages. (Based on Cranor [2008].)

Cranor's model is based on the Communication-Human Information Processing (C-HIP) model developed by Wogalter that attempts to explain why warning signs are sometimes ineffective [Wogalter, 2006]. Cranor extends this model with a recognition that any given human receiver may not have the necessary capability to act upon a security message that is received. The methodology provides a process for designers of systems and security mechanisms to consider human behavior and UPS issues.

However, such methodologies need to be paired with concrete *guidelines* towards the design of such systems. More work also needs to be done to distill all the lessons learned through research and observations into such guidelines. For example, Microsoft [2012] compiled advice for privacy and security warnings for use by developers at Microsoft, reducing them to the acronyms "NEAT" and "SPRUCE"(Figure 5.2). The card's purpose is to prevent developers from creating unusable security-critical dialogues that might themselves become sources of vulnerability.

UPS *metrics* would provide means for comparing one approach with another. One of the more common metrics reported in this review has been the number of individuals that fell for an attack in a laboratory or field environment. The problem with this metric is that it is utterly dependent upon experimental design. With little effort, an experimenter can easily design their experiment so that all users will succumb, or so that none of them will. It's generally more useful to perform a within-subjects or between-subjects study that varies an underlying condition and observes the results of changing a test condition. Sadly, such an approach makes it harder to compare the results of different studies.

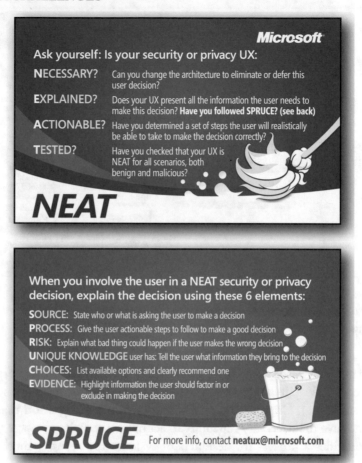

Figure 5.2: Microsoft's NEAT and SPRUCE guidelines are distributed on a wallet-sized card that the company hands out at developer meetings. (Based on Microsoft [2012].)

For those attempting to teach UPS or initiate collaborative research with others, the lack of UPS frameworks, taxonomies, conceptual models, methodologies, guidelines, and metrics is a serious stumbling block. Teaching is made harder by the lack of a textbook and general classroom resources. Cranor and Garfinkel [2005] wrote the only significant book in the field; although the introductory chapters are still relevant in a teaching environment, many of the other chapters are now only valuable for their historical perspective. Several course syllabi are available online (particularly from Carnegia Mellon University); however, these also rely on research papers organized around themes similar to this survey. While this survey attempts to pull together the various themes within the field, it does not yet re-organize these themes into curricular knowledge units.

There are still very few usable security courses taught that we are aware of, and no requirements for security programs to teach them. While the U.S. National Security Agency's "Academic Requirements for Designation as a Center of Academic Excellence in Cyber Operations" [National Security Agency, 2012] lists usable security as an optional knowledge unit, the requirements for a Center of Academic Excellence in Information Assurance does not. Instead, usability is merely mentioned as one sub topic of one knowledge unit on Security Design Principles. This is somewhat surprising, considering that phishing attacks and social engineering remain two of the most effective ways for compromising the security of organizations with hardened networks. Given the extensive list of knowledge units that are part of the IA requirements, universities also have little incentive to offer additional usable security education. We hope that this book provides a stepping stone towards the organization of the UPS body of knowledge for education and training.

CHAPTER 6

Conclusion: The Next Ten Years

For more than two decades there has been a growing realization that building secure computer systems requires attention not just to security mechanisms and underlying implementations, but also, to user interfaces and psychological issues. Although one would expect evolutionary pressure from market forces to slowly improve the usability of security systems over time, focused research on important usable privacy and security (UPS) topics has the ability to accelerate the development and adoption of secure systems that people can use.

In 1999, two seminal papers pointed out the problems of a lack of focus on usability. "Why Johnny Can't Encrypt" [Whitten and Tygar, 1999] and "Users Are Not The Enemy" [Adams and Sasse, 1999] demonstrated that without usability, security systems and software will in fact not be very secure. Since then, the UPS community has accumulated a substantial body of research demonstrating the usability issues with a range of security and privacy mechanisms, as well as proposing potential solutions to these issues. The community has matured, with an established conference as well as work appearing regularly in the top venues in security and Human Computer Interaction. There are now multiple academic research labs throughout the world, as well as increasing research being performed within industrial organizations.

Yet, despite this growth, progress can at times feel slow. As we have discussed in this book, passwords have not yet been replaced by a more usable mechanism. Phishing remains a problem. Users struggle to understand the privacy implications of their online activities, and manage the explosion of controls they now have. The majority of email sent has no end-to-end encryption or signature, and users still send unencrypted data over insecure public Wi-Fi networks.

As we have solved easier problems, attackers have gotten more sophisticated, requiring more advanced solutions. In addition, technology itself has changed dramatically in the past 15 years, with the security and privacy problems growing as consumers have more devices, more accounts, more shared information, and more online activities. That technological landscape is continually changing, making it more difficult to produce generalizable results, and then directly transition those results into practice.

Our hope for the future is that we will be able to leverage connectivity, social computing, technical gains in computation and interface technology, and artificial intelligence to overcome the increasing advantages and prowess of our adversaries. We also hope that our increased understanding of these issues will create new opportunities to inform developers and policymakers.

With this in mind, we will end this book with our predictions for the next ten years of usable security research.

More UPS Research Centers: Over the past decade, the majority of UPS research has been done at a relatively small number of academic and industrial research labs: Carnegie Mellon University, Carlton University in Canada, University College London, Google, and Microsoft Research. Some of the students to come out of these labs have now established their own labs at other institutions. As a result, we expect there to be an increase in the amount of UPS work as the number of research centers increases. We believe that funding from both government and industry will be a key element of growing and sustaining such centers.

More UPS Research Targets: Most academic usable-security research has been focused on a relatively limited number of tasks that are performed with traditional desktop computers or smart phones. This is unfortunate, because important, generalizable insights can come from working in other environments. Bauer et al. [2008]'s experience with the Grey electronic lock system provided deep insights into the importance of delegation and limiting access for a specific duration or even to a specific time-of-day. Likewise, there has been relatively little research done on improving the UPS associated with Automatic Teller Machines (ATMs), even though poor security interfaces provide opportunities for both theft and bodily harm to ATM users.

We therefore expect that opportunities for UPS research will increase at a greater rate than the number of researchers needed to carry out that research. We also expect that researchers will increasingly target their work to specific problems in order to remain relevant. We expect that the research challenges we outlined above will continue to be valuable research areas in the next ten years, and there will likely be more than what we can currently predict, as a result of new technologies and applications.

For example, we expect that there will be more work on usable security and privacy in domains such as the home [Little et al., 2009], the cloud, health care settings, and devices with integrated technology, such as cars and entertainment systems. Expanding into these domains will be challenging, as the adversary models will change, and may involve broader social issues, such as attitudes towards child rearing, care of elderly relatives, and safety. We expect that secure software development will become a focus area.

We also expect that the broader security research community will engage more with UPS researchers when developing and evaluating security mechanisms. Although industry now seems aware that usability is critically important for systems that are secure in practice, many security researchers still see usability as a requirement that can be addressed late in the development of algorithms and implementing technology. As the UPS field continues to mature, and educational opportunities for current students grow, we hope that these perceptions will be reduced.

More UPS Education: We likewise expect that there will be greater emphasis on integrating usability concepts into security curricula. Today, there is an awareness among some security educators that usability is important, but that awareness frequently stops with the statement "security systems must be usable"—not a significant advancement over Saltzer and Schroeder [1975]'s identification of "psychological acceptability" as a key principle for securing computer systems. Educators know that usability is important, but they rarely teach the basis of usability engineering, such as the importance of testing mechanisms on actual users before deploying them to a user population, or even the advantage of using consistent terminology and visual vocabulary within an application program. The UPS research community can help to advance this effort by developing and sharing course materials, teaching, and curricular strategies, and investigating a variety of ways to integrate these materials into existing programs.

Increased Research on Persuasion and Incentives: Focusing on making security interfaces more usable will only solve part of the challenge. Users need to also be motivated and incentivized to use those interfaces and make sound decisions. This requires additional research into mechanisms that influence users, using "nudges" that can help to persuade them towards secure or private behavior, without necessarily requiring it [Acquisti, 2009].

There have been several mechanisms proposed to persuade users towards stronger passwords, such as through password meters for text passwords [Egelman et al., 2013, Ur et al., 2012b]. Forget et al. [2008] investigated inserting random characters into users' passwords, allowing users to shuffle the added characters and positions until they were satisfied with the password. Another more subtle nudge is showing users photos of those they are about to email or post [Wang et al., 2014]. This provides additional concrete context to helps users reflect on whether they are communicating with a wider audience than intended. Improved defaults and options for configuration settings can also influence users towards more secure and private options [Ho et al., 2010]. Likewise, graphical passwords can be improved by using persuasion to encourage users to broaden their chosen points, removing "hotspots" chosen by multiple users [Chiasson et al., 2012].

More Field Studies: Field studies remain rare; in the future, we expect that there will be many more, especially as computing platforms become even more widely deployed in the environment. The growing use of application platforms, on both mobile devices and social network sites, is also allowing for easier deployment of experimental software and data collection of real behavior over longer periods of time. Organizations are also performing experiments on their own systems and interfaces, in an effort to improve them, and publishing their results. We hope to see data collection from field studies become the norm, yet, also note that such experimentation comes with its own challenges, including ethical considerations, such as informed consent and voluntary participation.

Increased Use of Crowd-Sourced Experiments, Data-Mining, and Machine Learning: We expect to see increased use of crowd-sourcing platforms, such as Amazon Mechnical Turk (AMT) and downloadable mobile apps, to allow researchers to collect information from thousands to hundreds of thousands of users. To process this data, we expect to see greater use of statistical techniques, such as data mining and machine learning for finding patterns. Crowd-sourced data collection and clustered analysis seems particularly well suited to UPS, since both good and poor security practices seem to cluster. Indeed, Lin et al. [2012] used crowd sourcing to explore expectations that AMT workers had for mobile apps. Lin [2013] describes a system that extends crowd-sourced collection of user privacy preferences with clustering, to derive different privacy preferences for different categories of users, with the raw data for the crowd-sourced collection coming from a static analysis of more than 100,000 applications downloaded from Google Play. These techniques will be useful to both deepen our understanding of users' current behaviors, as well as provide data to develop and compare solutions.

Personalization: The increase in large-scale data-driven research will also allow the pursuit of more customized and personal security solutions. As we have discussed, security and privacy can be highly contextual, dependent on the person, the information, the problem, and use. This means there are likely few instances of one-size-fits-all solutions. Currently, the user must intervene to make the appropriate security and privacy policy decisions. Personalization techniques would enable computer systems to make recommendations and decisions on behalf of the user that take more of this context into account.

* * *

We hope this review of the field helps to highlight the interesting results UPS researchers have so far achieved and the exciting challenges that remain. We believe that the future is one in which many of today's UPS questions will be resolved in ways that will seem obvious to future system designers and users. After all, "[m]ost really breakthrough conceptual advances are opaque in foresight and transparent in hindsight." [Cooper, 1999]

Bibliography

M. Abadi, L. Bharat, and A. Marais. 1997. US Patent 6141760. (1997). 39

Mark S. Ackerman, Lorrie Faith Cranor, and Joseph Reagle. 1999. Privacy in e-Commerce: Examining User Scenarios and Privacy Preferences. In *Proceedings of the 1st ACM Conference on Electronic Commerce (EC '99)*. ACM, New York, NY, USA, 1–8. DOI: 10.1145/336992.336995. 18

Alessandro Acquisti. 2009. Nudging Privacy: The Behavioral Economics of Personal Information. *IEEE Security & Privacy* 7, 6 (2009), 82–85. DOI: 10.1109/MSP.2009.163. 107

Alessandro Acquisti and Ralph Gross. 2006. Imagined Communities: Awareness, Information Sharing, and Privacy on the Facebook. In *Privacy Enhancing Technologies*, George Danezis and Philippe Golle (Eds.). Lecture Notes in Computer Science, Vol. 4258. Springer Berlin Heidelberg, 36–58. DOI: 10.1007/11957454_3. 81

Alessandro Acquisti and Ralph Gross. 2009. Predicting Social Security numbers from public data. *Proceedings of the National Academy of Sciences* 106, 27 (2009), 10975–10980. DOI: 10.1073/pnas.0904891106. 84

Anne Adams and Martina Angela Sasse. 1999. Users Are Not The Enemy. *Commun. ACM* 42 (1999), 41–46. Issue 12. 15, 105

Lalit Agarwal, Nisheeth Shrivastava, Sharad Jaiswal, and Saurabh Panjwani. 2013. Do Not Embarrass: Re-examining User Concerns for Online Tracking and Advertising. In *Proceedings of the Ninth Symposium on Usable Privacy and Security (SOUPS '13)*. ACM, New York, NY, USA, Article 8, 13 pages. DOI: 10.1145/2501604.2501612. 74

Gaurav Aggarwal, Elie Bursztein, Collin Jackson, and Dan Boneh. 2010. An analysis of private browsing modes in modern browsers. In *Proceedings of the 19th USENIX conference on Security (USENIX Security'10)*. USENIX Association, Berkeley, CA, USA, 6–6. http://dl.acm.org/citation.cfm?id=1929820.1929828 8

Luis Ahn, Manuel Blum, NicholasJ. Hopper, and John Langford. 2003. CAPTCHA: Using Hard AI Problems for Security. In *Advances in Cryptology — EUROCRYPT 2003*, Eli Biham (Ed.). Lecture Notes in Computer Science, Vol. 2656. Springer Berlin Heidelberg, 294–311. DOI: 10.1007/3-540-39200-9_18. 48

Devdatta Akhawe and Adrienne Porter Felt. 2013. Alice in Warningland: A Large-scale Field Study of Browser Security Warning Effectiveness. In *Proceedings of the 22Nd USENIX Conference on Security (SEC'13)*. USENIX Association, Berkeley, CA, USA, 257–272. `http://dl.acm.org/citation.cfm?id=2534766.2534789` 62, 63

M. Alsaleh, M. Mannan, and P. Van Oorschot. 2012. Revisiting Defenses against Large-Scale Online Password Guessing Attacks. *Dependable and Secure Computing, IEEE Transactions on* 9, 1 (Jan 2012), 128–141. DOI: 10.1109/TDSC.2011.24. 50

Irwin Altman. 1974. *The environment and social behavior: privacy, personal space, territory, crowding*. Brooks/Cole Pub. Co. 256 pages. 10, 84

Adam J Aviv, Katherine Gibson, Evan Mossop, Matt Blaze, and Jonathan M Smith. 2010a. Smudge attacks on smartphone touch screens. In *Proceedings of the 4th USENIX conference on Offensive technologies*. USENIX Association, Usenix, Washington, DC, 1–7. 43

Adam J. Aviv, Katherine Gibson, Evan Mossop, Matt Blaze, and Jonathan M. Smith. 2010b. Smudge attacks on smartphone touch screens. In *Proceedings of the 4th USENIX conference on Offensive technologies (WOOT'10)*. USENIX Association, Washington, DC, 1–7. `http://dl.acm.org/citation.cfm?id=1925004.1925009` 99

Oshrat Ayalon and Eran Toch. 2013. Retrospective Privacy: Managing Longitudinal Privacy in Online Social Networks. In *Proceedings of the Ninth Symposium on Usable Privacy and Security (SOUPS '13)*. ACM, New York, NY, USA, Article 4, 13 pages. DOI: 10.1145/2501604.2501608. 96

Rebecca Balebako, Jaeyeon Jung, Wei Lu, Lorrie Faith Cranor, and Carolyn Nguyen. 2013. "Little Brothers Watching You": Raising Awareness of Data Leaks on Smartphones. In *Proceedings of the Ninth Symposium on Usable Privacy and Security (SOUPS '13)*. ACM, New York, NY, USA, Article 12, 11 pages. DOI: 10.1145/2501604.2501616. 80

Dirk Balfanz, Glenn Durfee, Rebecca E. Grinter, D. K. Smetters, and Paul Stewart. 2004. Network-in-a-box: How to Set Up a Secure Wireless Network in Under a Minute. In *Proceedings of the 13th Conference on USENIX Security Symposium - Volume 13 (SSYM'04)*. USENIX Association, Berkeley, CA, USA, 15–15. `http://dl.acm.org/citation.cfm?id=1251375.1251390` 67

Susan B. Barnes. 2006. A privacy paradox: Social networking in the United States. *First Monday* 11, 9 (2006). `http://firstmonday.org/ojs/index.php/fm/article/view/1394` 81

Lujo Bauer, Lorrie Faith Cranor, Robert W. Reeder, Michael K. Reiter, and Kami Vaniea. 2008. A User Study of Policy Creation in a Flexible Access-control System. In *Proceedings of the SIGCHI Conference on Human Factors in Computing Systems (CHI '08)*. ACM, New York, NY, USA, 543–552. DOI: 10.1145/1357054.1357143. 77, 106

Lujo Bauer, Lorrie Faith Cranor, Robert W. Reeder, Michael K. Reiter, and Kami Vaniea. 2009. Real life challenges in access-control management. In *Proceedings of the SIGCHI Conference on Human Factors in Computing Systems (CHI '09)*. ACM, New York, NY, USA, 899–908. DOI: 10.1145/1518701.1518838. 77

Adam Beautement, M. Angela Sasse, and Mike Wonham. The Compliance Budget: Managing Security Behavior in Organisations. In *Proceedings of the 2008 Workshop on New Security Paradigms Workshop (NSPW '08)*. 2008, ACM, New York, NY. 2, 4

Michael Benisch, PatrickGage Kelley, Norman Sadeh, and LorrieFaith Cranor. 2011. Capturing location-privacy preferences: quantifying accuracy and user-burden tradeoffs. *Personal and Ubiquitous Computing* 15, 7 (2011), 679–694. DOI: 10.1007/s00779-010-0346-0. 79

Michael S. Bernstein, Eytan Bakshy, Moira Burke, and Brian Karrer. 2013. Quantifying the Invisible Audience in Social Networks. In *Proceedings of the SIGCHI Conference on Human Factors in Computing Systems (CHI '13)*. ACM, New York, NY, USA, 21–30. DOI: 10.1145/2470654.2470658. 82

Andrew Besmer and Heather Richter Lipford. 2010. Users' (Mis)Conceptions of Social Applications. In *Proceedings of Graphics Interface 2010 (GI '10)*. Canadian Information Processing Society, Toronto, Ont., Canada, Canada, 63–70. http://dl.acm.org/citation.cfm?id=1839214.1839226 84

Andrew Besmer, Heather Richter Lipford, Mohamed Shehab, and Gorrell Cheek. 2009. Social Applications: Exploring a More Secure Framework. In *Proceedings of the 5th Symposium on Usable Privacy and Security (SOUPS '09)*. ACM, New York, NY, USA, Article 2, 10 pages. DOI: 10.1145/1572532.1572535. 84, 98

Andrew Besmer and Heather Richter Lipford. 2010. Moving Beyond Untagging: Photo Privacy in a Tagged World. In *Proceedings of the SIGCHI Conference on Human Factors in Computing Systems (CHI '10)*. ACM, New York, NY, USA, 1563–1572. DOI: 10.1145/1753326.1753560. 81, 83

Andrew Besmer, Jason Watson, and Heather Richter Lipford. 2010. The impact of social navigation on privacy policy configuration. In *SOUPS '10: Proceedings of the Sixth Symposium on Usable Privacy and Security*. ACM, New York, NY, USA, 1–10. DOI: 10.1145/1837110.1837120. 19

Robert Biddle, Sonia Chiasson, and P. C. van Oorschot. 2012. Graphical passwords: Learning from the first twelve years. *ACM Comput. Surv.* 44, 4, Article 19 (Sept. 2012), 41 pages. DOI: 10.1145/2333112.2333114. 7, 11, 40, 42

Robert Biddle, P. C. van Oorschot, Andrew S. Patrick, Jennifer Sobey, and Tara Whalen. 2009. Browser Interfaces and Extended Validation SSL Certificates: An Empirical Study. In *Proceedings of the 2009 ACM Workshop on Cloud Computing Security (CCSW '09)*. ACM, New York, NY, USA, 19–30. DOI: 10.1145/1655008.1655012. 61

M. Bishop. 2003. What is computer security? *Security Privacy, IEEE* 1, 1 (Jan 2003), 67–69. DOI: 10.1109/MSECP.2003.1176998. 8

Matt Bishop and Daniel Klein. 1995. Improving System Security Through Proactive Password Checking. *Computers and Security* 14, 3 (May/June 1995), 233–249. 26

G. Blonder. 1996. Graphical password. (1996). US Patent 5,559,961, filed August 30, 1995, issued September 1996. 40

Rakesh Bobba, Joe Muggli, Meenal Pant, Jim Basney, and Himanshu Khurana. 2009. Usable Secure Mailing Lists with Untrusted Servers. In *Proceedings of the 8th Symposium on Identity and Trust on the Internet (IDtrust '09)*. ACM, New York, NY, USA, 103–116. DOI: 10.1145/1527017.1527032. 53

Joseph Bonneau. 2012. The Science of Guessing: Analyzing an Anonymized Corpus of 70 Million Passwords. In *Proceedings of the 2012 IEEE Symposium on Security and Privacy (SP '12)*. IEEE Computer Society, Washington, DC, USA, 538–552. DOI: 10.1109/SP.2012.49. 36

Joseph Bonneau, Cormac Herley, Paul C. van Oorschot, and Frank Stajano. 2012a. *The quest to replace passwords: a framework for comparative evaluation of Web authentication schemes*. Technical Report UCAM-CL-TR-817. University of Cambridge, Computer Laboratory. http://www.cl.cam.ac.uk/techreports/UCAM-CL-TR-817.pdf 36, 37

J. Bonneau, C. Herley, P.C. van Oorschot, and F. Stajano. 2012b. The Quest to Replace Passwords: A Framework for Comparative Evaluation of Web Authentication Schemes. In *Security and Privacy (SP), 2012 IEEE Symposium on*. IEEE, San Francisco, CA, 553–567. DOI: 10.1109/SP.2012.44. 11, 36, 38

Joseph Bonneau, Sörenn Preibusc, and Ross Anderson. 2012c. A birthday present every eleven wallets? The security of customer-chosen banking PINs. In *Financial Cryptography 2012*. Springer-Verlag, Bonaire. 29

Joseph Bonneau and Sören Preibusch. 2010. The password thicket: technical and market failures in human authentication on the web. In *The Ninth Workshop on the Economics of Information Security (WEIS)*. Arlington, VA. 29

Joseph Bonneau and Ekaterina Shutova. 2012. Linguistic properties of multi-word passphrases. In *Proceedings of the 16th international conference on Financial Cryptography and Data Security (FC'12)*. Springer-Verlag, Berlin, Heidelberg, 1–12. DOI: 10.1007/978-3-642-34638-5_1. 30, 33

David Botta, Kasia Muldner, Kirstie Hawkey, and Konstantin Beznosov. 2011. Toward understanding distributed cognition in IT security management: the role of cues and norms. *Cognition, Technology & Work* 13, 2 (2011), 121–134. DOI: 10.1007/s10111-010-0159-y. 85

David Botta, Rodrigo Werlinger, and André Gagné. 2007a. Studying IT Security Professionals: Research Design and Lessons Learned. In *Workshop on Security User Studies: Methodologies and Best practices (WSUS '07)*. ACM. http://lersse-dl.ece.ubc.ca/record/126/files/126.pdf 95, 96

David Botta, Rodrigo Werlinger, André Gagné, Konstantin Beznosov, Lee Iverson, Sidney Fels, and Brian Fisher. 2007b. Towards understanding IT security professionals and their tools. In *SOUPS '07: Proceedings of the 3rd symposium on Usable privacy and security*. ACM, New York, NY, USA, 100–111. DOI: 10.1145/1280680.1280693. 85

D. Boyd and J. Heer. 2006. Profiles as Conversation: Networked Identity Performance on Friendster. In *System Sciences, 2006. HICSS '06. Proceedings of the 39th Annual Hawaii International Conference on*, Vol. 3. IEEE Computer Society Press, Hawaii, 59c–59c. DOI: 10.1109/HICSS.2006.394. 82

Alex Braunstein, Laura Granka, and Jessica Staddon. 2011. Indirect content privacy surveys: measuring privacy without asking about it. In *SOUPS '11: Proceedings of the Seventh Symposium on Usable Privacy and Security*. ACM, New York, NY, USA, 1–14. DOI: 10.1145/2078827.2078847. 97

Cristian Bravo-Lillo, Lorrie Faith Cranor, Julie Downs, Saranga Komanduri, and Manya Sleeper. 2011. Improving Computer Security Dialogs. In *Proceedings of the 13th IFIP TC 13 International Conference on Human-computer Interaction - Volume Part IV (INTER-ACT'11)*. Springer-Verlag, Berlin, Heidelberg, 18–35. http://dl.acm.org/citation.cfm?id=2042283.2042286 62

Cristian Bravo-Lillo, Saranga Komanduri, Lorrie Faith Cranor, Robert W. Reeder, Manya Sleeper, Julie Downs, and Stuart Schechter. 2013. Your Attention Please: Designing Security-decision UIs to Make Genuine Risks Harder to Ignore. In *Proceedings of the Ninth Symposium on Usable Privacy and Security (SOUPS '13)*. ACM, New York, NY, USA, Article 6, 12 pages. DOI: 10.1145/2501604.2501610. 95

Carolyn Brodie, Clare-Marie Karat, John Karat, and Jinjuan Feng. 2005. Usable security and privacy: a case study of developing privacy management tools. In *SOUPS '05: Proceedings of the 2005 symposium on Usable privacy and security*. ACM, New York, NY, USA, 35–43. DOI: 10.1145/1073001.1073005. 77

Carolyn A. Brodie, Clare-Marie Karat, and John Karat. 2006. An empirical study of natural language parsing of privacy policy rules using the SPARCLE policy workbench. In *SOUPS*

'06: Proceedings of the second symposium on Usable privacy and security. ACM, New York, NY, USA, 8–19. DOI: 10.1145/1143120.1143123. 77

Sacha Brostoff, Philip Inglesant, and M. Angela Sasse. 2010. Evaluating the Usability and Security of a Graphical One-time PIN System. In *Proceedings of the 24th BCS Interaction Specialist Group Conference (BCS '10).* British Computer Society, Swinton, UK, UK, 88–97. `http://dl.acm.org/citation.cfm?id=2146303.2146317` 47, 48

Sacha Brostoff and M. Angela Sasse. 2003. Ten strikes and you're out: Increasing the number of login attempts can improve password usability. In *Workshop on Human-Computer Interaction and Security Systems, part of CHI2003.* ACM Press. `citeseer.ist.psu.edu/618589.html` 25

José Carlos Brustoloni and Ricardo Villamarín-Salomón. 2007. Improving security decisions with polymorphic and audited dialogs. In *SOUPS '07: Proceedings of the 3rd symposium on Usable privacy and security.* ACM, New York, NY, USA, 76–85. DOI: 10.1145/1280680.1280691. 62

Michael Buhrmester, Tracy Kwang, and Samuel D. Gosling. 2011. Amazon's Mechanical Turk: A New Source of Inexpensive, Yet High-Quality, Data? *Perspectives on Psychological Science* 6, 1 (2011), 3–5. DOI: 10.1177/1745691610393980. 20

Ulrich Burgbacher and Klaus Hinrichs. 2014. An Implicit Author Verification System for Text Messages Based on Gesture Typing Biometrics. In *Proceedings of the SIGCHI Conference on Human Factors in Computing Systems (CHI '14).* ACM, New York, NY, USA, 2951–2954. DOI: 10.1145/2556288.2557346. 45, 81

E. Bursztein, S. Bethard, C. Fabry, J.C. Mitchell, and D. Jurafsky. 2010. How Good Are Humans at Solving CAPTCHAs? A Large Scale Evaluation. In *Security and Privacy (SP), 2010 IEEE Symposium on.* IEEE, Oakland, CA, 399–413. DOI: 10.1109/SP.2010.31. 49

Elie Bursztein, Matthieu Martin, and John Mitchell. 2011. Text-based CAPTCHA Strengths and Weaknesses. In *Proceedings of the 18th ACM Conference on Computer and Communications Security (CCS '11).* ACM, New York, NY, USA, 125–138. DOI: 10.1145/2046707.2046724. 49

Elie Bursztein, Angelique Moscicki, Celine Fabry, Steven Bethard, John C. Mitchell, and Dan Jurafsky. 2014. Easy Does It: More Usable CAPTCHAs. In *Proceedings of the SIGCHI Conference on Human Factors in Computing Systems (CHI '14).* ACM, New York, NY, USA, 2637–2646. DOI: 10.1145/2556288.2557322. 19, 49

Simon Byers. 2003. Scalable Exploitation of, and Responses to Information Leakage Through Hidden Data in Published Documents. (April 2003). `http://www.user-agent.org/word_docs.pdf` 66

L.J. Camp. 2009. Mental models of privacy and security. *Technology and Society Magazine, IEEE* 28, 3 (Fall 2009), 37–46. DOI: 10.1109/MTS.2009.934142. 90

D.D. Caputo, S.L. Pfleeger, J.D. Freeman, and M.E. Johnson. 2014. Going Spear Phishing: Exploring Embedded Training and Awareness. *Security Privacy, IEEE* 12, 1 (Jan 2014), 28–38. DOI: 10.1109/MSP.2013.106. 64, 65

John M. Carroll and Caroline Carrithers. 1984. Training Wheels in a User Interface. *Commun. ACM* 27, 8 (Aug. 1984), 800–806. DOI: 10.1145/358198.358218. 52

Fred H. Cate. 2010. The Limits of Notice and Choice. *IEEE Security and Privacy* 8, 2 (March 2010), 59–62. DOI: 10.1109/MSP.2010.84. 74

William Cheswick. 2013. Rethinking passwords. *Commun. ACM* 56, 2 (Feb. 2013), 40–44. DOI: 10.1145/2408776.2408790. 25

Sonia Chiasson, Elizabeth Stobert, Alain Forget, Robert Biddle, and Paul C. van Oorschot. 2012. Persuasive Cued Click-Points: Design, Implementation, and Evaluation of a Knowledge-Based Authentication Mechanism. *IEEE Transactions on Dependable and Secure Computing* 9, 2 (2012), 222–235. DOI: 10.1109/TDSC.2011.55. 42, 107

Sonia Chiasson, P. C. van Oorschot, and Robert Biddle. 2006. A Usability Study and Critique of Two Password Managers. In *Proceedings of the 15th Conference on USENIX Security Symposium - Volume 15 (USENIX-SS'06)*. USENIX Association, Berkeley, CA, USA, Article 1. http://dl.acm.org/citation.cfm?id=1267336.1267337 39

Erika Chin, Adrienne Porter Felt, Vyas Sekar, and David Wagner. 2012. Measuring user confidence in smartphone security and privacy. In *SOUPS '12: Proceedings of the Eighth Symposium on Usable Privacy and Security*. ACM, New York, NY, USA, 1–16. DOI: 10.1145/2335356.2335358. 80, 81

Jim Chow, Ben Pfaff, Tal Garfinkel, and Mendel Rosenblum. 2005. Shredding Your Garbage: Reducing Data Lifetime. In *Proc. 14th USENIX Security Symposium*. Usenix, Baltimore, MD. 66

Jeremy Clark, P. C. van Oorschot, and Carlisle Adams. 2007. Usability of anonymous web browsing: an examination of Tor interfaces and deployability. In *SOUPS '07: Proceedings of the 3rd symposium on Usable privacy and security*. ACM, New York, NY, USA, 41–51. DOI: 10.1145/1280680.1280687. 88

Dwaine E. Clarke, Blaise Gassend, Thomas Kotwal, Matt Burnside, Marten van Dijk, Srinivas Devadas, and Ronald L. Rivest. 2002. The Untrusted Computer Problem and Camera-Based Authentication. In *Proceedings of the First International Conference on Pervasive Computing (Pervasive '02)*. Springer-Verlag, London, UK, UK, 114–124. http://dl.acm.org/citation.cfm?id=646867.706695 68

Sunny Consolvo, Ian E. Smith, Tara Matthews, Anthony LaMarca, Jason Tabert, and Pauline Powledge. 2005. Location Disclosure to Social Relations: Why, when, & What People Want to Share. In *Proceedings of the SIGCHI Conference on Human Factors in Computing Systems (CHI '05)*. ACM, New York, NY, USA, 81–90. DOI: 10.1145/1054972.1054985. 78

Gregory Conti, Kulsoom Abdullah, Julian Grizzard, John Stasko, John A. Copeland, Mustaque Ahamad, Henry L. Owen, and Chris Lee. 2006. Countering Security Information Overload Through Alert and Packet Visualization. *IEEE Comput. Graph. Appl.* 26, 2 (March 2006), 60–70. DOI: 10.1109/MCG.2006.30. 86

Gregory Conti, Mustaque Ahamad, and John Stasko. 2005. Attacking information visualization system usability overloading and deceiving the human. In *SOUPS '05: Proceedings of the 2005 symposium on Usable privacy and security*. ACM, New York, NY, USA, 89–100. DOI: 10.1145/1073001.1073010. 86

Alan Cooper. 1999. *The Inmates Are Running The Asylum*. Sams, Indianapolis, Indiana. 108

K. Coronges, Ronald Dodge, C. Mukina, Z. Radwick, J. Shevchik, and E. Rovira. 2012. The Influences of Social Networks on Phishing Vulnerability. In *System Science (HICSS), 2012 45th Hawaii International Conference on*. IEEE, Maui, Hawaii, 2366–2373. DOI: 10.1109/HICSS.2012.657. 100

Lynne Coventry. 2005. Usable Biometrics. In *Security and Usability*, Lorrie Cranor and Simson Garfinkel (Eds.). O'Reilly, Cambridge, MA. 43

Lynne Coventry, Antonella De Angeli, and Graham Johnson. 2003. Usability and biometric verification at the ATM interface. In *Proceedings of the SIGCHI Conference on Human Factors in Computing Systems (CHI '03)*. ACM, New York, NY, USA, 153–160. DOI: 10.1145/642611.642639. 19, 44

2003. *Four Grand Challenges in Trustworthy Computing*. Computing Research Association. http://archive.cra.org/reports/trustworthy.computing.pdf 1

Lorie Cranor. 1999. Agents of Choice: Tools that Facilitate Notice and Choice about Web Site Data Practices. In *Proceedings of the 21st International Conference on Privacy and Personal Data Protection*. Office of the Privacy Commissioner for Personal Data, Hong Kong, Hong Kong SAR, China, 19–25. 70

L.F. Cranor and S. Garfinkel. 2004. Guest Editors' Introduction: Secure or Usable? *Security Privacy, IEEE* 2, 5 (2004), 16–18. DOI: 10.1109/MSP.2004.69. 19

Lorrie Cranor and Simson Garfinkel. 2005. *Security and Usability*. O'Reilly, Cambridge, MA. 19, 102

Lorrie Faith Cranor. 2008. A framework for reasoning about the human in the loop. In *Proceedings of the 1st Conference on Usability, Psychology, and Security (UPSEC'08)*. USENIX Association, San Francisco, California, Article 1, 15 pages. `http://dl.acm.org/citation.cfm?id=1387649.1387650` 57, 88, 100, 101

Lorrie Faith Cranor. 2012. Necessary But Not Sufficient: Standardized Mechanisms for Privacy Notice and Choice. *Journal of Telecommunications and High Technology Law* 10, 2 (Dec. 2 2012). `http://papers.ssrn.com/sol3/papers.cfm?abstract_id=2184059` 74

Lorrie Faith Cranor, Serge Egelman, Steve Sheng, Aleecia M. McDonald, and Abdur Chowdhury. 2008. P3P Deployment on Websites. *Electron. Commer. Rec. Appl.* 7, 3 (Nov. 2008), 274–293. DOI: 10.1016/j.elerap.2008.04.003. 73

Lorrie Faith Cranor, Praveen Guduru, and Manjula Arjula. 2006. User Interfaces for Privacy Agents. *ACM Trans. Comput.-Hum. Interact.* 13, 2 (June 2006), 135–178. DOI: 10.1145/1165734.1165735. 71, 73

H. Crawford. 2010. Keystroke dynamics: Characteristics and opportunities. In *Privacy Security and Trust (PST), 2010 Eighth Annual International Conference on*. IEEE, Ottawa, ON, 205–212. DOI: 10.1109/PST.2010.5593258. 45

Matthew J. C. Crump, John V. McDonnell, and Todd M. Gureckis. 2013. Evaluating Amazon's Mechanical Turk as a Tool for Experimental Behavioral Research. *PLoS ONE* 8, 3 (03 2013), e57410. DOI: 10.1371/journal.pone.0057410. 20

Brinda Dalal, Les Nelson, Diana Smetters, Nathaniel Good, and Ame Elliot. 2008. Ad-hoc Guesting: When Exceptions Are the Rule. In *Proceedings of the 1st Conference on Usability, Psychology, and Security (UPSEC'08)*. USENIX Association, Berkeley, CA, USA, Article 9, 5 pages. `http://dl.acm.org/citation.cfm?id=1387649.1387658` 75

Sauvik Das, Eiji Hayashi, and Jason I. Hong. 2013. Exploring Capturable Everyday Memory for Autobiographical Authentication. In *Proceedings of the 2013 ACM International Joint Conference on Pervasive and Ubiquitous Computing (UbiComp '13)*. ACM, New York, NY, USA, 211–220. DOI: 10.1145/2493432.2493453. 81

Darren Davis, Fabian Monrose, and Michael K. Reiter. 2004. On User Choice in Graphical Password Schemes. In *Proceedings of the 13th Conference on USENIX Security Symposium - Volume 13 (SSYM'04)*. USENIX Association, Berkeley, CA, USA, 11–11. `http://dl.acm.org/citation.cfm?id=1251375.1251386` 40

Matteo Dell'Amico, Pietro Michiardi, and Yves Roudier. 2010. Password strength: an empirical analysis. In *Proceedings of the 29th conference on Information communications (INFO-COM'10)*. IEEE Press, Piscataway, NJ, USA, 983–991. `http://dl.acm.org/citation.cfm?id=1833515.1833671` 29

Rachna Dhamija. 2007. Usable Security (USEC'07). (2007). `http://www.usablesecurity` `.org/` 20

Rachna Dhamija and Adrian Perrig. 2000. Déjà Vu: A User Study Using Images for Authentication. In *Proceedings of the 9th USENIX Security Symposium*. Usenix, Denver, CO. `citeseer.ist.psu.edu/326534.html` 40

Rachna Dhamija and J. D. Tygar. 2005. The battle against phishing: Dynamic Security Skins. In *SOUPS '05: Proceedings of the 2005 symposium on Usable privacy and security*. ACM, New York, NY, USA, 77–88. DOI: 10.1145/1073001.1073009. 59, 60

Rachna Dhamija, J. D. Tygar, and Marti Hearst. 2006. Why Phishing Works. In *Proceedings of the SIGCHI Conference on Human Factors in Computing Systems (CHI '06)*. ACM, New York, NY, USA, 581–590. DOI: 10.1145/1124772.1124861. 57

A. Dieberger, P. Dourish, K. Höök, P. Resnick, and A. Wexelblat. 2000. Social Navigation: Techniques for Building More Usable Systems. *interactions* 7, 6 (Nov. 2000), 36–45. DOI: 10.1145/352580.352587. 98

Whitfield Diffie and Martin E. Hellman. 1976. New Directions in Cryptography. *IEEE Transactions on Information Theory* IT-22, 6 (1976), 644–654. `citeseer.ist.psu.edu/diffie76n` `ew.html` 51

Roger Dingledine and Nick Mathewson. 2005. Anonymity Loves Company: Usability and the Network Effect. In *Security and Usability*, Lorrie Cranor and Simson L. Garfinkel (Eds.). O'Reilly, Cambridge, MA. 88

DOD 1985. *Department of Defense Passowrd Management Guideline*. Technical Report CSC-STD-002-85. Department of Defense Computer Security Center, Fort George G. Meade, Maryland 20755. 25

DoD 1995. Cleaning and Sanitization Matrix. (Jan. 1995). `www.dss.mil/isec/nispom_` `0195.htm` Chapter 8. 65

G. Doddington, W. Liggett, A. Martin, M. Przybocki, and D. Reynolds. 1998. Sheep, Goats, Lambs and Wolves: A Statistical Analysis of Speaker Performance in the NIST 1998 Speaker Recognition Evaluation. In *Proc. Int'l Conf. Spoken Language Processing*. 94

Paul Dourish, E. Grinter, Jessica Delgado de la Flor, and Melissa Joseph. 2004. Security in the wild: user strategies for managing security as an everyday, practical problem. *Personal Ubiquitous Comput.* 8, 6 (Nov. 2004), 391–401. DOI: 10.1007/s00779-004-0308-5. 4

Julie S. Downs, Mandy B. Holbrook, and Lorrie Faith Cranor. 2006. Decision strategies and susceptibility to phishing. In *SOUPS '06: Proceedings of the second symposium on Usable privacy and security*. ACM, New York, NY, USA, 79–90. DOI: 10.1145/1143120.1143131. 63

Julie S. Downs, Mandy B. Holbrook, Steve Sheng, and Lorrie Faith Cranor. 2010. Are Your Participants Gaming the System?: Screening Mechanical Turk Workers. In *Proceedings of the SIGCHI Conference on Human Factors in Computing Systems (CHI '10)*. ACM, New York, NY, USA, 2399–2402. DOI: 10.1145/1753326.1753688. 20

W. Keith Edwards, Erika Shehan Poole, and Jennifer Stoll. 2008. Security Automation Considered Harmful?. In *Proceedings of the 2007 Workshop on New Security Paradigms (NSPW '07)*. ACM, New York, NY, USA, 33–42. DOI: 10.1145/1600176.1600182. 55, 88

Serge Egelman, Lorrie Faith Cranor, and Jason Hong. 2008a. You've Been Warned: An Empirical Study of the Effectiveness of Web Browser Phishing Warnings. In *Proceedings of the SIGCHI Conference on Human Factors in Computing Systems (CHI '08)*. ACM, New York, NY, USA, 1065–1074. DOI: 10.1145/1357054.1357219. 62, 93

Serge Egelman, Lorrie Faith Cranor, and Jason Hong. 2008b. You've been warned: an empirical study of the effectiveness of web browser phishing warnings. In *CHI '08: Proceeding of the twenty-sixth annual SIGCHI conference on Human factors in computing systems*. ACM, New York, NY, USA, 1065–1074. DOI: 10.1145/1357054.1357219. 95

Serge Egelman, Adrienne Porter Felt, and David Wagner. 2012. Choice Architecture and Smartphone Privacy: There's a Price for That. In *Proc. of the 11th Annual Workshop on the Economics of Information Security (WEIS '12)*. Springer-Verlag, Berlin, Germany. https://www.eecs.berkeley.edu/~daw/papers/choice-weis12.pdf 80

Serge Egelman, Andrew Oates, and Shriram Krishnamurthi. 2011. Oops, I Did It Again: Mitigating Repeated Access Control Errors on Facebook. In *Proceedings of the SIGCHI Conference on Human Factors in Computing Systems (CHI '11)*. ACM, New York, NY, USA, 2295–2304. DOI: 10.1145/1978942.1979280. 82, 83

Serge Egelman, Andreas Sotirakopoulos, Ildar Muslukhov, Konstantin Beznosov, and Cormac Herley. 2013. Does My Password Go Up to Eleven?: The Impact of Password Meters on Password Selection. In *Proceedings of the SIGCHI Conference on Human Factors in Computing Systems (CHI '13)*. ACM, New York, NY, USA, 2379–2388. DOI: 10.1145/2470654.2481329. 107

Serge Egelman, Janice Tsai, Lorrie Faith Cranor, and Alessandro Acquisti. 2009. Timing is everything?: the effects of timing and placement of online privacy indicators. In *Proceedings of the SIGCHI Conference on Human Factors in Computing Systems (CHI '09)*. ACM, New York, NY, USA, 319–328. DOI: 10.1145/1518701.1518752. 71

Carl Ellison. 2007. Ceremony Design and Analysis. (2007). http://eprint.iacr.org/2007/399.pdf 52

Carl Ellison and Bruce Schneier. 2000. Ten Risks of PKI: What You're not Being Told about Public Key Infrastructure. *Computer Security Journal* XVI, 1 (2000). 52

Sascha Fahl, Marian Harbach, Yasemin Acar, and Matthew Smith. 2013. On the Ecological Validity of a Password Study. In *Proceedings of the Ninth Symposium on Usable Privacy and Security (SOUPS '13)*. ACM, New York, NY, USA, Article 13, 13 pages. DOI:
10.1145/2501604.2501617. 5, 34

Sascha Fahl, Marian Harbach, Thomas Muders, Matthew Smith, and Uwe Sander. 2012. Helping Johnny 2.0 to encrypt his Facebook conversations. In *SOUPS '12: Proceedings of the
Eighth Symposium on Usable Privacy and Security*. ACM, New York, NY, USA, 1–17. DOI:
10.1145/2335356.2335371. 54

Adrienne Porter Felt, Serge Egelman, and David Wagner. 2012a. I've Got 99 Problems, but
Vibration Ain'T One: A Survey of Smartphone Users' Concerns. In *Proceedings of the Second
ACM Workshop on Security and Privacy in Smartphones and Mobile Devices (SPSM '12)*. ACM,
New York, NY, USA, 33–44. DOI: 10.1145/2381934.2381943. 80

Adrienne Porter Felt, Elizabeth Ha, Serge Egelman, Ariel Haney, Erika Chin, and David Wagner. 2012b. Android permissions: user attention, comprehension, and behavior. In *SOUPS
'12: Proceedings of the Eighth Symposium on Usable Privacy and Security*. ACM, New York, NY,
USA, 1–14. DOI: 10.1145/2335356.2335360. 80, 89

Adrienne Porter Felt, Robert W. Reeder, Hazim Almuhimedi, and Sunny Consolvo. 2014. Ex-
perimenting at Scale with Google Chrome's SSL Warning. In *Proceedings of the SIGCHI Conference on Human Factors in Computing Systems (CHI '14)*. ACM, New York, NY, USA, 2667–
2670. DOI: 10.1145/2556288.2557292. 63

G.A. Fink, C.L. North, Alex Endert, and S. Rose. 2009. Visualizing cyber security: Usable
workspaces. In *Visualization for Cyber Security, 2009. VizSec 2009. 6th International Workshop
on*. IEEE, Atlantic City, CA, 45–56. DOI: 10.1109/VIZSEC.2009.5375542. 86

Drew Fisher, Leah Dorner, and David Wagner. 2012. Short Paper: Location Privacy: User
Behavior in the Field. In *Proceedings of the Second ACM Workshop on Security and Privacy in
Smartphones and Mobile Devices (SPSM '12)*. ACM, New York, NY, USA, 51–56. DOI:
10.1145/2381934.2381945. 79

Dinei Florencio and Cormac Herley. 2007. A large-scale study of web password habits. In *Proceedings of the 16th international conference on World Wide Web (WWW '07)*. ACM, New York,
NY, USA, 657–666. DOI: 10.1145/1242572.1242661. 27, 35

Dinei Florêncio and Cormac Herley. 2010. Where do security policies come from?. In *SOUPS
'10: Proceedings of the Sixth Symposium on Usable Privacy and Security*. ACM, New York, NY,
USA, 1–14. DOI: 10.1145/1837110.1837124. 28

Dinei Florêncio, Cormac Herley, and Paul van Oorschot. 2014a. Password Portfolios and the Fintie-Effort User: Sustainably Managing Large Numbers of Accounts. In *Usenix Security*. Usenix, San Diego, CA. 28

Dinei Florêncio, Cormac Herley, and Paul C. van Oorschot. 2014b. An Administrator's Guide to Internet Password Research. In *Proceedings of the Usenix LISA 2014 (LISA '14)*. USENIX, Seattle, WA. 24, 25, 29

Alain Forget, Sonia Chiasson, P. C. van Oorschot, and Robert Biddle. 2008. Improving text passwords through persuasion. In *SOUPS '08: Proceedings of the 4th symposium on Usable privacy and security*. ACM, New York, NY, USA, 1–12. DOI: 10.1145/1408664.1408666. 42, 107

Anthony Y. Fu, Xiaotie Deng, Liu Wenyin, and Greg Little. 2006. The methodology and an application to fight against Unicode attacks. In *SOUPS '06: Proceedings of the second symposium on Usable privacy and security*. ACM, New York, NY, USA, 91–101. DOI: 10.1145/1143120.1143132. 56

Eran Gabber, Phillip B. Gibbons, Yossi Matias, and Alain J. Mayer. 1997. How to Make Personalized Web Browsing Simple, Secure, and Anonymous. In *Proceedings of the First International Conference on Financial Cryptography (FC '97)*. Springer-Verlag, London, UK, UK, 17–32. http://dl.acm.org/citation.cfm?id=647501.728165 39

Alexander Gallego, Nitesh Saxena, and Jonathan Voris. 2011. Playful Security: A Computer Game for Secure Pairing of Wireless Devices. In *The 16th International Computer Games Conference (CGames): AI, Animation, Mobile, Interactive Multimedia, Educational & Serious Games*. IEEE, Louisville, Kentucky. 68

S.L. Garfinkel. 2014. Leaking Sensitive Information in Complex Document Files–and How to Prevent It. *Security Privacy, IEEE* 12, 1 (Jan 2014), 20–27. DOI: 10.1109/MSP.2013.131. 66

Simson Garfinkel and Abhi Shelat. 2003. Remembrance of Data Passed. *IEEE Security and Privacy* 1, 1 (Jan. 2003), 17–27. 65

Simson L. Garfinkel. 1995. Illegal program troubles America Online. *The Boston Globe* (April 21 1995). http://simson.net/clips/1995/95.Globe.AOHell.pdf 56

Simson L. Garfinkel. 2003. Enabling Email Confidentiality Through the Use of Opportunistic Encryption. In *Proceedings of the 2003 Annual National Conference on Digital Government Research (dg.o '03)*. Digital Government Society of North America, Boston, MA, 1–4. http://dl.acm.org/citation.cfm?id=1123196.1123245 53

Simson L. Garfinkel. 2005. *Design Principles and Patterns for Computer Systems that are Simultaneously Secure and Usable*. Ph.D. Dissertation. MIT, Cambridge, MA. 56, 66

Simson L. Garfinkel, David Margrave, Jeffrey I. Schiller, Erik Nordlander, and Robert C. Miller. 2005. How to Make Secure Email Easier to Use. In *Proceedings of the SIGCHI Conference on Human Factors in Computing Systems (CHI '05)*. ACM, New York, NY, USA, 701–710. DOI: 10.1145/1054972.1055069. 52

Simson L. Garfinkel and Robert C. Miller. 2005. Johnny 2: a user test of key continuity management with S/MIME and Outlook Express. In *SOUPS '05: Proceedings of the 2005 symposium on Usable privacy and security*. ACM, New York, NY, USA, 13–24. DOI: 10.1145/1073001.1073003. 52, 61, 95

Shirley Gaw and Edward W. Felten. 2006. Password management strategies for online accounts. In *SOUPS '06: Proceedings of the second symposium on Usable privacy and security*. ACM, New York, NY, USA, 44–55. DOI: 10.1145/1143120.1143127. 2

Shirley Gaw, Edward W. Felten, and Patricia Fernandez-Kelly. 2006. Secrecy, Flagging, and Paranoia: Adoption Criteria in Encrypted Email. In *Proceedings of the SIGCHI Conference on Human Factors in Computing Systems (CHI '06)*. ACM, New York, NY, USA, 591–600. DOI: 10.1145/1124772.1124862. 54

Georgia Tech Graphic, Visualization, and Usability Center. 1998. GVU's 10th WWW User Survey. (1998). http://www.cc.gatech.edu/gvu/user_surveys/survey-1998-10/ 18

Jeremy Goecks and Elizabeth D. Mynatt. 2005. Social Approaches to End-User Privacy Management. In *Security and Usability*, Lorrie Cranor and Simson Garfinkel (Eds.). O'Reilly, Cambridge, MA. 98

Nathaniel Good, Rachna Dhamija, Jens Grossklags, David Thaw, Steven Aronowitz, Deirdre Mulligan, and Joseph Konstan. 2005. Stopping spyware at the gate: a user study of privacy, notice and spyware. In *SOUPS '05: Proceedings of the 2005 symposium on Usable privacy and security*. ACM, New York, NY, USA, 43–52. DOI: 10.1145/1073001.1073006. 71, 79

Nathaniel S. Good and Aaron Krekelberg. 2003. Usability and privacy: a study of Kazaa P2P file-sharing. In *Proceedings of the conference on Human factors in computing systems*. ACM Press, Ft. Lauderdale, Florida, 137–144. DOI: 10.1145/642611.642636. 19

Google. 2012. google-authenticator. (May 2012). https://code.google.com/p/google-authenticator/ 69

Jens Grossklags and Nathan Good. 2007. Empirical Studies on Software Notices to Inform Policy Makers and Usability Designers. In *Proceedings of the 11th International Conference on Financial Cryptography and 1st International Conference on Usable Security (FC'07/USEC'07)*. Springer-Verlag, Berlin, Heidelberg, 341–355. http://dl.acm.org/citation.cfm?id=1785594. 1785637 70

Peter Gutmann. 2004. Why isn't the Internet Secure Yet, Dammit. In *AusCERT Asia Pacific Information Technology Security Conference 2004; Computer Security: Are we there yet?* AusCERT, RACV Royal Pines Resort, Gold Coast, Australia. http://www.cs.auckland.ac.nz/~pgut001/pubs/dammit.pdf 61

Eben M. Haber and John Bailey. 2007. Design Guidelines for System Administration Tools Developed Through Ethnographic Field Studies. In *Proceedings of the 2007 Symposium on Computer Human Interaction for the Management of Information Technology (CHIMIT '07)*. ACM, New York, NY, USA. DOI: 10.1145/1234772.1234774. 85

Eben M. Haber and Eser Kandogan. 2007. Security Administrators: A Breed Apart. In *Proc. of Workshop on Usable IT Security Management*. Carnegie Mellon University, Pittsburgh, PA. http://cups.cs.cmu.edu/soups/2007/workshop/Security_Admins.pdf 85

J. Alex Halderman, Brent Waters, and Edward W. Felten. 2005. A Convenient Method for Securely Managing Passwords. In *Proceedings of the 14th International Conference on World Wide Web (WWW '05)*. ACM, New York, NY, USA, 471–479. DOI: 10.1145/1060745.1060815. 39

Kirstie Hawkey, David Botta, Rodrigo Werlinger, Kasia Muldner, Andre Gagne, and Konstantin Beznosov. 2008. Human, Organizational, and Technological Factors of IT Security. In *CHI '08 Extended Abstracts on Human Factors in Computing Systems (CHI EA '08)*. ACM, New York, NY, USA, 3639–3644. DOI: 10.1145/1358628.1358905. 85

Eiji Hayashi, Sauvik Das, Shahriyar Amini, Jason Hong, and Ian Oakley. 2013. CASA: Context-aware Scalable Authentication. In *Proceedings of the Ninth Symposium on Usable Privacy and Security (SOUPS '13)*. ACM, New York, NY, USA, Article 3, 10 pages. DOI: 10.1145/2501604.2501607. 81

R.V. Head. 2002. Getting Sabre off the ground. *Annals of the History of Computing, IEEE* 24, 4 (2002), 32–39. DOI: 10.1109/MAHC.2002.1114868. 25

Rosa R. Heckle, Andrew S. Patrick, and Ant Ozok. 2007. Perception and acceptance of fingerprint biometric technology. In *SOUPS '07: Proceedings of the 3rd symposium on Usable privacy and security*. ACM, New York, NY, USA, 153–154. DOI: 10.1145/1280680.1280704. 45

Cormac Herley. 2009. So Long, and No Thanks for the Externalities: The Rational Rejection of Security Advice by Users. In *Proceedings of the 2009 Workshop on New Security Paradigms Workshop (NSPW '09)*. ACM, New York, NY, USA, 133–144. DOI: 10.1145/1719030.1719050. 93

Cormac Herley and Dinei Florêncio. 2008. A profitless endeavor: phishing as tragedy of the commons. In *Proceedings of the 2008 workshop on New security paradigms (NSPW '08)*. ACM, Lake Tahoe, California, 59–70. DOI: 10.1145/1595676.1595686. 57

Cormac Herley and Paul van Oorschot. 2012. A Research Agenda Acknowledging the Persistence of Passwords. *IEEE Security and Privacy* 10, 1 (Jan. 2012), 28–36. http://dl.acm.org/citation.cfm?id=2360743.2360824 37

Amir Herzberg and Ahmad Jbara. 2008. Security and Identification Indicators for Browsers Against Spoofing and Phishing Attacks. *ACM Trans. Internet Technol.* 8, 4, Article 16 (Oct. 2008), 36 pages. DOI: 10.1145/1391949.1391950. 58

José María Gómez Hidalgo and Gonzalo Alvarez. 2011. CAPTCHAs: An Artificial Intelligence Application to Web Security. In *Advances in Computers*, Vol. 83. Elsevier, 109–181. 11, 49

Justin T. Ho, David Dearman, and Khai N. Truong. 2010. Improving users' security choices on home wireless networks. In *SOUPS '10: Proceedings of the Sixth Symposium on Usable Privacy and Security*. ACM, New York, NY, USA, 1–12. DOI: 10.1145/1837110.1837126. 2, 107

Mark Hochhauser. 2001. Lost in the Fine Print: Readability of Financial Privacy Notices. (1 July 2001). https://www.privacyrights.org/ar/GLB-Reading.htm 70

Harry Hochheiser. 2002. The Platform for Privacy Preference As a Social Protocol: An Examination Within the U.S. Policy Context. *ACM Trans. Internet Technol.* 2, 4 (Nov. 2002), 276–306. DOI: 10.1145/604596.604598. 18

Lance J. Hoffman. 1969. Computers and Privacy: A Survey. *ACM Comput. Surv.* 1, 2 (June 1969), 85–103. DOI: 10.1145/356546.356548. 25

P. Hoffman. 2002. SMTP Service Extension for Secure SMTP over Transport Layer Security. RFC 3207 (Proposed Standard). (Feb. 2002). http://www.ietf.org/rfc/rfc3207.txt 53

Jason Hong. 2012. The State of Phishing Attacks. *Commun. ACM* 55, 1 (Jan. 2012), 74–81. DOI: 10.1145/2063176.2063197. 57

Jeffrey Hunker. 2008. A Privacy Expectations and Security Assurance Offer System. In *Proceedings of the 2007 Workshop on New Security Paradigms (NSPW '07)*. ACM, New York, NY, USA, 15–22. DOI: 10.1145/1600176.1600179. 71

Giovanni Iachello and Jason Hong. 2007. End-User Privacy in Human–Computer Interaction. *Foundations and Trends in Human-Computer Interaction* 1, 1 (2007), 1–137. http://ww.sbejournal.com/media/Journal-Article-PDFs/1100000004.pdf 10

Giovanni Iachello, Ian E. Smith, Sunny Consolvo, Gregory D. Abowd, Jeff Hughes, James Howard, Fred Potter, James Scott, Timothy Sohn, Jeffrey Hightower, and Anthony LaMarca. 2005. Control, Deception, and Communication: Evaluating the Deployment of a Location-Enhanced Messaging Service.. In *Ubicomp* (2005-09-06) *(Lecture Notes in Computer Science)*, Michael Beigl, Stephen S. Intille, Jun Rekimoto, and Hideyuki Tokuda (Eds.), Vol. 3660. Springer, 213–231. http://dblp.uni-trier.de/db/conf/huc/ubicomp2005.html 78

Iulia Ion, Marc Langheinrich, Ponnurangam Kumaraguru, and Srdjan Čapkun. 2010. Influence of user perception, security needs, and social factors on device pairing method choices. In *SOUPS '10: Proceedings of the Sixth Symposium on Usable Privacy and Security*. ACM, New York, NY, USA, 1–13. DOI: 10.1145/1837110.1837118. 69

Iulia Ion, Niharika Sachdeva, Ponnurangam Kumaraguru, and Srdjan Čapkun. 2011. Home is safer than the cloud!: privacy concerns for consumer cloud storage. In *SOUPS '11: Proceedings of the Seventh Symposium on Usable Privacy and Security*. ACM, New York, NY, USA, 1–20. DOI: 10.1145/2078827.2078845. 66

ISO/IEC 1998. ISO/IEC 2382-8: Information technology—Vocabulary— Part 8:Security. (1998). 9

ISO/IEC 2012. ISO/IEC 27000: Information technology—Security techniques—Informaiton security management systems—Overview and vocabulary. (2012). 8

Pooya Jaferian, David Botta, Kirstie Hawkey, and Konstantin Beznosov. 2009. A Case Study of Enterprise Identity Management System Adoption in an Insurance Organization. In *Proceedings of the Symposium on Computer Human Interaction for the Management of Information Technology (CHiMiT '09)*. ACM, New York, NY, USA, Article 7, 10 pages. DOI: 10.1145/1641587.1641594. 85

Pooya Jaferian, David Botta, Fahimeh Raja, Kirstie Hawkey, and Konstantin Beznosov. 2008. Guidelines for Designing IT Security Management Tools. In *Proceedings of the 2Nd ACM Symposium on Computer Human Interaction for Management of Information Technology (CHiMiT '08)*. ACM, New York, NY, USA, Article 7, 10 pages. DOI: 10.1145/1477973.1477983. 85

Pooya Jaferian, Kirstie Hawkey, Andreas Sotirakopoulos, Maria Velez-Rojas, and Konstantin Beznosov. 2011. Heuristics for evaluating IT security management tools. In *SOUPS '11: Proceedings of the Seventh Symposium on Usable Privacy and Security*. ACM, New York, NY, USA, 1–20. DOI: 10.1145/2078827.2078837. 6

Tom N. Jagatic, Nathaniel A. Johnson, Markus Jakobsson, and Filippo Menczer. 2007. Social phishing. *Commun. ACM* 50, 10 (Oct. 2007), 94–100. DOI: 10.1145/1290958.1290968. 64, 100

A.K. Jain, A. Ross, and S. Pankanti. 2006. Biometrics: a tool for information security. *Information Forensics and Security, IEEE Transactions on* 1, 2 (June 2006), 125–143. DOI: 10.1109/TIFS.2006.873653. 44

Markus Jakobsson and Steven Myers. 2006. *Phishing and Countermeasures: Understanding the Increasing Problem of Electronic Identity Theft*. Wiley-Interscience, Hoboken, NJ. 736 pages. 2, 57

Markus Jakobsson and Jacob Ratkiewicz. 2006. Designing Ethical Phishing Experiments: A Study of (ROT13) rOnl Query Features. In *Proceedings of the 15th International Conference on World Wide Web (WWW '06)*. ACM, New York, NY, USA, 513–522. DOI: 10.1145/1135777.1135853. rOnl is the ROT13 transformation of eBay. 57

Carlos Jensen and Colin Potts. 2004. Privacy Policies As Decision-making Tools: An Evaluation of Online Privacy Notices. In *Proceedings of the SIGCHI Conference on Human Factors in Computing Systems (CHI '04)*. ACM, New York, NY, USA, 471–478. DOI: 10.1145/985692.985752. 70, 71

Carlos Jensen, Colin Potts, and Christian Jensen. 2005. Privacy practices of Internet users: Self-reports versus observed behavior. *International Journal of Human-Computer Studies* 63, 1–2 (2005), 203 – 227. DOI: 10.1016/j.ijhcs.2005.04.019. {HCI} research in privacy and security. 71

Ian Jermyn, Alain Mayer, Fabian Monrose, Michael K. Reiter, and Aviel D. Rubin. 1999. The Design and Analysis of Graphical Passwords. In *8th USENIX Security Symposium*. Usenix, Washington, DC. http://citeseer.ist.psu.edu/jermyn99design.html 16, 17, 40, 81, 99

Maritza Johnson, Serge Egelman, and Steven M. Bellovin. 2012. Facebook and privacy: it's complicated. In *SOUPS '12: Proceedings of the Eighth Symposium on Usable Privacy and Security*. ACM, New York, NY, USA, 1–15. DOI: 10.1145/2335356.2335369. 82, 83

Maritza Johnson, John Karat, Clare-Marie Karat, and Keith Grueneberg. 2010. Optimizing a policy authoring framework for security and privacy policies. In *SOUPS '10: Proceedings of the Sixth Symposium on Usable Privacy and Security*. ACM, New York, NY, USA, 1–9. DOI: 10.1145/1837110.1837121. 77

Maritza L. Johnson, Steven M. Bellovin, Robert W. Reeder, and Stuart E. Schechter. 2009. Laissez-faire File Sharing: Access Control Designed for Individuals at the Endpoints. In *Proceedings of the 2009 Workshop on New Security Paradigms Workshop (NSPW '09)*. ACM, New York, NY, USA, 1–10. DOI: 10.1145/1719030.1719032. 76

Simon Jones and Eamonn O'Neill. 2010. Feasibility of structural network clustering for group-based privacy control in social networks. In *SOUPS '10: Proceedings of the Sixth Symposium on Usable Privacy and Security*. ACM, New York, NY, USA, 1–13. DOI: 10.1145/1837110.1837122. 83

Jaeyeon Jung, Seungyeop Han, and David Wetherall. 2012. Short Paper: Enhancing Mobile Application Permissions with Runtime Feedback and Constraints. In *Proceedings of the Second ACM Workshop on Security and Privacy in Smartphones and Mobile Devices (SPSM '12)*. ACM, New York, NY, USA, 45–50. DOI: 10.1145/2381934.2381944. 80

Mike Just. 2005. Designing Authentication Systems with Challenge Questions. In *Security and Usability*, Lorrie Cranor and Simson Garfinkel (Eds.). O'Reilly, Cambridge, MA. 50

Mike Just and David Aspinall. 2009. Personal choice and challenge questions: a security and usability assessment. In *SOUPS '09: Proceedings of the 5th Symposium on Usable Privacy and Security*. ACM, New York, NY, USA, 1–11. DOI: 10.1145/1572532.1572543. 50

Sanjay Kairam, Mike Brzozowski, David Huffaker, and Ed Chi. 2012. Talking in Circles: Selective Sharing in Google+. In *Proceedings of the SIGCHI Conference on Human Factors in Computing Systems (CHI '12)*. ACM, New York, NY, USA, 1065–1074. DOI: 10.1145/2207676.2208552. 83

Eser Kandogan and Eben M. Haber. 2005. Security Administration Tools and Practices. In *Security and Usability*, Lorrie Cranor and Simson Garfinkel (Eds.). O'Reilly, Cambridge, MA. 85

Clare-Marie Karat. 1989. Iterative Usability Testing of a Security Application. In *Proceedings of the Human Factors Society 33rd Annual Meeting*. Human Factors & Ergonomics Society, Denver, CO, 273–277. 1, 14

Matthew Kay and Michael Terry. 2010. Textured agreements: re-envisioning electronic consent. In *SOUPS '10: Proceedings of the Sixth Symposium on Usable Privacy and Security*. ACM, New York, NY, USA, 1–13. DOI: 10.1145/1837110.1837127. 71

Patrick Gage Kelley. 2009. Designing a Privacy Label: Assisting Consumer Understanding of Online Privacy Practices. In *CHI EA '09: CHI '09 Extended Abstracts on Human Factors in Computing Systems*. ACM, New York, NY, USA. 608095. 71

Patrick Gage Kelley, Michael Benisch, Lorrie Faith Cranor, and Norman Sadeh. 2011. When Are Users Comfortable Sharing Locations with Advertisers?. In *Proceedings of the SIGCHI Conference on Human Factors in Computing Systems (CHI '11)*. ACM, New York, NY, USA, 2449–2452. DOI: 10.1145/1978942.1979299. 79

Patrick Gage Kelley, Joanna Bresee, Lorrie Faith Cranor, and Robert W. Reeder. 2009. A "nutrition label" for privacy. In *SOUPS '09: Proceedings of the 5th Symposium on Usable Privacy and Security*. ACM, New York, NY, USA, 1–12. DOI: 10.1145/1572532.1572538. 71, 78

Patrick Gage Kelley, Robin Brewer, Yael Mayer, Lorrie Faith Cranor, and Norman M. Sadeh. 2011. An Investigation into Facebook Friend Grouping.. In *INTERACT (3) (Lecture Notes in Computer Science)*, Pedro Campos, T. C. Nicholas Graham, Joaquim A. Jorge, Nuno Jardim Nunes, Philippe A. Palanque, and Marco Winckler (Eds.), Vol. 6948. Springer, 216–233. http://dblp.uni-trier.de/db/conf/interact/interact2011-3.html 83

Patrick Gage Kelley, Lucian Cesca, Joanna Bresee, and Lorrie Faith Cranor. 2010. Standardiz-
ing Privacy Notices: An Online Study of the Nutrition Label Approach. In *Proceedings of the
SIGCHI Conference on Human Factors in Computing Systems (CHI '10)*. ACM, New York, NY,
USA, 1573–1582. DOI: 10.1145/1753326.1753561. 71, 72

Patrick Gage Kelley, Sunny Consolvo, Lorrie Faith Cranor, Jaeyeon Jung, Norman Sadeh, and
David Wetherall. 2012. A Conundrum of Permissions: Installing Applications on an Android
Smartphone. In *Proceedings of the 16th International Conference on Financial Cryptography and
Data Security (FC'12)*. Springer-Verlag, Berlin, Heidelberg, 68–79. DOI: 10.1007/978-3-
642-34638-5_6. 80

Patrick Gage Kelley, Lorrie Faith Cranor, and Norman Sadeh. 2013a. Privacy As Part of
the App Decision-making Process. In *Proceedings of the SIGCHI Conference on Human Factors in Computing Systems (CHI '13)*. ACM, New York, NY, USA, 3393–3402. DOI:
10.1145/2470654.2466466. 80

Patrick Gage Kelley, Saranga Komanduri, MichelleL. Mazurek, Richard Shay, Timothy Vidas, Lujo Bauer, Nicolas Christin, and Lorrie Faith Cranor. 2013b. The Impact of Length
and Mathematical Operators on the Usability and Security of System-Assigned One-Time
PINs. In *Financial Cryptography and Data Security*, AndrewA. Adams, Michael Brenner, and
Matthew Smith (Eds.). Lecture Notes in Computer Science, Vol. 7862. Springer Berlin Heidelberg, Okinawa, Japan, 34–51. DOI: 10.1007/978-3-642-41320-9_3. 47, 48

Patrick Gage Kelley, Saranga Komanduri, Michelle L. Mazurek, Richard Shay, Timothy Vidas, Lujo Bauer, Nicolas Christin, Lorrie Faith Cranor, and Julio Lopez. 2012. Guess Again
(and Again and Again): Measuring Password Strength by Simulating Password-Cracking Algorithms. In *Proceedings of the 2012 IEEE Symposium on Security and Privacy (SP '12)*. IEEE
Computer Society, Washington, DC, USA, 523–537. DOI: 10.1109/SP.2012.38. 19, 29, 32,
33

Jonathan Kent. 2005. Malaysia car thieves steal finger. (31 March 2005). `http://news.bbc.c`
`o.uk/2/hi/asia-pacific/4396831.stm` 44

Jennifer King, Airi Lampinen, and Alex Smolen. 2011. Privacy: is there an app for that?. In
SOUPS '11: Proceedings of the Seventh Symposium on Usable Privacy and Security. ACM, New
York, NY, USA, 1–20. DOI: 10.1145/2078827.2078843. 84

Richard Kissel, Matthew Scholl, Steven Skolochenko, and Xing Li. 2006. *Guidelines for Media Sanitization*. Technical Report SP800-88. National Institute of Standards and Technology. `http://csrc.nist.gov/publications/nistpubs/800-88/NISTSP800-88_with-`
`errata.pdf` 65

Aniket Kittur, Ed H. Chi, and Bongwon Suh. 2008. Crowdsourcing User Studies with Mechanical Turk. In *Proceedings of the SIGCHI Conference on Human Factors in Computing Systems (CHI '08)*. ACM, New York, NY, USA, 453–456. DOI: 10.1145/1357054.1357127. 19

Kurt Alfred Kluever and Richard Zanibbi. 2009. Balancing usability and security in a video CAPTCHA. In *SOUPS '09: Proceedings of the 5th Symposium on Usable Privacy and Security*. ACM, New York, NY, USA, 1–11. DOI: 10.1145/1572532.1572551. 49

Alfred Kobsa, Rahim Sonawalla, Gene Tsudik, Ersin Uzun, and Yang Wang. 2009. Serial hookups: a comparative usability study of secure device pairing methods. In *SOUPS '09: Proceedings of the 5th Symposium on Usable Privacy and Security*. ACM, New York, NY, USA, 1–12. DOI: 10.1145/1572532.1572546. 69

Loren M. Kohnfelder. 1978. Towards a practical public-key cryptosystem. (May 1978). Undergraduate thesis supervised by L. Adleman. 51

Saranga Komanduri, Richard Shay, Patrick Gage Kelley, Michelle L. Mazurek, Lujo Bauer, Nicolas Christin, Lorrie Faith Cranor, and Serge Egelman. 2011. Of passwords and people: measuring the effect of password-composition policies. In *Proceedings of the SIGCHI Conference on Human Factors in Computing Systems (CHI '11)*. ACM, New York, NY, USA, 2595–2604. DOI: 10.1145/1978942.1979321. 30

Hanna Krasnova, Elena Kolesnikova, and Oliver Guenther. 20009. "It Won't Happen to Me!" Self-Disclosure in Online Social Networks. In *Proceedings of the Americas Conference on Information Systems (AMCIS 2009)*. Associate for Information Systems, San Francisco, CA. http://www.icsi.berkeley.edu/pubs/other/itwont09.pdf 81

A. Kumar, N. Saxena, G. Tsudik, and E. Uzun. 2009. Caveat eptor: A comparative study of secure device pairing methods. In *Pervasive Computing and Communications, 2009. PerCom 2009. IEEE International Conference on*. IEEE, Galveston, TX, 1–10. DOI: 10.1109/PERCOM.2009.4912753. 69

Ponnurangam Kumaraguru, Justin Cranshaw, Alessandro Acquisti, Lorrie Cranor, Jason Hong, Mary Ann Blair, and Theodore Pham. 2009. School of phish: a real-world evaluation of anti-phishing training. In *SOUPS '09: Proceedings of the 5th Symposium on Usable Privacy and Security*. ACM, New York, NY, USA, 1–12. DOI: 10.1145/1572532.1572536. 64

Ponnurangam Kumaraguru, Yong Rhee, Alessandro Acquisti, Lorrie Faith Cranor, Jason Hong, and Elizabeth Nunge. 2007. Protecting People from Phishing: The Design and Evaluation of an Embedded Training Email System. In *Proceedings of the SIGCHI Conference on Human Factors in Computing Systems (CHI '07)*. ACM, New York, NY, USA, 905–914. DOI: 10.1145/1240624.1240760. 33

Ponnurangam Kumaraguru, Steve Sheng, Alessandro Acquisti, Lorrie Faith Cranor, and Jason Hong. 2010. Teaching Johnny Not to Fall for Phish. *ACM Trans. Internet Technol.* 10, 2, Article 7 (June 2010), 31 pages. DOI: 10.1145/1754393.1754396. 64

Cynthia Kuo, Sasha Romanosky, and Lorrie Faith Cranor. 2006. Human selection of mnemonic phrase-based passwords. In *SOUPS '06: Proceedings of the second symposium on Usable privacy and security.* ACM, New York, NY, USA, 67–78. DOI: 10.1145/1143120.1143129. 32

Stan Kurkovsky and Ewa Syta. 2010. Digital natives and mobile phones: A survey of practices and attitudes about privacy and security. In *Proceedings of the 2010 IEEE International Symposium on Technology and Society (ISTAS).* IEEE, Wollongong, Australia, 441–449. DOI: 10.1109/istas.2010.5514610. 2, 81

Kiran Lakkaraju, William Yurcik, and Adam J. Lee. 2004. NVisionIP: Netflow Visualizations of System State for Security Situational Awareness. In *Proceedings of the 2004 ACM Workshop on Visualization and Data Mining for Computer Security (VizSEC/DMSEC '04).* ACM, New York, NY, USA, 65–72. DOI: 10.1145/1029208.1029219. 86

Airi Lampinen, Vilma Lehtinen, Asko Lehmuskallio, and Sakari Tamminen. 2011. We're in It Together: Interpersonal Management of Disclosure in Social Network Services. In *Proceedings of the SIGCHI Conference on Human Factors in Computing Systems (CHI '11).* ACM, New York, NY, USA, 3217–3226. DOI: 10.1145/1978942.1979420. 82, 83

Phil Lapsey. 2013. *Exploding the Phone.* Grove Press. 56

Scott Lederer, Jennifer Mankoff, and Anind K. Dey. 2003. Who Wants to Know What when? Privacy Preference Determinants in Ubiquitous Computing. In *CHI '03 Extended Abstracts on Human Factors in Computing Systems (CHI EA '03).* ACM, New York, NY, USA, 724–725. DOI: 10.1145/765891.765952. 78

Pedro Leon, Blase Ur, Richard Shay, Yang Wang, Rebecca Balebako, and Lorrie Cranor. 2012. Why Johnny Can't Opt out: A Usability Evaluation of Tools to Limit Online Behavioral Advertising. In *Proceedings of the SIGCHI Conference on Human Factors in Computing Systems (CHI '12).* ACM, New York, NY, USA, 589–598. DOI: 10.1145/2207676.2207759. 74

Pedro Giovanni Leon, Blase Ur, Yang Wang, Manya Sleeper, Rebecca Balebako, Richard Shay, Lujo Bauer, Mihai Christodorescu, and Lorrie Faith Cranor. 2013. What Matters to Users?: Factors That Affect Users' Willingness to Share Information with Online Advertisers. In *Proceedings of the Ninth Symposium on Usable Privacy and Security (SOUPS '13).* ACM, New York, NY, USA, Article 7, 12 pages. DOI: 10.1145/2501604.2501611. 74

Shujun Li, S. Amier Haider Shah, M. Asad Usman Khan, Syed Ali Khayam, Ahmad-Reza Sadeghi, and Roland Schmitz. 2010. Breaking e-Banking CAPTCHAs. In *Proceedings of the*

26th Annual Computer Security Applications Conference (ACSAC '10). ACM, New York, NY, USA, 171–180. DOI: 10.1145/1920261.1920288. 49

Zhou Li, Kehuan Zhang, Yinglian Xie, Fang Yu, and XiaoFeng Wang. 2012. Knowing your enemy: understanding and detecting malicious web advertising. In *Proceedings of the 2012 ACM conference on Computer and communications security (CCS '12)*. ACM, New York, NY, USA, 674–686. DOI: 10.1145/2382196.2382267. 2

Eric Lieberman and Robert C. Miller. 2007. Facemail: showing faces of recipients to prevent misdirected email. In *SOUPS '07: Proceedings of the 3rd symposium on Usable privacy and security*. ACM, New York, NY, USA, 122–131. DOI: 10.1145/1280680.1280696. 76, 89

Eric Lin, Saul Greenberg, Eileah Trotter, David Ma, and John Aycock. 2011b. Does Domain Highlighting Help People Identify Phishing Sites?. In *Proceedings of the SIGCHI Conference on Human Factors in Computing Systems (CHI '11)*. ACM, New York, NY, USA, 2075–2084. DOI: 10.1145/1978942.1979244. 61

Felix Xiaozhu Lin, Daniel Ashbrook, and Sean White. 2011a. RhythmLink: Securely Pairing I/O-constrained Devices by Tapping. In *Proceedings of the 24th Annual ACM Symposium on User Interface Software and Technology (UIST '11)*. ACM, New York, NY, USA, 263–272. DOI: 10.1145/2047196.2047231. 68

Jialiu Lin. 2013. *UNDERSTANDING AND CAPTURING PEOPLE'S MOBILE APP PRI-VACY PREFERENCES*. Technical Report CMU-CS-13-127. Carnegie Mellon University. 107

Jialiu Lin, Shahriyar Amini, Jason I. Hong, Norman Sadeh, Janne Lindqvist, and Joy Zhang. 2012. Expectation and Purpose: Understanding Users' Mental Models of Mobile App Privacy Through Crowdsourcing. In *Proceedings of the 2012 ACM Conference on Ubiquitous Computing (UbiComp '12)*. ACM, New York, NY, USA, 501–510. DOI: 10.1145/2370216.2370290. 80, 107

Janne Lindqvist, Justin Cranshaw, Jason Wiese, Jason Hong, and John Zimmerman. 2011. I'M the Mayor of My House: Examining Why People Use Foursquare - a Social-driven Location Sharing Application. In *Proceedings of the SIGCHI Conference on Human Factors in Computing Systems (CHI '11)*. ACM, New York, NY, USA, 2409–2418. DOI: 10.1145/1978942.1979295. 79

Heather Richter Lipford, Jason Watson, Michael Whitney, Katherine Froiland, and Robert W. Reeder. 2010. Visual vs. Compact: A Comparison of Privacy Policy Interfaces. In *Proceedings of the SIGCHI Conference on Human Factors in Computing Systems (CHI '10)*. ACM, New York, NY, USA, 1111–1114. DOI: 10.1145/1753326.1753492. 78, 82

Heather Richter Lipford and Mary Ellen Zurko. 2012. Someone to Watch over Me. In *Proceedings of the 2012 Workshop on New Security Paradigms (NSPW '12)*. ACM, New York, NY, USA, 67–76. DOI: 10.1145/2413296.2413303. 99

Eden Litt. 2012. Knock, Knock. Who's There? The Imagined Audience. *Journal of Broadcasting & Electronic Media* 56, 3 (2012), 330–345. DOI: 10.1080/08838151.2012.705195. 82

Linda Little, Elizabeth Sillence, and Pam Briggs. 2009. Ubiquitous systems and the family: thoughts about the networked home. In *SOUPS '09: Proceedings of the 5th Symposium on Usable Privacy and Security*. ACM, New York, NY, USA, 1–9. DOI: 10.1145/1572532.1572540. 106

Tao Lu and Jie Bao. 2012. A Systematic Approach to Context Aware Service Design. *Journal of Computers* 7, 1 (2012). http://ojs.academypublisher.com/index.php/jcp/article/view/jcp0701207217 85

Ronald J. Mann. 2003. Regulating Internet payment intermediaries. In *Proceedings of the 5th international conference on Electronic commerce (ICEC '03)*. ACM, New York, NY, USA, 376–386. DOI: 10.1145/948005.948053. 56

Winter Mason and Siddharth Suri. 2012. Conducting behavioral research on Amazon's Mechanical Turk. *Behavior Research Methods* 44, 1 (2012), 1–23. DOI: 10.3758/s13428-011-0124-6. 20

Max-Emanuel Maurer, Alexander De Luca, and Sylvia Kempe. 2011. Using data type based security alert dialogs to raise online security awareness. In *SOUPS '11: Proceedings of the Seventh Symposium on Usable Privacy and Security*. ACM, New York, NY, USA, 1–13. DOI: 10.1145/2078827.2078830. 89

R. Mayrhofer and H. Gellersen. 2009. Shake Well Before Use: Intuitive and Secure Pairing of Mobile Devices. *Mobile Computing, IEEE Transactions on* 8, 6 (June 2009), 792–806. DOI: 10.1109/TMC.2009.51. 68

Michelle L. Mazurek, J. P. Arsenault, Joanna Bresee, Nitin Gupta, Iulia Ion, Christina Johns, Daniel Lee, Yuan Liang, Jenny Olsen, Brandon Salmon, Richard Shay, Kami Vaniea, Lujo Bauer, Lorrie Faith Cranor, Gregory R. Ganger, and Michael K. Reiter. 2010. Access Control for Home Data Sharing: Attitudes, Needs and Practices. In *Proceedings of the SIGCHI Conference on Human Factors in Computing Systems (CHI '10)*. ACM, New York, NY, USA, 645–654. DOI: 10.1145/1753326.1753421. 75, 77

Michelle L. Mazurek, Peter F. Klemperer, Richard Shay, Hassan Takabi, Lujo Bauer, and Lorrie Faith Cranor. 2011. Exploring Reactive Access Control. In *Proceedings of the SIGCHI Conference on Human Factors in Computing Systems (CHI '11)*. ACM, New York, NY, USA, 2085–2094. DOI: 10.1145/1978942.1979245. 77

Michelle L. Mazurek, Saranga Komanduri, Timothy Vidas, Lujo Bauer, Nicolas Christin, Lorrie Faith Cranor, Patrick Gage Kelley, Richard Shay, and Blase Ur. 2013. Measuring Password Guessability for an Entire University. In *Proceedings of the 2013 ACM SIGSAC Conference on Computer and Communications Security (CCS '13)*. ACM, New York, NY, USA, 173–186. DOI: 10.1145/2508859.2516726. 20, 32, 36

Alessandra Mazzia, Kristen LeFevre, and Eytan Adar. 2012. The PViz comprehension tool for social network privacy settings. In *SOUPS '12: Proceedings of the Eighth Symposium on Usable Privacy and Security*. ACM, New York, NY, USA, 1–12. DOI: 10.1145/2335356.2335374. 82

Daniel McCarney, David Barrera, Jeremy Clark, Sonia Chiasson, and Paul C. van Oorschot. 2012. Tapas: design, implementation, and usability evaluation of a password manager. In *Proceedings of the 28th Annual Computer Security Applications Conference (ACSAC '12)*. ACM, New York, NY, USA, 89–98. DOI: 10.1145/2420950.2420964. 39, 41

Jonathan M. McCune, Adrian Perrig, and Michael K. Reiter. 2004. *Seeing-Is-Believing: Using Camera Phones for Human-Verifiable Authentication*. Technical Report CMU-CS-04-174. Carnegie Mellon University, Pittsburgh, PA. http://reports-archive.adm.cs.cmu.edu/anon/2004/CMU-CS-04-174.pdf 68

J. M. McCune, A. Perrig, and M. K. Reiter. 2005. Seeing-is-believing: using camera phones for human-verifiable authentication. In *Security and Privacy, 2005 IEEE Symposium on*. IEEE, Oakland, CA, 110–124. DOI: 10.1109/SP.2005.19. 68

Jonathan M. McCune, Adrian Perrig, and Michael K. Reiter. 2009. Seeing-Is-Believing: using camera phones for human-verifiable authentication. *Int. J. Secur. Netw.* 4, 1/2 (Feb. 2009), 43–56. DOI: 10.1504/IJSN.2009.023425. 68

Aleecia M. McDonald and Lorrie F. Cranor. 2008. The Cost of Reading Privacy Policies. *I/S: A Journal of Law and Policy for the Information Society* 4, 3 (2008), 540–565. http://www.is-journal.org/files/2012/02/Cranor_Formatted_Final.pdf 71

Aleecia M. McDonald and Lorrie Faith Cranor. 2010. Americans' Attitudes About Internet Behavioral Advertising Practices. In *Proceedings of the 9th Annual ACM Workshop on Privacy in the Electronic Society (WPES '10)*. ACM, New York, NY, USA, 63–72. DOI: 10.1145/1866919.1866929. 74

L. McLaughlin. 2003. Online fraud gets sophisticated. *Internet Computing, IEEE* 7, 5 (2003), 6–8. DOI: 10.1109/MIC.2003.1232512. 56

Robert McMillan. 2012. The World's First Computer Password? It Was Useless Too. *Wired* (Jan. 27 2012). http://www.wired.com/wiredenterprise/2012/01/computer-password/ 25

R.M. Metcalfe. 1973. "The stockings were hung by the chimney with care". RFC 602. (Dec. 1973). http://www.ietf.org/rfc/rfc602.txt 25

Microsoft 2012. NEAT. (Oct. 2012). 101, 102

Fabian Monrose and Michael K. Reiter. 2005. Graphical Passwords. In *Security and Usability*, Lorrie Cranor and Simson L. Garfinkel (Eds.). O'Reilly, Cambridge, MA. 40

J. Moody. 2004. Public perceptions of biometric devices: The effect of misinformation on acceptance and use. *Journal of Issues in Informing Science and Information Technology* 1 (2004), 753–761. 45

Robert Morris and Ken Thompson. 1979. Password security: a case history. *Commun. ACM* 22, 11 (1979), 594–597. DOI: 10.1145/359168.359172. 1, 13, 25, 26

Marti Motoyama, Damon McCoy, Kirill Levchenko, Stefan Savage, and Geoffrey M. Voelker. 2011. Dirty Jobs: The Role of Freelance Labor in Web Service Abuse. In *Proceedings of the 20th USENIX Conference on Security (SEC'11)*. USENIX Association, Berkeley, CA, USA, 14–14. http://dl.acm.org/citation.cfm?id=2028067.2028081 49

2008. *Grand Challenges for Engineering*. National Academy of Engineering, Washington, DC. http://www.engineeringchallenges.org/cms/8996/9221.aspx 1

National Security Agency. 2012. Academic Requirements for Designation as a Center of Academic Excellence in Cyber Operations. (Sept. 2012). http://www.nsa.gov/academia/nat _cae_cyber_ops/nat_cae_co_requirements.shtml 103

C. Newman. 1999. Using TLS with IMAP, POP3 and ACAP. RFC 2595 (Proposed Standard). (June 1999). http://www.ietf.org/rfc/rfc2595.txt Updated by RFC 4616. 53

Jakob Nielsen. 1993. *Usability Engineering*. Academic Press, Waltham, MA. 13

Helen Nissenbaum. 2004. Privacy as contextual integrity. *Wash. L. Rev.* 79 (2004), 119. 10

Greg Norcie, Kelly Caine, and L. Jean Camp. 2012. Eliminating Stop-Points in the Installation and Use of Anonymity Systems: a Usability Evaluation of the Tor Browser Bundle. In *5th Workshop on Hot Topics in Privacy Enhancing Technologies (HotPETs 2012)*. Springer, Vigo, Spain. http://petsymposium.org/2012/papers/hotpets12-1-usability.pdf 88

Donald A. Norman. 1983. Design Rules Based on Analyses of Human Error. *Commun. ACM* 26, 4 (April 1983), 254–258. 13

W3C Working Group Note. 2006. *The platform for privacy preferences 1.1 (P3P1.1) specification*. Technical Report P3P11. World Wide Web Consortium. http://www.w3.org/TR/P3P11/ 71

Jon Oberheide and Farnam Jahanian. 2010. When mobile is harder than fixed (and vice versa): demystifying security challenges in mobile environments. In *Proceedings of the Eleventh Workshop on Mobile Computing Systems & Applications (HotMobile '10)*. ACM, New York, NY, USA, 43–48. DOI: 10.1145/1734583.1734595. 2

P. C. van Oorschot and Julie Thorpe. 2008. On Predictive Models and User-drawn Graphical Passwords. *ACM Trans. Inf. Syst. Secur.* 10, 4, Article 5 (Jan. 2008), 33 pages. DOI: 10.1145/1284680.1284685. 16, 42

Leysia Palen and Paul Dourish. 2003. Unpacking "Privacy" for a Networked World. In *Proceedings of the SIGCHI Conference on Human Factors in Computing Systems (CHI '03)*. ACM, New York, NY, USA, 129–136. DOI: 10.1145/642611.642635. 96

Sameer Patil, Greg Norcie, Apu Kapadia, and Adam J. Lee. 2012. Reasons, rewards, regrets: privacy considerations in location sharing as an interactive practice. In *SOUPS '12: Proceedings of the Eighth Symposium on Usable Privacy and Security*. ACM, New York, NY, USA, 1–15. DOI: 10.1145/2335356.2335363. 78, 79

Andrew Patrick. 2008. Fingerprint Concerns: Performance, Usability, and Acceptance of Fingerprint Biometric Systems. (2 July 2008). http://www.andrewpatrick.ca/essays/fi ngerprint-concerns-performance-usability-and-acceptance-of-fingerprint- biometric-systems 44

Andrew Patrick, A. Chris Long, and Scott Flinn (Eds.). 2003. *Workshop on Human-Computer Interaction and Security Systems, part of CHI2003*. ACM Press, Fort Lauderdale, Florida. http: //www.andrewpatrick.ca/CHI2003/HCISEC/ 2, 19

A. Peacock, Xian Ke, and M. Wilkerson. 2004. Typing patterns: a key to user identification. *Security Privacy, IEEE* 2, 5 (Sept 2004), 40–47. DOI: 10.1109/MSP.2004.89. 45

Trevor Pering, Murali Sundar, John Light, and Roy Want. 2003. Photographic Authentication through Untrusted Terminals. *IEEE Pervasive Computing* 2, 1 (Jan. 2003), 30–36. DOI: 10.1109/MPRV.2003.1186723. 40

Adrian Perrig and Dawn Song. 1999. Hash Visualization: a New Technique to improve Real-World Security. In *Cryptographic Techniques and E-COmmerce: Proceedings of the 1999 International Workshop on Cryptographic Techniques and E-Commerce (CryTEC '99)*, Manuel Blum and C. H. Lee (Eds.). City University of Hong Kong Press, 131–138. citeseer.ist.psu.e du/perrig99hash.html 68

Ugo Piazzalunga, Paolo Salvaneschi, and Paolo Coffetti. 2005. The Usability of Security Devices. In *Security and Usability*, Lorrie Cranor and Simson L. Garfinkel (Eds.). O'Reilly, Cambridge, MA. 46

Alexander P. Pons and Peter Polak. 2008. Understanding User Perspectives on Biometric Technology. *Commun. ACM* 51, 9 (Sept. 2008), 115–118. DOI: 10.1145/1378727.1389971. 45

Marc Prensky. 2001. Digital Natives, Digital Immigrants. *On the Horizon* 9, 5 (Oct. 2001). `http://www.albertomattiacci.it/docs/did/Digital_Natives_Digital_Imm igrants.pdf` 2

Ariel Rabkin. 2008. Personal knowledge questions for fallback authentication: security questions in the era of Facebook. In *SOUPS '08: Proceedings of the 4th symposium on Usable privacy and security*. ACM, New York, NY, USA, 13–23. DOI: 10.1145/1408664.1408667. 84

Emilee Rader, Rick Wash, and Brandon Brooks. 2012. Stories as informal lessons about security. In *SOUPS '12: Proceedings of the Eighth Symposium on Usable Privacy and Security*. ACM, New York, NY, USA, 1–17. DOI: 10.1145/2335356.2335364. 5, 98

Fahimeh Raja, Kirstie Hawkey, Steven Hsu, Kai-Le Clement Wang, and Konstantin Beznosov. 2011. A brick wall, a locked door, and a bandit: a physical security metaphor for firewall warnings. In *SOUPS '11: Proceedings of the Seventh Symposium on Usable Privacy and Security*. ACM, New York, NY, USA, 1–20. DOI: 10.1145/2078827.2078829. 90

B. Ramsdell and S. Turner. 2010. Secure/Multipurpose Internet Mail Extensions (S/MIME) Version 3.2 Message Specification. RFC 5751 (Proposed Standard). (Jan. 2010). `http://ww w.ietf.org/rfc/rfc5751.txt` 51

Ramprasad Ravichandran, Michael Benisch, Patrick Gage Kelley, and Norman M. Sadeh. 2009. Capturing Social Networking Privacy Preferences. In *Proceedings of the 9th International Symposium on Privacy Enhancing Technologies (PETS '09)*. Springer-Verlag, Berlin, Heidelberg, 1–18. DOI: 10.1007/978-3-642-03168-7_1. 79

Patricia Reaney. 2012. Most of world interconnected through email and social media. (March 27 2012). `http://www.reuters.com/article/2012/03/27/uk-socialmedia-online- poll-idUSLNE82Q02120120327` 2

Ian Reay, Scott Dick, and James Miller. 2009. A Large-scale Empirical Study of P3P Privacy Policies: Stated Actions vs. Legal Obligations. *ACM Trans. Web* 3, 2, Article 6 (April 2009), 34 pages. DOI: 10.1145/1513876.1513878. 73

David Recordon and Drummond Reed. 2006. OpenID 2.0: A Platform for User-centric Identity Management. In *Proceedings of the Second ACM Workshop on Digital Identity Management (DIM '06)*. ACM, New York, NY, USA, 11–16. DOI: 10.1145/1179529.1179532. 37

R.W. Reeder and S. Schechter. 2011. When the Password Doesn't Work: Secondary Authentication for Websites. *Security Privacy, IEEE* 9, 2 (March 2011), 43–49. DOI: 10.1109/MSP.2011.1. 50

Robert W. Reeder. 2008. *Expandable Grids: A user interface visualization technique and a policy semantics to support fast, accurate security and privacy policy authoring.* Ph.D. Dissertation. Pittsburgh, PA. 78

Robert W. Reeder, Lujo Bauer, Lorrie Faith Cranor, Michael K. Reiter, Kelli Bacon, Keisha How, and Heather Strong. 2008a. Expandable Grids for Visualizing and Authoring Computer Security Policies. In *Proceedings of the SIGCHI Conference on Human Factors in Computing Systems (CHI '08)*. ACM, New York, NY, USA, 1473–1482. DOI: 10.1145/1357054.1357285. 77

Robert W. Reeder, Patrick Gage Kelley, Aleecia M. McDonald, and Lorrie Faith Cranor. 2008b. A User Study of the Expandable Grid Applied to P3P Privacy Policy Visualization. In *Proceedings of the 7th ACM Workshop on Privacy in the Electronic Society (WPES '08)*. ACM, New York, NY, USA, 45–54. DOI: 10.1145/1456403.1456413. 78

Paul Resnick and James Miller. 1996. PICS: Internet Access Controls Without Censorship. *Commun. ACM* 39, 10 (Oct. 1996), 87–93. DOI: 10.1145/236156.236175. 70

Jens Riegelsberger, M. Angela Sasse, and John D. McCarthy. 2003. The researcher's dilemma: evaluating trust in computer-mediated communication. *Int. J. Hum.-Comput. Stud.* 58, 6 (June 2003), 759–781. DOI: 10.1016/S1071-5819(03)00042-9. 19

R. L. Rivest, A. Shamir, and L. M. Adelman. 1977. *A Method For Obtaining Digital Signatures And Public-Key Cryptosystems.* Technical Report MIT/LCS/TM-82. Massachusetts Institute of Technology. 15 pages. http://citeseer.ist.psu.edu/rivest78method.html 51

Blake Ross, Collin Jackson, Nick Miyake, Dan Boneh, and John C. Mitchell. 2005. Stronger Password Authentication Using Browser Extensions. In *Proceedings of the 14th Conference on USENIX Security Symposium - Volume 14 (SSYM'05)*. USENIX Association, Berkeley, CA, USA, 2–2. http://dl.acm.org/citation.cfm?id=1251398.1251400 39

Volker Roth, Wolfgang Polak, Eleanor Rieffel, and Thea Turner. 2008. Simple and Effective Defense Against Evil Twin Access Points. In *Proceedings of the First ACM Conference on Wireless Network Security (WiSec '08)*. ACM, New York, NY, USA, 220–235. DOI: 10.1145/1352533.1352569. 68

RSA Security. 2008. Annual RSA Wireless Security Survey: with Encrypted Wi-Fi Vulnerable, How Companies and Individuals Are Risking Their Assets and Reputations. (2008). http://www.emc.com/about/news/press/2008/20081027-03.htm 2

Scott Ruoti, Nathan Kim, Ben Burgon, Timothy van der Horst, and Kent Seamons. 2013. Confused Johnny: When Automatic Encryption Leads to Confusion and Mistakes. In *Proceedings of the Ninth Symposium on Usable Privacy and Security (SOUPS '13)*. ACM, New York, NY, USA, Article 5, 12 pages. DOI: 10.1145/2501604.2501609. 53, 54, 88

Norman Sadeh, Jason Hong, Lorrie Cranor, Ian Fette, Patrick Kelley, Madhu Prabaker, and Jinghai Rao. 2009. Understanding and Capturing People's Privacy Policies in a Mobile Social Networking Application. *Personal Ubiquitous Comput.* 13, 6 (Aug. 2009), 401–412. DOI: 10.1007/s00779-008-0214-3. 79

Napa Sae-Bae, Kowsar Ahmed, Katherine Isbister, and Nasir Memon. 2012. Biometric-rich Gestures: A Novel Approach to Authentication on Multi-touch Devices. In *Proceedings of the SIGCHI Conference on Human Factors in Computing Systems (CHI '12)*. ACM, New York, NY, USA, 977–986. DOI: 10.1145/2207676.2208543. 45, 81

Jerome H. Saltzer and M. Frans Kaashoek. 2009. *Principles of Computer System Design: An Introduction*. Morgan Kaufmann Publishers Inc., San Francisco, CA, USA. 13

Jerome H. Saltzer and Michael D. Schroeder. 1975. The Protection of Information in Computer Systems. *Proc. IEEE* 63 (Sept. 1975), 1278–1308. Issue 9. 1, 13, 88, 106

M. Angela Sasse, Clare-Marie Karat, and Roy Maxion. 2009. Designing and evaluating usable security and privacy technology. In *SOUPS '09: Proceedings of the 5th Symposium on Usable Privacy and Security*. ACM, New York, NY, USA, 1–1. DOI: 10.1145/1572532.1572554. 77

N. Saxena, J.-E. Ekberg, K. Kostiainen, and N. Asokan. 2011. Secure Device Pairing Based on a Visual Channel: Design and Usability Study. *Information Forensics and Security, IEEE Transactions on* 6, 1 (March 2011), 28–38. DOI: 10.1109/TIFS.2010.2096217. 67

Florian Schaub, Marcel Walch, Bastian Könings, and Michael Weber. 2013. Exploring the Design Space of Graphical Passwords on Smartphones. In *Proceedings of the Ninth Symposium on Usable Privacy and Security (SOUPS '13)*. ACM, New York, NY, USA, Article 11, 14 pages. DOI: 10.1145/2501604.2501615. 42, 43

Stuart Schechter, A. J. Bernheim Brush, and Serge Egelman. 2009. It's No Secret. Measuring the Security and Reliability of Authentication via "Secret” Questions. In *Proceedings of the 2009 30th IEEE Symposium on Security and Privacy (SP '09)*. IEEE Computer Society, Washington, DC, USA, 375–390. DOI: 10.1109/SP.2009.11. 50

Stuart Schechter, Serge Egelman, and Robert W. Reeder. 2009. It's Not What You Know, but Who You Know: A Social Approach to Last-resort Authentication. In *Proceedings of the SIGCHI Conference on Human Factors in Computing Systems (CHI '09)*. ACM, New York, NY, USA, 1983–1992. DOI: 10.1145/1518701.1519003. 99

Stuart Schechter, Cormac Herley, and Michael Mitzenmacher. 2010. Popularity is everything: a new approach to protecting passwords from statistical-guessing attacks. In *Proceedings of the 5th USENIX conference on Hot topics in security (HotSec'10)*. USENIX Association, Berkeley, CA, USA, 1–8. http://dl.acm.org/citation.cfm?id=1924931.1924935 28

Stuart Schechter and Robert W. Reeder. 2009.   1 + 1 = you: measuring the comprehensi-
bility of metaphors for configuring backup authentication. In *SOUPS '09: Proceedings of the
5th Symposium on Usable Privacy and Security*. ACM, New York, NY, USA, 1–31.   DOI:
10.1145/1572532.1572544. 50

Stuart E. Schechter, Rachna Dhamija, Andy Ozment, and Ian Fischer. 2007. The Emperor's New
Security Indicators. In *Proceedings of the 2007 IEEE Symposium on Security and Privacy (SP '07)*.
IEEE Computer Society, Washington, DC, USA, 51–65.   DOI: 10.1109/SP.2007.35. 35, 60,
95

Roman Schlegel, Apu Kapadia, and Adam J. Lee. 2011.   Eyeing your exposure: quantifying and
controlling information sharing for improved privacy. In *SOUPS '11: Proceedings of the Seventh Symposium on Usable Privacy and Security*. ACM, New York, NY, USA, 1–14.   DOI:
10.1145/2078827.2078846. 83

Neil Selwyn. 2009.   The digital native - myth and reality.   *Aslib Proceedings: new information
perspectives* 61, 4 (2009), 364–379.   DOI: 10.1108/00012530910973776. 2

Richard Shay, Patrick Gage Kelley, Saranga Komanduri, Michelle L. Mazurek, Blase Ur, Timothy Vidas, Lujo Bauer, Nicolas Christin, and Lorrie Faith Cranor. 2012.   Correct horse battery
staple: exploring the usability of system-assigned passphrases. In *SOUPS '12: Proceedings of the
Eighth Symposium on Usable Privacy and Security*. ACM, New York, NY, USA, 1–20.   DOI:
10.1145/2335356.2335366. 30, 31, 33

Richard Shay, Saranga Komanduri, Adam L. Durity, Phillip (Seyoung) Huh, Michelle L.
Mazurek, Sean M. Segreti, Blase Ur, Lujo Bauer, Nicolas Christin, and Lorrie Faith Cranor.
2014.   Can Long Passwords Be Secure and Usable?. In *Proceedings of the SIGCHI Conference
on Human Factors in Computing Systems (CHI '14)*. ACM, New York, NY, USA, 2927–2936.
DOI: 10.1145/2556288.2557377. 30

Steve Sheng, Mandy Holbrook, Ponnurangam Kumaraguru, Lorrie Faith Cranor, and Julie
Downs. 2010.   Who falls for phish?: a demographic analysis of phishing susceptibility and effectiveness of interventions. In *Proceedings of the SIGCHI Conference on Human
Factors in Computing Systems (CHI '10)*. ACM, Atlanta, Georgia, USA, 373–382.   DOI:
10.1145/1753326.1753383. 7, 57, 64

Steve Sheng, Bryant Magnien, Ponnurangam Kumaraguru, Alessandro Acquisti, Lorrie Faith
Cranor, Jason Hong, and Elizabeth Nunge. 2007.   Anti-Phishing Phil: the design and evaluation of a game that teaches people not to fall for phish. In *SOUPS '07: Proceedings of the
3rd symposium on Usable privacy and security*. ACM, New York, NY, USA, 88–99.   DOI:
10.1145/1280680.1280692. 64

Ben Shneiderman. 2003. *Designing the user interface*. Pearson Education India. 9

Meredith M. Skeels and Jonathan Grudin. 2009. When Social Networks Cross Boundaries: A Case Study of Workplace Use of Facebook and Linkedin. In *Proceedings of the ACM 2009 International Conference on Supporting Group Work (GROUP '09)*. ACM, New York, NY, USA, 95–104. DOI: 10.1145/1531674.1531689. 81, 83

Dirk Balfanz Smetters, Dirk Balfanz, D. K. Smetters, Paul Stewart, and H. Chi Wong. 2002. Talking To Strangers: Authentication in Ad-Hoc Wireless Networks. In *Network and Distributed System Security Symposium (NDSS)*. The Internet Society, Palo Alto, CA. 67

D. K. Smetters and Nathan Good. 2009. How users use access control. In *SOUPS '09: Proceedings of the 5th Symposium on Usable Privacy and Security*. ACM, New York, NY, USA, 1–12. DOI: 10.1145/1572532.1572552. 75, 76

Claudio Soriente, Gene Tsudik, and Ersin Uzun. 2008. HAPADEP: Human-Assisted Pure Audio Device Pairing. In *Proceedings of the 11th International Conference on Information Security (ISC '08)*. Springer-Verlag, Berlin, Heidelberg, 385–400. DOI: 10.1007/978-3-540-85886-7_27. 67, 69

Andreas Sotirakopoulos, Kirstie Hawkey, and Konstantin Beznosov. 2011. On the challenges in usable security lab studies: lessons learned from replicating a study on SSL warnings. In *SOUPS '11: Proceedings of the Seventh Symposium on Usable Privacy and Security*. ACM, New York, NY, USA, 1–18. DOI: 10.1145/2078827.2078831. 93

Sukamol Srikwan and Markus Jakobsson. 2008. Using Cartoons to Teach Internet Security. *Cryptologia* 32, 2 (April 2008), 137–154. DOI: 10.1080/01611190701743724. 33

Jessica Staddon, David Huffaker, Larkin Brown, and Aaron Sedley. 2012. Are privacy concerns a turn-off?: engagement and privacy in social networks. In *SOUPS '12: Proceedings of the Eighth Symposium on Usable Privacy and Security*. ACM, New York, NY, USA, 1–13. DOI: 10.1145/2335356.2335370. 82

Frank Stajano and Ross J. Anderson. 2000. The Resurrecting Duckling: Security Issues for Ad-hoc Wireless Networks. In *Proceedings of the 7th International Workshop on Security Protocols*. Springer-Verlag, London, UK, UK, 172–194. http://dl.acm.org/citation.cfm?id=647217.760118 67

Douglas Stebila. 2010. Reinforcing Bad Behaviour: The Misuse of Security Indicators on Popular Websites. In *Proceedings of the 22Nd Conference of the Computer-Human Interaction Special Interest Group of Australia on Computer-Human Interaction (OZCHI '10)*. ACM, New York, NY, USA, 248–251. DOI: 10.1145/1952222.1952275. 60

Steering Committe on the Usability, Security, and Privacy of Computer Systems. 2010. *Toward Better Usability, Security, and Privacy of Information Technology: Report of a Workshop*. National

Academies Press, Washington, DC. 70 pages. http://www.nap.edu/catalog.php?record_id=12998 11

Marc Stiegler. 2005. An Introduction to Petname Systems. (Feb. 2005). http://www.skyhunter.com/marcs/petnames/IntroPetNames.html 60

Katherine Strater and Heather Richter Lipford. 2008. Strategies and Struggles with Privacy in an Online Social Networking Community. In *Proceedings of the 22Nd British HCI Group Annual Conference on People and Computers: Culture, Creativity, Interaction - Volume 1 (BCS-HCI '08)*. British Computer Society, Swinton, UK, UK, 111–119. http://dl.acm.org/citation.cfm?id=1531514.1531530 82

William H. Stufflebeam, Annie I. Antón, Qingfeng He, and Neha Jain. 2004. Specifying Privacy Policies with P3P and EPAL: Lessons Learned. In *Proceedings of the 2004 ACM Workshop on Privacy in the Electronic Society (WPES '04)*. ACM, New York, NY, USA, 35–35. DOI: 10.1145/1029179.1029190. 73

Fred Stutzman, Ralph Gross, and Alessandro Acquisti. 2013. Silent listeners: The evolution of privacy and disclosure on Facebook. *Journal of privacy and confidentiality* 4, 2 (2013), 2. 82

Frederic Stutzman and Woodrow Hartzog. 2012. Boundary Regulation in Social Media. In *Proceedings of the ACM 2012 Conference on Computer Supported Cooperative Work (CSCW '12)*. ACM, New York, NY, USA, 769–778. DOI: 10.1145/2145204.2145320. 82

Fred Stutzman and Jacob Kramer-Duffield. 2010. Friends Only: Examining a Privacy-enhancing Behavior in Facebook. In *Proceedings of the SIGCHI Conference on Human Factors in Computing Systems (CHI '10)*. ACM, New York, NY, USA, 1553–1562. DOI: 10.1145/1753326.1753559. 82

San-Tsai Sun, Eric Pospisil, Ildar Muslukhov, Nuray Dindar, Kirstie Hawkey, and Konstantin Beznosov. 2011. What makes users refuse web single sign-on?: an empirical investigation of OpenID. In *SOUPS '11: Proceedings of the Seventh Symposium on Usable Privacy and Security*. ACM, New York, NY, USA, 1–20. DOI: 10.1145/2078827.2078833. 5

Joshua Sunshine, Serge Egelman, Hazim Almuhimedi, Neha Atri, and Lorrie Faith Cranor. 2009. Crying Wolf: An Empirical Study of SSL Warning Effectiveness. In *Proceedings of the 18th Conference on USENIX Security Symposium (SSYM'09)*. USENIX Association, Berkeley, CA, USA, 399–416. http://dl.acm.org/citation.cfm?id=1855768.1855793 61, 62, 63

Furkan Tari, A. Ant Ozok, and Stephen H. Holden. 2006. A comparison of perceived and real shoulder-surfing risks between alphanumeric and graphical passwords. In *SOUPS '06: Proceedings of the second symposium on Usable privacy and security*. ACM, New York, NY, USA, 56–66. DOI: 10.1145/1143120.1143128. 42

Christopher Thompson, Maritza Johnson, Serge Egelman, David Wagner, and Jennifer King. 2013. When It's Better to Ask Forgiveness Than Get Permission: Attribution Mechanisms for Smartphone Resources. In *Proceedings of the Ninth Symposium on Usable Privacy and Security (SOUPS '13)*. ACM, New York, NY, USA, Article 1, 14 pages. DOI: 10.1145/2501604.2501605. 80

Ramona Su Thompson, Esa M. Rantanen, William Yurcik, and Brian P. Bailey. 2007. Command Line or Pretty Lines?: Comparing Textual and Visual Interfaces for Intrusion Detection. In *Proceedings of the SIGCHI Conference on Human Factors in Computing Systems (CHI '07)*. ACM, New York, NY, USA, 1205–. DOI: 10.1145/1240624.1240807. 86

Julie Thorpe and P. C. van Oorschot. 2004. Graphical Dictionaries and the Memorable Space of Graphical Passwords. In *Proceedings of the 13th Conference on USENIX Security Symposium - Volume 13 (SSYM'04)*. USENIX Association, Berkeley, CA, USA, 10–10. http://dl.acm.org/citation.cfm?id=1251375.1251385 16

Eran Toch, Justin Cranshaw, Paul Hankes Drielsma, Janice Y. Tsai, Patrick Gage Kelley, James Springfield, Lorrie Cranor, Jason Hong, and Norman Sadeh. 2010. Empirical Models of Privacy in Location Sharing. In *Proceedings of the 12th ACM International Conference on Ubiquitous Computing (Ubicomp '10)*. ACM, New York, NY, USA, 129–138. DOI: 10.1145/1864349.1864364. 79

Win Treese. 2004. The state of security on the internet. *netWorker* 8, 3 (Sept. 2004), 13–15. DOI: 10.1145/1016961.1016971. 56

Janice Y. Tsai, Serge Egelman, Lorrie Cranor, and Alessandro Acquisti. 2011. The Effect of Online Privacy Information on Purchasing Behavior: An Experimental Study. *Info. Sys. Research* 22, 2 (June 2011), 254–268. DOI: 10.1287/isre.1090.0260. 71

Janice Y. Tsai, Patrick Kelley, Paul Drielsma, Lorrie Faith Cranor, Jason Hong, and Norman Sadeh. 2009. Who's Viewed You?: The Impact of Feedback in a Mobile Location-sharing Application. In *Proceedings of the SIGCHI Conference on Human Factors in Computing Systems (CHI '09)*. ACM, New York, NY, USA, 2003–2012. DOI: 10.1145/1518701.1519005. 79

Zeynep Tufekci. 2008. Can You See Me Now? Audience and Disclosure Regulation in Online Social Network Sites. *Bulletin of Science, Technology & Society* 28, 1 (2008), 20–36. DOI: 10.1177/0270467607311484. 81, 82

UPSEC 20008. (20008). https://www.usenix.org/legacy/events/upsec08/index.html 20

Blase Ur, Patrick Gage Kelley, Saranga Komanduri, Joel Lee, Michael Maass, Michelle Mazurek, Timothy Passaro, Richard Shay, Timothy Vidas, Lujo Bauer, and others. 2012b. How does your password measure up? The effect of strength meters on password creation. In *Proc. USENIX Security*. USENIX, Belleveu, WA. 107

Blase Ur, Patrick Gage Kelley, Saranga Komanduri, Joel Lee, Michael Maass, Michelle L. Mazurek, Timothy Passaro, Richard Shay, Timothy Vidas, Lujo Bauer, Nicolas Christin, and Lorrie Faith Cranor. 2012a. How Does Your Password Measure Up? The Effect of Strength Meters on Password Creation. In *Proceedings of the 21st USENIX Conference on Security Symposium (Security'12)*. USENIX Association, Berkeley, CA, USA, 5–5. http://dl.acm.org/citation.cfm?id=2362793.2362798 20, 30, 31

Blase Ur, Pedro Giovanni Leon, Lorrie Faith Cranor, Richard Shay, and Yang Wang. 2012c. Smart, useful, scary, creepy: perceptions of online behavioral advertising. In *SOUPS '12: Proceedings of the Eighth Symposium on Usable Privacy and Security*. ACM, New York, NY, USA, 1–15. DOI: 10.1145/2335356.2335362. 70, 73

US Department of Commerce. 1985. *Password Usage*. Technical Report FIPS PUB 112. US Department of Commerce / National Bureau of Standards. 55 pages. 25

US Department of Homeland Security. 2009. A Roadmap for Cybersecurity Research. (Nov. 2009). http://www.cyber.st.dhs.gov/docs/DHS-Cybersecurity-Roadmap.pdf 1, 11

US HHS. 2009. 45 CFR Part 46: Protection of Human Subjects Subpart A: Basic HHS Policy for Protection of Human Research Subjects. (Jan. 15 2009). http://www.hhs.gov/ohrp/humansubjects/guidance/45cfr46.html 100

Paul C. Van Oorschot and Stuart Stubblebine. 2006. On Countering Online Dictionary Attacks with Login Histories and Humans-in-the-loop. *ACM Trans. Inf. Syst. Secur.* 9, 3 (Aug. 2006), 235–258. DOI: 10.1145/1178618.1178619. 50

Paul C van Oorschot and Julie Thorpe. 2011. Exploiting predictability in click-based graphical passwords. *Journal of Computer Security* 19, 4 (2011), 669–702. 42

Kami Vaniea, Lujo Bauer, Lorrie Faith Cranor, and Michael K. Reiter. 2012. Out of sight, out of mind: Effects of displaying access-control information near the item it controls. *2012 Tenth Annual International Conference on Privacy, Security and Trust* 0 (2012), 128–136. DOI: 10.1109/PST.2012.6297929. 77

Kami Vaniea, Clare-Marie Karat, Joshua B. Gross, John Karat, and Carolyn Brodie. 2008. Evaluating assistance of natural language policy authoring. In *SOUPS '08: Proceedings of the 4th symposium on usable privacy and security*. ACM, New York, NY, USA, 65–73. DOI: 10.1145/1408664.1408674. 77

Serge Vaudenay. 2005.   Secure Communications over Insecure Channels Based on Short Authenticated Strings. In *Proceedings of the 25th Annual International Conference on Advances in Cryptology (CRYPTO'05)*. Springer-Verlag, Berlin, Heidelberg, 309–326. DOI: 10.1007/11535218_19. 67

Stephen Voida, W. Keith Edwards, Mark W. Newman, Rebecca E. Grinter, and Nicolas Ducheneaut. 2006. Share and Share Alike: Exploring the User Interface Affordances of File Sharing. In *Proceedings of the SIGCHI Conference on Human Factors in Computing Systems (CHI '06)*. ACM, New York, NY, USA, 221–230. DOI: 10.1145/1124772.1124806. 75, 77

Luis von Ahn, Ben Maurer, Colin McMillen, David Abraham, and Manuel Blum.   re-CAPTCHA: Human-Based Character Recognition via Web Security Measures. *Science* 321 (2008) 1465–1468. Issue 5895. 49

Emanuel von Zezschwitz, Paul Dunphy, and Alexander De Luca. 2013. Patterns in the Wild: A Field Study of the Usability of Pattern and Pin-based Authentication on Mobile Devices. In *Proceedings of the 15th International Conference on Human-computer Interaction with Mobile Devices and Services (MobileHCI '13)*. ACM, New York, NY, USA, 261–270. DOI: 10.1145/2493190.2493231. 43

Na Wang, Heng Xu, and Jens Grossklags. 2011b. Third-party Apps on Facebook: Privacy and the Illusion of Control. In *Proceedings of the 5th ACM Symposium on Computer Human Interaction for Management of Information Technology (CHIMIT '11)*. ACM, New York, NY, USA, Article 4, 10 pages. DOI: 10.1145/2076444.2076448. 84

Yang Wang, Pedro Giovanni Leon, Alessandro Acquisti, Lorrie Faith Cranor, Alain Forget, and Norman Sadeh. 2014. A Field Trial of Privacy Nudges for Facebook. In *Proceedings of the SIGCHI Conference on Human Factors in Computing Systems (CHI '14)*. ACM, New York, NY, USA, 2367–2376. DOI: 10.1145/2556288.2557413. 107

Yang Wang, Gregory Norcie, Saranga Komanduri, Alessandro Acquisti, Pedro Giovanni Leon, and Lorrie Faith Cranor. 2011a. "I regretted the minute I pressed share": a qualitative study of regrets on Facebook. In *SOUPS '11: Proceedings of the Seventh Symposium on Usable Privacy and Security*. ACM, New York, NY, USA, 1–16. DOI: 10.1145/2078827.2078841. 81

Roy Want, Andy Hopper, Veronica Falcão, and Jonathan Gibbons. 1992.   The Active Badge Location System.   *ACM Trans. Inf. Syst.* 10, 1 (Jan. 1992), 91–102. DOI: 10.1145/128756.128759. 78

Samuel D. Warren and Louis D. Brandeis. 1890. The Right to Privacy. *Harward Law Review* 4, 5 (December 1890), 193–220. 9

Rick Wash. 2010. Folk models of home computer security. In *SOUPS '10: Proceedings of the Sixth Symposium on Usable Privacy and Security*. ACM, New York, NY, USA, 1–16. DOI: 10.1145/1837110.1837125. 6, 91

Jason Watson, Andrew Besmer, and Heather Richter Lipford. 2012. +Your circles: sharing behavior on Google+. In *SOUPS '12: Proceedings of the Eighth Symposium on Usable Privacy and Security*. ACM, New York, NY, USA, 1–9. DOI: 10.1145/2335356.2335373. 83

Jason Watson, Michael Whitney, and Heather Richter Lipford. 2009. Configuring Audience-oriented Privacy Policies. In *Proceedings of the 2Nd ACM Workshop on Assurable and Usable Security Configuration (SafeConfig '09)*. ACM, New York, NY, USA, 71–78. DOI: 10.1145/1655062.1655076. 82

Nicholas Weaver, Vern Paxson, Stuart Staniford, and Robert Cunningham. 2003. A taxonomy of computer worms. In *Proceedings of the 2003 ACM workshop on rapid malcode (WORM '03)*. ACM, New York, NY, USA, 11–18. DOI: 10.1145/948187.948190. 55

Catherine S. Weir, Gary Douglas, Martin Carruthers, and Mervyn Jack. 2009b. User perceptions of security, convenience and usability for ebanking authentication tokens. *Computers and Security* 28, 1–2 (2009), 47 – 62. DOI: 10.1016/j.cose.2008.09.008. 46

Matt Weir, Sudhir Aggarwal, Breno de Medeiros, and Bill Glodek. 2009a. Password Cracking Using Probabilistic Context-Free Grammars. In *Proceedings of the 2009 30th IEEE Symposium on Security and Privacy (SP '09)*. IEEE Computer Society, Washington, DC, USA, 391–405. DOI: 10.1109/SP.2009.8. 32, 36

Rodrigo Werlinger, Kirstie Hawkey, and Konstantin Beznosov. 2008. Security Practitioners in Context: Their Activities and Interactions. In *CHI '08 Extended Abstracts on Human Factors in Computing Systems (CHI EA '08)*. ACM, New York, NY, USA, 3789–3794. DOI: 10.1145/1358628.1358931. 85

Rodrigo Werlinger, Kirstie Hawkey, David Botta, and Konstantin Beznosov. 2009. Security practitioners in context: Their activities and interactions with other stakeholders within organizations. *International Journal of Human-Computer Studies* 67, 7 (2009), 584 – 606. DOI: 10.1016/j.ijhcs.2009.03.002. 85

Rodrigo Werlinger, Kirstie Hawkey, Kasia Muldner, Pooya Jaferian, and Konstantin Beznosov. 2008. The challenges of using an intrusion detection system: is it worth the effort?. In *SOUPS '08: Proceedings of the 4th symposium on Usable privacy and security*. ACM, New York, NY, USA, 107–118. DOI: 10.1145/1408664.1408679. 85

A.F. Westin. 1970. *Privacy and Freedom*. Bodley Head. http://books.google.com/books?id=rapOSAAACAAJ 10, 17

Tara Whalen, Diana K. Smetters, and Elizabeth F. Churchill. 2006. User experiences with sharing and access control.. In *CHI Extended Abstracts* (2006-09-27), Gary M. Olson and Robin Jeffries (Eds.). ACM, 1517–1522. `http://dblp.uni-trier.de/db/conf/chi/chi2006a.html` 75, 77

Alma Whitten. 2004. *Making Security Usable*. Ph.D. Dissertation. School of Computer Science, Carnegie Mellon University. 52

Alma Whitten and J. D. Tygar. 1999. Why Johnny can't encrypt: A usability evaluation of PGP 5.0. In *8th USENIX Security Symposium*. Usenix, 169–184. `citeseer.nj.nec.com/whitten99why.html` 3, 15, 51, 52, 93, 95, 105

Susan Wiedenbeck, Jim Waters, Jean-Camille Birget, Alex Brodskiy, and Nasir Memon. 2005. PassPoints: Design and Longitudinal Evaluation of a Graphical Password System. *Int. J. Hum.-Comput. Stud.* 63, 1-2 (July 2005), 102–127. DOI: 10.1016/j.ijhcs.2005.04.010. 42

M. V. Wilkes. 1968. *Time-Sharing Computer Systems*. American Elsevier, New York. 26

Stephen Wilson. 2008. Public Key Superstructure "It's PKI Jim, but Not As We Know It!". In *Proceedings of the 7th Symposium on Identity and Trust on the Internet (IDtrust '08)*. ACM, New York, NY, USA, 72–88. DOI: 10.1145/1373290.1373301. 52

Shomir Wilson, Justin Cranshaw, Norman Sadeh, Alessandro Acquisti, Lorrie Faith Cranor, Jay Springfield, Sae Young Jeong, and Arun Balasubramanian. 2013. Privacy Manipulation and Acclimation in a Location Sharing Application. In *Proceedings of the 2013 ACM International Joint Conference on Pervasive and Ubiquitous Computing (UbiComp '13)*. ACM, New York, NY, USA, 549–558. DOI: 10.1145/2493432.2493436. 79

Pamela Wisniewski, Heather Lipford, and David Wilson. 2012. Fighting for My Space: Coping Mechanisms for Sns Boundary Regulation. In *Proceedings of the SIGCHI Conference on Human Factors in Computing Systems (CHI '12)*. ACM, New York, NY, USA, 609–618. DOI: 10.1145/2207676.2207761. 82, 84

M. S. Wogalter. 2006. *Communication-Human Information Processing (C-HIP) Model*. Lawrence Erlbaum Associates, Mahwah, NJ, 3–9. 101

Charles C. Wood. 1984. Logging, Security Experts Data Base, and Crypto Key Management. In *Proceedings of the 1984 Annual Conference of the ACM on The Fifth Generation Challenge (ACM '84)*. ACM, New York, NY, USA, 248–252. DOI: 10.1145/800171.809640. 53

Min Wu, Robert C. Miller, and Simson L. Garfinkel. 2006a. Do Security Toolbars Actually Prevent Phishing Attacks?. In *Proceedings of the SIGCHI Conference on Human Factors in Computing Systems (CHI '06)*. ACM, New York, NY, USA, 601–610. DOI: 10.1145/1124772.1124863. 58

Min Wu, Robert C. Miller, and Greg Little. 2006b. Web wallet: preventing phishing attacks by revealing user intentions. In *SOUPS '06: Proceedings of the second symposium on Usable privacy and security*. ACM, New York, NY, USA, 102–113. DOI: 10.1145/1143120.1143133. 65

Yi Xu, Gerardo Reynaga, Sonia Chiasson, Jan-Michael Frahm, Fabian Monrose, and Paul Van Oorschot. 2013. Security Analysis and Related Usability of Motion-based CAPTCHAs: Decoding Codewords in Motion. *IEEE Transactions on Dependable and Secure Computing* 99, PrePrints (2013), 1. DOI: 10.1109/TDSC.2013.52. 49

Jeff Yan, Alan Blackwell, Ross Anderson, and Alasdair Grant. 2004. Password Memorability and Security: Empirical Results. *IEEE Security and Privacy* 2, 5 (Sept. 2004), 25–31. DOI: 10.1109/MSP.2004.81. 32

Jeff Yan and Ahmad Salah El Ahmad. 2008. Usability of CAPTCHAs or usability issues in CAPTCHA design. In *SOUPS '08: Proceedings of the 4th symposium on Usable privacy and security*. ACM, New York, NY, USA, 44–52. DOI: 10.1145/1408664.1408671. 49

Ka-Ping Yee and Kragen Sitaker. 2006. Passpet: convenient password management and phishing protection. In *SOUPS '06: Proceedings of the second symposium on Usable privacy and security*. ACM, New York, NY, USA, 32–43. DOI: 10.1145/1143120.1143126. 60

T. Ylonen. 1996. SSH - Secure login connections over the Internet. In *Proceedings of the 6th Security Symposium) (USENIX Association: Berkeley, CA)*. Usenix, 37. http://citeseer.nj.nec.com/ylonen96ssh.html 52, 61

William Yurcik. 2006. Tool Update: NVisionIP Improvements (Difference View, Sparklines, and Shapes). In *Proceedings of the 3rd International Workshop on Visualization for Computer Security (VizSEC '06)*. ACM, New York, NY, USA, 65–66. DOI: 10.1145/1179576.1179589. 86

Yinqian Zhang, Fabian Monrose, and Michael K. Reiter. 2010. The Security of Modern Password Expiration: An Algorithmic Framework and Empirical Analysis. In *Proceedings of the 17th ACM Conference on Computer and Communications Security (CCS '10)*. ACM, New York, NY, USA, 176–186. DOI: 10.1145/1866307.1866328. 24, 35

Mary Ellen Zurko. 2005. Lotus Notes/Domino: Embedding Security in Collaborative Applications. In *Security and Usability*, Lorrie Cranor and Simson Garfinkel (Eds.). O'Reilly, Cambridge, MA. 51

Mary Ellen Zurko and Richard T. Simon. 1996. User-centered security. In *NSPW '96: Proceedings of the 1996 workshop on new security paradigms*. ACM Press, New York, NY, USA, 27–33. DOI: 10.1145/304851.304859. 14, 21

Authors' Biographies

SIMSON GARFINKEL

Simson Garfinkel is an Associate Professor at the Naval Post-graduate School. Based in Arlington VA, Garfinkel's research interests include digital forensics, usable security, data fusion, information policy, and terrorism. He holds seven US patents and has published dozens of research articles on security and digital forensics. He is an ACM Fellow and an IEEE Senior Member, as well as a member of the National Association of Science Writers.

Garfinkel is the author of 14 books on computing. He is perhaps best known for his book *Database Nation: The Death of Privacy in the 21st Century*, http://www.databasenation.com/. Garfinkel's most successful book, *Practical UNIX and Internet Security* (co-authored with Gene Spafford), has sold more than 250,000 copies and been translated into many languages since the first edition in 1991.

Garfinkel is also a journalist and has written more than a thousand articles about science, technology, and technology policy. He has won numerous journalism awards, including the Jesse H. Neal National Business Journalism Award for his "Machine shop" series in *CSO* magazine. Today he writes for *Technology Review Magazine* and the www.technologyreview.com website.

As an entrepreneur, Garfinkel founded five companies, including Vineyard.NET, which provided Internet service on Martha's Vineyard from 1995–2005, and Sandstorm Enterprises, an early developer of commercial computer forensic tools.

Garfinkel received three Bachelor of Science degrees from MIT in 1987, a Master's of Science in Journalism from Columbia University in 1988, and a Ph.D. in Computer Science from MIT in 2005.

HEATHER RICHTER LIPFORD

Heather Richter Lipford is an Associate Professor in the Department of Software and Information Systems at the University of North Carolina at Charlotte. Lipford's research interests are in Human Computer Interaction, with a focus in usable privacy and security, secure programming, and social computing. She has published dozens of research articles in these areas at premiere HCI and usable security venues. She has also previously done research in the areas of ubiquitous computing and software engineering.

At UNC Charlotte, Lipford co-directs the HCI Lab and is a member of the UNCC Cyber Defense and Network Assurability Center, the Charlotte Visualization Center, and the UNCC Cognitive Science Academy. She regularly teaches and mentors students in the areas of HCI and usable privacy and security. She is also heavily involved in efforts to broaden participation in computing, and increase the recruitment and retention of under-represented groups in computing degree programs.

Lipford received a Bachelor of Science degree from Michigan State University in 1995, and a Ph.D. from the College of Computing at the Georgia Institute of Technology in 2005.

Printed in the United States
by Baker & Taylor Publisher Services